The Catholic Thing

Other Titles of interest from St. Augustine's Press

The Catholic Thing
Five Years of a Singular Website

Edited by Robert Royal

Foreword by Archbishop Charles J. Chaput OFM Cap

ST. AUGUSTINE'S PRESS
South Bend, Indiana

Manufactured in the United States of America

1 2 3 4 5 6   19 18 17 16 15 14 13

Library of Congress Control Number: 2013940810

∞ The paper used in this publication meets the minimum requirements of the American National Standard for Information Sciences Permanence of Paper for Printed Materials, ANSI Z39.481984.

ST. AUGUSTINE'S PRESS
www.staugustine.net

Contents

Contents

No Higher Vocation, No Greater Joy

Life as a bishop—or at least the life of *this* bishop—doesn't leave much time to spend on poetry. But a few years ago a friend loaned me a volume of Rainer Maria Rilke, and of course, Rilke's work can be quite beautiful. In it, I found these lines of his verse:

> *Slowly now the evening changes his garments*
> *held for him by a rim of ancient trees;*
> *you gaze: and the landscape divides and leaves you*
> *one sinking and one rising toward the stars.*
>
> *And you are left, to none belonging wholly,*
> *not so dark as a silent house, nor quite*
> *so surely pledged unto eternity*
> *as that which grows to star and climbs the night.*
>
> *To you is left (unspeakably confused)*
> *your life, gigantic, ripening, full of fears,*
> *so that it, now hemmed in, now grasping all,*
> *is changed in you by turns to stone and stars.*[1]

Philosophers and psychologists have offered a lot of different theories about the nature of the human person. But few have captured the human condition better than Rilke does in those twelve lines. We are creatures made for heaven; but we are born of this earth. We love the beauty of this world; but we sense there is something more behind that beauty. Our longing for that something pulls us outside of ourselves.

Striving for "something more" is part of the greatness of the human spirit, even when it involves failure and suffering. In the words of Blessed John Paul II, something in the artist, and by extension in all human beings, "mirrors the image of God as Creator."[2] We have an instinct to create beauty and new life that comes from our Creator. Yet the cruelty in today's world is *also* the work of human hands. So if we are troubled by the spirit of our age, if we really want to change the current course of our culture and challenge its guiding ideas, then we need to start with the author of that culture. That means examining man himself.

Culture exists because man exists. Men and women think, imagine, believe, and act. The mark they leave on the world is what we call culture. That includes in a special way what we consciously choose to create; things like art, literature, technology, music, and architecture. We are social animals. Culture is the framework within which we locate ourselves in relationship to other people, find meaning in the world and then transmit meaning to others.

For believers, culture flows naturally from their faith. Christianity is an incarnational religion. We believe that God became man. This has huge implications for how we live and think. When God tells our first parents, "be fruitful and multiply, and fill the earth and subdue it" (Gen 1:28), he invites us to take part, in a small but powerful way, in the life of God himself.

The results of that fertility surround us. We see it in the immense Christian heritage that still underpins the modern world. Christian faith has inspired much of the greatest scholarship, painting, music, architecture, and literature in human experience. For Christians, these are holy vocations with the power to elevate the human spirit and lead men and women toward God.

And yet, we still face a problem. God has never been more absent from the Western mind than he is today. And we live in an age when almost every scientific advance seems to be matched by some increase of cruelty in our entertainment, cynicism in our politics, ignorance of the past, consumer greed, little genocides posing as "rights" like the cult of abortion, and a basic confusion about what—if anything at all—it means to be "human."

In such a time, every seed of sane reflection and Christian hope becomes precious; every source of moral insight and Catholic intellectual renewal becomes water in a desert. For the past five years, against the odds, *The Catholic Thing* has offered day after day of consistently invaluable Catholic commentary on the world around us and the issues we face as believers. The 100 essays included in this volume are far more than just "useful aids" in understanding our times; they're also filled with the beauty of truth, and the elegance of wonderful intellects writing wonderfully. *The Catholic Thing* is the kind of little miracle that ripples out to touch lives in powerful ways. The evidence is in these pages. I'm blessed to know Robert Royal as a friend; but more importantly, the Church is blessed to have him and his colleagues as superior minds in the Gospel's service. There is no higher vocation, and in the end, no greater joy.

+Charles J. Chaput, O.F.M. Cap.
Archbishop of Philadelphia
May 15, 2013

1   Rilke quotations are from *Rilke: Selected Poems*, with English translations and notes by C.F. MacIntyre; Los Angeles, University of California Press, 1968 edition. Cited poems are *Evening (Abend)* and *The Angels (Die Engel)*.

2   *Letter of His Holiness Pope John Paul II to Artists*, Vatican City, 1999.

A Thing Not a Theory

The name *The Catholic Thing* has a distinguished pedigree—as does the reality to which it refers. In 1930, G. K. Chesterton wrote a still incisive little book, *The Thing: Why I Am a Catholic*. He was remembering, it may have been, a passage in a letter from his friend and co-belligerent Hilaire Belloc, shortly after Chesterton was received into the Catholic Church: "I am by all my nature of mind skeptical, by all my nature of body exceedingly sensual. So sensual that the virtues restrictive of sense are but phrases to me. But I accept these phrases as true and act upon them as well as a struggling man can. And as to the doubt of the soul, I discover it to be false: a mood: not a conclusion. My conclusion—and that of all men who have ever once *seen* it—is the Faith. Corporate, organised, a personality, teaching. A thing, not a theory. It."

When *The Catholic Thing* was founded in 2008 by a small group of old friends who had long been individually occupied in Catholic things, this concrete presence of Catholicism in the world—continuous across ages and resilient in the face of cultural upheavals—was very much present to our minds. It's not simply that the Catholic tradition has much to say about the many questions always troubling the human race: wars and rumors of wars, the relations of men and women, the just ordering of our lives together, economics and the claims of the poor in spirit, the place of the Beautiful alongside the True and the Good, and the many other realities, large and small, that must make up the *humanum*. It's that the Church, besides teaching propositions, is a living presence in the world, a "thing" as substantial as any other and more than vital to all the rest.

Introduction

Few people, even among Catholics, know this, and many of those who do might be inclined to doubt whether it's true today. The ever more rapid rise of non-Christian and anti-Christian tendencies in the twenty first century makes it appear that Catholicism is, at best, some abstract and unreal doctrine, less relevant to human lives than a discipline like astrophysics. When the Catholic Thing does put in a public appearance, it's usually in the context of some controversy like contraception, or abortion, or gay marriage that allegedly shows the Church is medieval or patriarchal or insular or sectarian—in any event, decidedly not the Church of What's Happening Now.

One of the reasons for founding *The Catholic Thing*, of course, was to enter into these burning controversies with the best evidence and arguments we could muster. There's quite a lot of evidence to back up controversial Catholic claims for those with eyes to see. Church teaching on marriage, family, and sex, for example, has been derided as hopelessly out of touch with modern realities. But the most superficial glance at the sociological literature would convince any reasonable person that those realities are hardly a standard by which to measure Christian principles—or mere social sanity. In fact, the evidence points entirely in the other direction. Sexual license and family breakdown has led to unprecedented numbers of children born out of wedlock, with all the disadvantages and social pathologies illegitimacy feeds: drug use, crime, poor health, and low educational levels. And indescribable damage to what Catholics still think of as the common good.

This is just one of the concrete sets of issues treated in the following pages—an important set but perhaps a helpful indicator of the way the Catholic Thing warrants careful attention on less obvious questions as well. This book starts with Fundamental Things because not all questions are merely "issues." The secular world has a very hard time understanding Catholicism, not least as to why Church teachings cannot merely be changed to suit the times, on the model of public policies. The notion of a community of longstanding remaining faithful to principles thousands of years old, rooted in divine revelation sounds to many like something guaranteed to go quickly out of date.

Many of the columns reproduced in the present volume address current issues, but you will not read very far in these pages before you understand that they are all embedded—even if they sometimes take positions at variance from one another—in a large common framework, to which they attest. It's difficult given current cultural trends to feel confident about the Catholic Thing, but behind much of the writing here lies the unspoken assumption that Macaulay was right when he wrote, memorably, of the Church:

> She saw the commencement of all the governments and of all the ecclesiastical establishments that now exist in the world; and we feel no assurance that she is not destined to see the end of them all. She was great and respected before the Saxon had set foot on Britain, before the Frank had passed the Rhine, when Grecian eloquence still flourished in Antioch, when idols were still worshipped in the temple of Mecca. And she may still exist in undiminished vigour when some traveller from New Zealand shall, in the midst of a vast solitude, take his stand on a broke arch of London Bridge to sketch the ruins of St Paul's.

One of the things that make the Catholic Thing so durable is the diversity of thought and life that springs from its fundamental unity. As editor of *The Catholic Thing*, I've been amazed again and again how our writers could be inspired to take up the quite necessary—and thankless—task of reforming the culture morning after morning. It was, therefore, both pleasurable and painful to put together this selection. Pleasurable in that it was inspiring to recall how much careful thought and good writing found its way onto *TCT*'s site for over half a decade now. Painful because there was much more of equal quality and even greater range that I would have liked to include.

So I thank our writers, who, walking by faith not sight, in the beginning worked for free and, more recently, for what can generously be described as slave wages. I thank those who helped start this *Thing* with me—especially the late Ralph McInerny, Michael Novak, George Marlin, Austin Ruse, and Hadley Arkes. Deep thanks to my dear colleagues over these years: Brad Miner, Hannah

Introduction

Russo, Maria Hungerford, Kirk Kramer, Christopher Wendt, Richard Lender, and Elizabeth McCoy. And to our partners in several foreign countries who have made it possible for *TCT* to appear, with varying degrees of regularity in French, Italian, Slovak, Spanish, and Portuguese.

And what can you say about our passionate, contentious, and rapidly growing band of readers?

Or of our publisher, and sometime contributor, Bruce Fingerhut who worked a minor miracle to produce this book in desperately short order for our anniversary?

We all owe a special debt of gratitude to Sean Fieler, Greg Pfundstein, Michele and Donald D'Amour, Jim Perry, Robert Odle, Chris Ruddy, Michael Crofton, George Marlin, Allen Roth, Joseph Starshak, and other generous souls who, during years of an unsettled economy, have helped keep body and spirit together.

We are all servants of a Word that no man born of woman follows perfectly or can claim for his own. But for five years we've sought to make this *Thing*, these our words, serve that Word *sicut erat in principio et nunc et semper.*

Robert Royal
Faith and Reason Institute

I. Fundamental Things

1. Implicit Philosophy

RALPH MCINERNY

Not long ago I noticed a sign in the office of an editor at a university press announcing that this was a "Thomist-Free Zone." That is a warning that could be posted over many philosophy departments in Catholic colleges and universities. The abandonment of Thomas Aquinas by so many Catholic philosophers and theologians in the wake of Vatican II is a story in itself. Many years ago, when the dismantling had just begun, I wrote a book called *Thomism in an Age of Renewal* in which I tried to understand what was going on around me.

Often the disenchantment was attributed to uninspired textbooks or awful representatives of Thomism and since most philosophy books are uninspired and most philosophers awful, this excuse had a certain plausibility. After all, the disenchantment might even have involved philosophical reasons, though these were in rather short supply among the disenchanted. Far more prominent was the assumption that things were much more intellectually lively in Thomist-Free Zones, that non-Thomists were a pretty impressive bunch and signing on with them was a matter of upward mobility.

Reading Thomas Nagel's *The Last Word*, in which this engaging NYU philosopher addresses the widespread tendency to

adopt some version of what might be called the Protagoras position—what's true for me is true for me, what's true for you is true
for you—it occurred to me that it must have come as a shock to
my erstwhile comrades to find that, no matter where they fled,
they would find the current condition of philosophy subjected to
fundamental criticism. Being discontented with prevailing opinion
is scarcely confined to Thomists. It is in a way the mark of the
philosopher.

Nagel set out to show that fundamental relativism is, as Plato
had argued long ago, self-destructive, ultimately incoherent. There
are inescapable fundamental truths that can be only verbally
denied. Now, as it happens, that is the key to the thought of
Thomas Aquinas as it was to Aristotle's before him. There are
starting points of human reasoning that are grounded in the way
things are and those starting points are indeed the principles of
philosophizing.

No wonder then that Pope John Paul II, in *Fides et Ratio*,
begins with them. Imagining that his reader would be alarmed to
find that he is reading an encyclical devoted to philosophy, the
Holy Father sought to allay that fear. Philosophy takes its rise
from questions that are inescapable for human beings—What
does it all mean? Is death the end? What is the difference
between good and evil? Sooner or later everyone will ask them in
one form or another. Human beings in a sense *are* those questions. But the pope goes on to say that there are *answers* to
them that are commonly held and those answers make up what
he calls an Implicit Philosophy. Only after that does he take up
the somewhat embarrassing fact that there are a large number of
rival philosophical systems. Implicit philosophy turns out to be a
means of appraising those systems. Philosophical systems that
are at odds with Implicit Philosophy are for that reason suspicious.

Descartes said of common sense that everyone is sure that he
has enough of it. This suggests that we should be wary of identifying Implicit Philosophy with common sense. The latter may be
merely prevailing opinion and include such oddities as that people

once thought the world was flat or that killing unborn babies is a natural right. A good deal of philosophizing consists in appraising candidates for the status of self-evident truths.

There is an old adage: *primum vivere, deinde philosophari.* One needs lived experience in order to philosophize. That order seems reversed when we are taught philosophy. A teacher takes us along for the ride and we learn to mimic the moves he makes but often this amounts to what Newman would call notional rather than real knowledge. After learning philosophy one must still assimilate it, make it one's own. A lot of people studied Thomas but didn't become Thomists. It was that realization that prompted, I think, the discontent among so many in the 1960s. Descartes had a similar epiphany in winter quarters. One reaction is to jettison what one has been taught but not really learned. The other is really to learn it.

In *Orthodoxy* Chesterton likened himself to a man who set sail from England on a voyage of discovery. Much later, sighting land, he stormed ashore only to find that he was planting his flag on the island he had left. Wandering Thomists may have a similar experience. The older we get, the more simple things engage us, starting points, principles. Getting right about those is to get right about the basis for Thomism. Or any other philosophy worthy of the name. In the end, there are no Thomist-Free Zones.

2. A Man Like No Other

ANTHONY ESOLEN

For the last several months I've been doing something that, for all I know, nobody else in the United States is doing. I've been learning to read Welsh by toddling through the New Testament.

That doesn't make me unique. People do *unusual* things all the time; being unusual in one way or another is as common as rain. But when you are handling the words of Jesus one by one, like riddles, even though you know what the verses will say, you see that words like *usual* and *unusual* do not describe Jesus.

It isn't as if Jesus stands at an extreme end of a spectrum of teachers in the ancient world. He teaches "with authority," as the people remarked, amazed, even bewildered. He defers to no prophet or king, not even to Moses. He does not reason people into a benignant way of life, like Buddha, nor does he embrace the traditions of a gentleman, like Confucius.

We are to imitate Jesus, but Jesus never imitates us. He knows the heart of man, says Saint John, and he is like us in all things but sin, says Saint Paul, and he feels for our weakness, says the writer to the Hebrews, but it would sound like blasphemy to give Jesus a compliment, to call Him unusually perceptive. It would be like saying that light is unusually illuminating, or that beauty is unusually attractive.

I'm struggling to say that there is no one in the history of the world whom Jesus resembles; although many a saint, by the grace of God, has come to resemble Jesus. The Lord is unique. So are the great things associated with Him. There's nothing in the ancient world that is like the Gospels—and that includes the foolish sham-gospels, flimsy and derivative things.

There's nothing in the world that is like the Person or the events they describe. The great letters of Saint Paul are unique. The transformation of ordinary people into saints on fire to spread the Good News, unique; the kinds of people they became, unique; even the Shroud of Turin is unique—there isn't any ancient artifact like it, and there isn't anything close.

So I'm reading the Gospels slowly, in Welsh, and am compelled to dwell upon words that pass me by too quickly in English. "When you give alms," says Jesus, "do not sound a trumpet before you, as the hypocrites do in the synagogues and in the streets, that they may have glory from men. Truly I say to you, they have their reward. But when you give alms, let not your left hand know what your right hand is doing." (Mt. 6:2–3)

If we hear those words aright, we'll experience the shock of something wholly unexpected, but which, when expressed, strikes us, if we are steeped in the wisdom of the law and the prophets, as fulfilling the whole of the Old Testament, *even though no one in the Old Testament ever says anything like it.*

And what of the ancient pagans? Aristotle praised the virtue of magnificence, the performing of visibly great deeds, especially by means of public generosity, because he took for granted that men desire honor. The lowliest mayor of a cow town wants to emulate Augustus Caesar—to find Farmville in brick, and leave it, if not in marble, at least in shiny slates, and with new sidewalks; and he wants to be seen and known for it too, with a nice plaque on the village commons.

But there is Jesus, saying, *Na wyped dy law aswy pa beth a wna dy law ddehau:* Let not your left hand know what your right hand is doing. No one ever said anything like it.

So let's pause. Let's not assume that it is an *unusual* metaphor expressing an *unusual* wisdom. Let's assume that this unique Jesus, in saying this never-said thing, has expressed it also in a unique way. Then we will not reduce the metaphor to anything resembling a "Christian" common sense.

We'll not then say, "Jesus recommends that we be quiet about it, when we give alms." After all, there's a way to win the approval of men quietly, so that you can double the glow of the pleasure, basking not only in the glory of your generosity, but in the knowledge that your beneficiaries cannot accuse you of pride.

No, if the left hand is not to know what the right hand is doing, we must take care to hide our good deeds from the most fawning and flattering audience there can be—ourselves. How is that possible? We accuse the disciples of being slow to understand Jesus, and we're right, they were slow. Are we any quicker? And did they not have cause to be slow? How can we hide ourselves from ourselves? How can we not know what we know?

I can't answer my own question, but Jesus does give us a hint at where the answer must lie. "Your Father," He says, "who sees in secret shall reward you openly." We are, He has said, to be like that Father who makes His rain to fall upon the just and the unjust, in the mysteries of His wisdom and providence.

This is the Father who sees the recesses of the heart. He is the

God who wishes to dwell in those recesses; to take away the heart of stone, even if it is gleaming marble stone, and replace it with a heart of flesh, a heart that beats with His life.

If we are to enjoy a reward, what better can it be than God Himself? So Jesus isn't simply warning against ostentation. He's inviting us into a complete surrender to the Father, so that we will not remain in our ignorant knowledge, and our alienating generosity. It is a call to be born again. And what is that? Can we toddle more than a step or two beyond the beginning of that?

3. The Grounds of Civilization

JAMES V. SCHALL, S.J.

The grounds of civilization are found in the *Apology* of Socrates: "It is not difficult to avoid death, gentlemen of the jury; it is much more difficult to avoid wickedness, for it runs faster than death." (39a) The principled foundation of worthy human living is asserted here. Lest wickedness rule, death is to be preferred. This terse statement was addressed particularly to politicians and judges. They had, if they willed, the power to enforce the wickedness to which, as Aristotle also said, human nature is prone.

Earlier in the *Apology*, Socrates had counseled: "Concentrate your attention on whether what I say is just or not, for the excellence of a judge lies in this, as that of a speaker lies in telling the truth." (18a) If these Socratic dicta, reaffirmed by the Hebrew and Christian tradition, are the foundations of civilization as such, the experiment of civilization based on truth, we may fear, is ending. Its grounds are rejected in those very traditions and lands that once accepted them. We need not be surprised at this. Wickedness does "run faster than death." Civilizations die in minds before they die in polities.

"The noble type of man," Nietzsche wrote headily in *Beyond Good and Evil*, "feels *himself* to be the determiner of values, he does not need to be approved of, he judges 'what harms me is harmful in itself,' he knows himself to be that which in general first accords honor to things, he *creates values*." Viewed from this position, no wickedness is possible. Anything can be justified. *Quod placuit principi legis habet vigorem*, as the Roman Law held. If it pleases the law-enforcer, it is the law.

However eloquently Nietzsche expressed this position, he was not the first to affirm it. Greek philosophers knew of this view. The Sophist could tell you how to get whatever you wanted, whatever it was. The principle was, as we saw, in the Roman law. The Muslim and medieval voluntarists saw nothing behind things but a will that could always be otherwise. Machiavelli made it famous in politics. Modern relativists, of whom Benedict XVI speaks, think they invented this transformational idea that Nietzsche propounded in the nineteenth century. Indeed, Nietzsche is often the source of their thinking.

Yet Nietzsche is not simply a modern relativist. His "value" revolution, now codified in much civil law, was the result of his shock at finding that neither believers believed nor thinkers explained. Nietzsche was easily scandalized. His many readers were uncritical of the power of pure will in a world empty of gods and natures.

Civilization itself, however, is not built on the supposition that the "noble" man "creates" his own values. Liberty is not "creative" of truth. It is the impetus to find truth, to rejoice in it. Truth exists in things before we discover it, especially in our own being.

We are creatures who indeed have the practical power to "make" and to "act" in this world, the arena of deciding our own destinies. Ever since Bacon, we wonder if we cannot even "make" or "remake" ourselves, "cure" ourselves by "research." We become the ultimate object of science. As we have no "truth" in our being, we are "free" to eliminate or refashion the being we are, as if we can indeed build a human being as we build a better mousetrap.

Once politics is free of anything higher than itself, it becomes the master science. No natural law, revelation, or tradition is left as a measure. The politician sees himself as the messiah, the "mortal god," a phrase Allan Bloom used of Caesar. The Socratic foundation of civilization always left the principle of truth intact precisely when the polity killed the philosopher.

Joseph Pieper once wrote: "No calamity causes more despair in this world than the unjust exercise of power. And yet, any power that could never be abused is ultimately no power at all—a fearful thought." Such are sage words. The "power" to create "values" exists. The alternative to the unjust use of power is not "no" power, but the just use of power, one that recognizes the measure.

The just use of power, however, rejects wickedness. We are to be defended against wickedness by first knowing that it exists and can be identified. It can likewise be chosen, even democratically, as a public policy.

Civilization depends on there being a truth to which those who suffer under unjust power can turn even in the face of established and enforced wickedness. It is this latter ground that relativism denies us. The central issue behind every public controversy and every threat against our national existence lies here. Yet this is the one threat to civilization that we choose not to recognize. We have "created" our own "values" in order to deny the truth in our being.

4. Two Mistakes on the Human in Nature

HADLEY ARKES

The mafia, we are told, brings forth its own version of charity in taking care of the dependants, the widows and children of those who have fallen in the service of "the common good" in their criminal enterprise. But that is not exactly what the rest of us mean by "charity." In the recent encyclical *Caritas in Veritate*, Benedict XVI reminds us that charity cannot be equated simply with benefits, detached from the kind of life that is truly rightful for human beings. And yet, in turn, that understanding of the ends true and rightful for mankind cannot be detached from an understanding of the ends, or purpose, contained in the Creation in which they find their place.

The Creation marks at least the judgment that there should be something rather than nothing. It is not a random happening. The whole thing makes little sense unless there is a telos or purpose in that Creation. Within the orders of Creation living things were higher than the lifeless stars, and among living things the peak would come with those moral beings, who could reason over right and wrong. If Creation has a purpose, life has a purpose, moral beings have a purpose, and a Creation with moral beings must contain a moral purpose.

The lesson is old but the connections may evade us: The human person cannot be understood apart from the Creation, but then neither can Nature be understood apart from the existence of those human creatures. It takes a certain perverse genius then to conceive of Nature in our own day detached from a moral purpose and from the existence of those creatures who alone bear a moral purpose. But in the scheme of environmentalism we are constantly enjoined to save the planet as though human beings were somehow not as much a part of that Nature as trees and rivers.

Benedict takes the occasion of the new encyclical to drive home the gravest point that has eluded them: The environmentalists seem serenely unaware that what they seek to do in the name of saving Nature may actually do damage to the integrity and character of "the human person," that moral being who is every bit a part of that Nature. And so, as Benedict writes: "In order to protect nature, it is not enough to intervene with economic incentives or deterrents . . . These are important steps, but *the decisive issue is the overall moral tenor of society*. If there is a lack of respect for the right to life and to a natural death, if human conception, gestation and birth are made artificial, if human embryos are sacrificed to research, the conscience of society ends up losing the concept of human ecology and, along with it, that of environmental ecology. . . The book of nature is one and indivisible: it takes in not only the environment but also life, sexuality, marriage, the family, social relations: in a word, integral human development."

In the name of preserving the planet we may disfigure the character of human beings. We can do that, in part, by inducing them to believe that they have a license to manufacture and discard human life to suit their own interests or advance a project in research, as though a human life had no intrinsic importance and a claim to our respect. We seek to extend the span of human life, while we gradually purge from ourselves any sense of reverence for those lives we profess to treasure.

But it is also one of the oddities of the moral life that people on different sides may back themselves into the same premises. This point struck me forcibly last week when I was involved in seminars on natural law and found some of my own allies, on the Catholic and Jewish side, arguing that there was something about marriage that is "pre-political." It is so grounded in nature that it can exist without the "laws," the distinct mark of political life. Their own political motive here is to persuade themselves that marriage, in its rightful sense, may be preserved in certain religious enclaves, even as the civil laws are remodeled to encompass same-sex marriage.

But my friends might be backing into another form of that fallacy of which Benedict was warning. The environmentalists remove the human person from the domain of nature, and now some of our allies in the defense of marriage imagine a human nature detached from "laws." But law springs distinctly from the nature of only one kind of creature, and what if it is the case that marriage, rightly understood, requires the kind of commitment that only law can provide? People can have sex at any time, even when governments break down. And yet if marriage is understood as the framework of a love meant to endure, a love that encompasses the begetting and nurturing of children, it makes the most profound difference that it is a framework of commitment made firm in the law: in the most emphatic way, the husband and wife have foregone their freedom to quit this relation, to each other and their children, as it suits their convenience. Nothing in this universe could be more distinctly human. And no account of Nature without this imprint of the things most distinctly human could be a true account.

5. The Book of Life

ROBERT ROYAL

A goodly portion of the history of Catholicism in the last forty years is a history of ignorance. Not ignorance stemming from dogmatism, as many outsiders think, but an ignorance of basic human things. Women who faithfully observed the Virgin's feast days years ago may have been unaware of much of the Bible or Church history, but they lived a true devotion. The men who fasted (or did not) from midnight to Communion on Sundays knew no ascetic theology, but they knew asceticism. When these Catholic practices were reduced or eliminated in the belief that they were old-fashioned or too difficult in modern circumstances, it did not make Catholicism more attractive. It made faith much less a part of life.

Nearly 250 cardinals, bishops, and invited guests met in Rome at the World Synod of Bishops on the Bible. Their mission, quite an urgent one, is to find ways to make knowledge of the Bible more widespread among Catholics and modern societies in general. As Chicago's Cardinal Francis George said, even formerly well-known Biblical figures like Moses or Job or Jonah (or Jesus?) are no longer the cultural backdrop for most people. Without an awareness of the basic shape of salvation history, how can people understand the meaning of faith?

Unless we have a general picture of God creating the world, of that world as going terribly wrong after we came on the scene, of the people of Israel as the special bearers of God's promise, of Christ as the Redeemer, and of the Church as the continuing vehicle for the graces that free us from sin and death, what could possibly motivate someone to get up on Sunday for Mass rather than brunch or the golf course? Something like two-thirds of Catholics in America—an even higher percentage in Europe—seem to believe that there is nothing of such urgency to be found there.

The Synod on the Bible is clearly part of Pope Benedict's larger aims at renewal, which include the liturgy, instruction in basics such as the theological virtues (he's already done two in encyclicals), and confronting our skeptical culture head-on with some very deft ideas. Several of the Synod bishops have also recommended better-focused homilies that stick to Biblical themes. All these are good suggestions. But absent real-life practices, it's hard to say what exactly Bible study will do.

We had some experience of that in the Reformation. One historian has discovered that within a century of Luther's appearance, there were 243 different interpretations of the Eucharist. Sects arose with multiple wives. Some believed the Bible forbade all government, others that kings held power by divine right. The Jesuits who were founded and worked effectively to counteract these centrifugal Protestant influences did not proceed so much by Bible lessons as by word and example.

One of the dangers in talk about Bible study is that we risk turning the Scriptures into just another book at a time when books of all kinds—literature, philosophy, history—have a smaller and smaller influence on the world. A Protestant group is about to publish a Bible that tries to be relevant by using news photos, among them the Rev. Martin Luther King, Jr. and Angelina Jolie (let's hope these are going to be images of justice and of the cult of celebrity). But even more sober approaches have to deal with the sheer fact that a text will have a hard time cutting through technological static. Some have proposed multimedia and other high-tech presentations of Scripture. But without proper preparation, the Bible then becomes just one more text message—good seed spread on poor ground.

Benedict, of course, is quite aware of this and said in his opening address to the gathering: "Exegesis, the true reading of Holy Scripture, is not only a literary phenomenon, not only reading a text. It is the movement of my existence. It is moving towards the Word of God in the human words. Only by conforming ourselves to the Mystery of God, to the Lord who is the Word, can we enter within the Word, can we truly find the Word of God in human words."

This gets to the heart of the matter. Yet how to get people not merely to recognize but to live this profound truth is another thing entirely. No one can do everything at once, and the participants in the Synod have made some quite astute proposals. But Catholics, with our belief in tradition and a life in communion with the Church correlated with the sacred texts, need to find an embodiment of Scripture in daily practices. Our whole tradition used to recognize that the vast majority of people do not have the gifts to be philosophers, or theologians, or Scripture scholars, but can lead rich, even saintly lives with basic instruction nonetheless.

Everyone who cares about the Catholic Church has a list of pet peeves about things that have gone wrong in the forty years since the Second Vatican Council. But somewhere near the top of the list has to be the notion that a superficial understanding of sacred things is an advance over longstanding practices that directly confront the evils we find in ourselves and in a fallen world. On the very first page of *The Imitation of Christ*, Thomas à Kempis writes: "I would rather feel compunction than know how to define it. For what would it profit us to know the whole Bible by heart and the principles of all the philosophers if we live without grace and the love of God?" That's the old Catholic wisdom, and it would be good if we listened to—and figured out how to follow it—again.

6. One God: No More, No Less

MICHAEL BARUZZINI

An ancient Chinese myth tells of ten Suns that existed in primordial times. Prideful and intemperate, as pagan gods are often wont to be, these Suns rode together over the surface of the Earth each day, their combined heat scorching it. Insensitive to the plight of the mortals, the Suns refused to take turns in the sky, and were eventually struck down until only one Sun remained.

I was reminded of this story when I read yet again another example of an atheist inviting religious believers to go "one god more" when critically evaluating their beliefs. For instance, here is noted skeptic Michael Shermer: "Ten thousand different religions, a thousand different gods. Our opponents agree with us that 999 of those gods are false gods. They are atheists like we are atheists. What I'm asking you to do is just go one God further with us."

This cannot be dignified with the label "argument." But as a clever rhetorical trick, it does deserve a response. It fails as an argument because it just does not follow that if nine propositions are false, a tenth, superficially similar one must also be false.

Back to the Chinese myth: if I were to claim that a new sun rose on each day of the week, but you demonstrated to me that the "Monday Sun" was the same as the "Tuesday Sun," and so on with the Suns on Wednesday, Thursday, and Friday, it would be an error to just "go one Sun further" and conclude that there was in fact *no* Sun at all.

We might also find an analogy in the history of science itself: no one believes in rudimentary, primitive accounts of physical motion anymore, because ever since Newton we have known that the laws of motion are universal—the Heavens are governed by the same physical laws as the Earth. That is, there are not different sets of laws of motion on Earth, in the solar system, in the stars, and so on. Yet we do not therefore conclude that there are therefore no sets of laws; instead, we look for a single, deeper account of what were once thought of as separated phenomena.

This is the correct answer to Shermer's suggestion. The Christian God is not the last hanger-on of a long line of fading divinities. He is the refinement of a previously vague and inchoate experience of the supernatural.

That reality has some supernatural aspect has been universally apparent to mankind, but the understanding of that dimension (just as with the understanding of the natural world) has usually been scattered, imprecise, unrigorous, and idiosyncratic.

With God's revelation of himself, however, as a singular, absolute God—first to the Jews and then in the person of Christ—the wild pantheon to which humanity has always been attracted is revealed to be under the domain of a single, absolute, yet loving Father.

Mythology has almost universally preserved a dim notion of this single Father God behind all, and the philosophers have been able to come to the same conclusion through the application of reason. The examination of reality and of knowledge leads to the conclusion that there is one Absolute Principle behind it all, and that this Absolute does not so much "exist" as rather encompass *existence itself* in some way—and "this all men call God."

This philosophical God, of course, remained distant and unreachable. It was in the Jewish and the Christian revelation of "I AM" that this mythical and intellectual notion of the "One God" Who was the God of gods, became recognized as real and as a Father with whom man can have a relationship. It is this more robust notion of God that conquered the ancient pagan world.

Thus, Shermer is right about one thing: the gods are gone because there has been a certain disenchantment that has occurred as our description of nature has been tested and refined. But the very reason that Shermer is right is also the reason he is wrong. This understanding of a universally ordered, rationally accessible nature developed because of, not despite, monotheism.

When the world was seen as an intentional Creation of God it was understood that Reason could be applied to it in order to figure things out—precisely because the world depends on a Reasonable Creator. The many gods have not vanished solely in the light of science. They have, more importantly, vanished in the light of one greater God.

Reasoned investigation and revelation together cast light on the mysterious workings of the reality in which we find ourselves. Shermer believes in the light of Reason, because he correctly judges that that light has dissipated many shadows. When he asks us to go "one God further," however, he is asking us to put out the ultimate source of the very light by which he sees.

Ten Suns is surely too many, but if the last Sun sets, all that is left is darkness.

7. Understanding First Philosophy

FRANCIS BECKWITH

William E. Carroll has remarked in these pages: "It's literally impossible to argue philosophically (about substance, accident, matter, body, change, etc.) with someone who refuses to accept the first principles of philosophy, or who reduces all first principles to the natural sciences." He is referring to thinkers like Richard Dawkins who maintain that rationality is equivalent to the deliverances of the natural sciences.

In this way, what was traditionally known as "first philosophy" cannot be a rational enterprise until its claims can be verified by the natural sciences. This, of course, is not possible, since first philosophy involves the first principles of thought and being, and thus any first principle that depends on a more fundamental truth or reality would not be a first principle. For this very reason, some philosophers, including some Christian philosophers, have abandoned first philosophy, choosing to model their intellectual projects after the natural sciences.

It is, undeniably, an attractive move, since the natural sciences have been so successful. But is that really a good reason to abandon first philosophy? After all, free markets have been incredibly successful in producing unparalleled prosperity in the developed world. Does that mean that we should extend its understandings of "goods" to account for the good of family life? If parents begin to think of their children as commodities whose value is determined by the free market, is that more rational than our immediate belief that our offspring, by virtue of being human persons, are intrinsically valuable beings of immeasurable worth?

But the critics of first philosophy are worse off than the free market reductionists. For first philosophy is literally undeniable. First, when a critic like Dawkins distinguishes rational enterprises (i.e., the natural sciences) from non-rational enterprises (i.e., religion), he grounds his judgment in what he believes are the necessary and sufficient conditions of what constitutes a rational enterprise. But that judgment is no more a deliverance of the natural sciences than the judgment that "hip hop is not poetry" is a deliverance of either hip hop or poetry. It is an exercise in philosophical reasoning about first principles of rational thought. It is first philosophy.

Second, critics often issue normative judgments that depend on the reasoning of first philosophy. Take, for example, Dawkins' criticism of the career path of paleontologist Kurt Wise. In *The God Delusion*, Dawkins laments that even after earning a bachelor's degree at the University of Chicago and a Ph.D. under the renowned Harvard paleontologist Stephen Jay Gould, Wise did not abandon his belief in young-earth creationism, the view that the first chapters of Genesis should be interpreted literally and that the Bible teaches that the earth is less than 10,000 years old.

Although I share Dawkins' puzzlement with Wise's tenacity, there is something strangely, and delightfully, non-scientific about Dawkins' lament. He writes: "I find that terribly sad . . . the Kurt Wise story is just plain pathetic—pathetic and contemptible. The wound, to his career and his life's happiness, was self-inflicted, so unnecessary, so easy to escape. . . . I am hostile to religion because of what it did to Kurt Wise. And if it did that to a Harvard educated geologist, just think what it can do to others less gifted and less well armed."

This is an odd lament for someone of Dawkins' philosophical leanings, for he denies that nature, which presumably includes Wise, has within it any intrinsic purposes from which we may draw conclusions about our moral obligations to not frustrate those ends. Dawkins claims that Darwin has shown us that natural teleology of any sort, including intrinsic purpose, is an illusion, and thus maintains that belief in teleology is "childish." (This, by the way, is rhetorical bluster of the worst sort, since as virtually anyone who has studied the subject knows, Darwinism may count against some versions of design but not all, as Ed Feser, Etienne Gilson, and my former professor, James Sadowsky, S.J., have convincingly argued.)

In order to issue his judgment, Dawkins must know something about the nature of the sort of creature Wise is and the obligations that such a creature has to his natural powers and their proper function. But since Dawkins cannot discover the human being's intrinsic purposes or our obligations to them by the methods and means of the natural sciences, he opines—when he is not lamenting another person's life choices—that these purposes and obligations must be illusory and to believe in them childish. Yet Dawkins' brief against Wise depends on these "childish" illusions.

The key to escaping such counter-intuitive dead ends is to abandon the failed project that the methods of the natural sciences are the model of rationality for all human endeavors. But don't just take my word for it. Just observe how Richard Dawkins does not practice what he preaches

8. The End of the Science/Religion War?

JOHN O'CALLAGHAN

When I was a physics major in college, my father happened to be a professor of Medieval Philosophy at the same institution. One day, after lecturing on Dante and the Music of the Spheres, he happened across my physics professor, Jim Lang: "Jim, can you hear the music of the spheres?" Lang: "Hear it? Hear it? Bill, I can't turn the damn stuff off!" That ought to be our attitude toward the ways in which the invisible things of God are made visible by the things of creation, which I think is the crux of the question, "Are we beyond the conflict between science and faith?"

The question seems factual, almost a kind of sociological investigation—is it or is it not the case that most of a certain group of what?—intellectuals?, citizens?, common persons on the street?, religious believers? scientists? are beyond the conflict between science and faith? But I am a philosopher, a believing and practicing Roman Catholic. I am not concerned primarily about that sociological question. My focus is and ought to be the tacit normative claim. Ought we to be beyond that conflict? The answer, of course, is yes.

Science provides us with an insight into the workings of

natural causality. Faith provides us with an insight into the workings of divine causality. A favorite tactic of people of faith and scientists alike to eliminate apparent conflicts between faith and science is an epistemological solution—science knows facts and truth, faith involves feeling and a kind of emotional response to the transcendent, where the transcendent is understood to be noumenal, beyond the realm of fact and truth. That solution is nonsense. It misunderstands both Catholic faith and natural science. Scientists often experience a kind of awe and wonder at the intelligibility of what they study, an intelligible reality that transcends them. And Catholics make claims of fact when they speak of God, claims that exclude their contradictory opposites as false. The divine transcends the natural; it does not transcend the factual and the true.

This epistemological armistice won't do. There can be no conflict between faith and science because of the factual truth claims about God that Christians ought to make, animated by faith. God is not a natural cause, and thus should not be understood within the context of natural sciences that study natural causes. In other words, the knowledge of God gained through philosophically informed faith ought not to be understood to be a kind of scientific hypothesis in competition with other scientific theories about the mundane workings of the natural world. This approach suggests that when naturalistic science fails we appeal to the God hypothesis as if to the God particle in cosmology, and when it succeeds we exclude God. But Catholic Christians ought to recognize God in the *success* of science, not its failure.

To see this one must adhere to and try to understand the Christian doctrine of creation *ex nihilo*. God is not a kind of natural cause, only a really really powerful one, perhaps an omnipotent natural cause, able in his power to do what we cannot, and yet doing it in pretty much the way we do it, interacting with an already existing world. If God truly created the world and its causes from nothing, then it is nonsense to suggest that God interacts with natural causes as we do. It is a kind of anthropomorphism for religious believers to see God as needing to intervene in nature to achieve his purposes, undermining the autonomy of natural causes, as if creating and sustaining all things in being from nothing isn't enough for God to do.

But it is equally anthropomorphic for other religious believers trying to uphold the autonomy of nature to say that God created it all and then left it to work itself out. Both views regard God as if he is a natural cause, only different from all the rest of the natural causes. Natural causes operate on presupposed material. But there is nothing presupposed that God acts upon in creation—that's why creation is *ex nihilo*, a doctrine that as a matter of history was a hard won victory of Christian orthodoxy over ancient Gnosticism and paganism. The gods of the pagans were always intervening and messing about with the world of nature and human beings, and the Gnostics broadly believed that the divine principle of light was always interacting with an uncreated material principle that it was not responsible for and that was presupposed to its action. Sometimes Gnostics included a divine demiurge who does what he can with the matter at hand, but whose action is also limited by it.

Those who think there is a conflict between faith and science, whether scientist or believer, have in effect regressed intellectually to a pagan, indeed Gnostic view of the world and God. But for Christians, God creates and sustains from nothing natural causes, and thus does not engage or interact with them as they do with each other. He is not an interacting cause, but an enabling cause.

There ought not to be a conflict between faith and science. If there is such a conflict it is only because religious believers and scientists alike do not consider well enough the nature of God, the nature of natural causes, the nature of faith, and the nature of science. The remedy for that sociological fact is the extraordinary gift that only religious institutions like Our Lady's University can give to the world, a setting for an education that pursues, indeed requires, greater understanding of all these things in peace. Only such an education informed by scientific knowledge and faith can teach us to hear that lovely music that moves the sun and other stars.

9. The First Freedom and the First Right

AUSTIN RUSE

The government of France has fined the Church of Scientology almost a million dollars for the regular practice of their "religion," which France says is not a religion at all but a criminal fraud. The government of France is very close to outlawing Scientology altogether.

The Organization of the Islamic Conference once more is intending to advance its now annual U.N. resolution calling for a ban on the "defamation of religion." It used to be a ban only on the defamation of Islam, but was expanded to include other religions in order to gather more support, which it has annually received in the U.N. General Assembly.

Every day there are reports of people being discriminated against for their religious beliefs. Churches are burned. People are murdered or imprisoned for their faith. It is illegal to convert from Islam in many countries, under penalty of death. A young American woman converted to Christianity here in the United States and she has had to ask the courts to protect her from her family.

In its annual report a few years ago, Freedom House—one of the premiere monitors of human rights worldwide—showed that you could walk from the western coast of Africa all the way to the east coast of China and never once set foot in a country that practices religious freedom. Religious freedom is in a deplorable state worldwide.

This situation is not just one problem among many. Man has an obligation under natural law to seek the truth and because of this he has a human right to seek that truth, as almost all people in every age have done, in the religious context. Freedom of religion is therefore the first freedom. It is arguably far more important than political self-determination, freedom of the press, or any other freedom.

That freedom also matters to notions of rights. In the field of humanitarian and human rights work, there are many vineyards.

Some work to feed the poor, aid the sick and dying. Others work on freeing prisoners held unjustly. Others work on issues of democracy, voting rights, governmental transparency. And others work on freedom of religion. People from all across the political spectrum are engaged in one or more of these issues and good for them. All of these questions fit neatly and perfectly into the category of basic human rights and the people who work to defend those rights are honored and applauded—and rightly so.

But what is missing in the usual understanding of human rights, both right and left, is that there is one right that is higher and more fundamental than all the rest. It is one that does not bring honor and praise and profiles in the *New York Times*. It is the right that eclipses them all: the right to life.

A few days ago a very good man from a prestigious Washington think-tank said that in the field of human rights there ought to be an organization comprised only of democracies that uphold human rights. Such an organization would exclude those countries that do not. Of course, he is thinking of the right to vote, to assemble, to worship, and all the generally recognized categories that the United States upholds and that Muslim states violate.

Think about this, though. The human-rights-loving Western countries account for the deliberate killing of millions of children annually. The United States alone accounts for the deliberate killing of 1.2 million children a year. According to the Alan Guttmacher Institute, America has the highest abortion rate in the Western world. Some will counter that these people are not killed under orders or direction from governments. True enough. They are private killings. But they are private killings that are protected by governments. The governments have said not only will we not protect these children; we will protect your right to kill them.

Which is the greater violator of human rights, the government that does not allow women to drive, makes them dress in head-to-toe coverings, does not allow them to vote, jails dissenters, controls the press, and all the rest? Or the government that allows and protects the private killing of millions of children?

I am not making excuses for thuggish states that violate the important human rights of religious freedom, political self-determination, and the usual list of basic human rights. What I am saying is there is something wrong in the human rights field—even the parts patrolled by conservatives—that ignores the deliberate killing of human beings and in fact does not even recognize this as a human rights violation.

Where religious freedom is the first freedom, the right to life is the first right. It is higher than all the rest because the right to life gives everyone at least a running and breathing chance at all the other rights and freedom. The dead do not have that opportunity. The dead do not have rights.

10. The Catholic Principle

ROBERT ROYAL

Here's a figure that might make you stop and think: 39 percent of Catholics in a 2002 Boston survey said they would support an American Catholic Church independent of the Vatican.

That was ten years ago, at the height of the priestly sex-abuse scandal, and the *Boston Globe*, which had published hundreds of articles exposing moral turpitude by priests and feckless oversight by bishops, was doing the polling with the obvious intention of getting precisely that answer.

Still, Boston used to be heavily Catholic and people in the area are among the most highly educated Americans. For almost 40 percent of respondents to say that they would be fine with a Church separate from Rome—even at a singularly emotional moment—is no small thing. So far as I know, no one has asked that question again, but I wouldn't be surprised if the results were basically the same now, or that the number was even higher.

We've seen other efforts to measure the beliefs of Catholics that are equally appalling. Mass goers—*Mass goers*, not the nominals—who think the Eucharist is a mere symbol; Catholic school *religion* teachers who don't believe in God; *Catholic* universities who drive more students away from the Church than do secular institutions.

But underlying all that, and of ultimately greater importance than the fact that Catholics are split in their political allegiances, is the fact that many have abandoned or, more likely, never heard of what I would call the "Catholic principle."

All other churches in America pretty much belong to what sociologists have called the "denominational mentality," that for public purposes there's no real difference what any religious group teaches so long as it falls in line with prevailing social mores.

Once you've given in to that, you essentially will stand for nothing anymore because, even within your own church, you're going to have people deciding what they will believe and what they won't. In fact, they will start to make the "right to choose" the central tenet of the faith.

The Catholic principle is quite different. All of us have the freedom of the sons and daughters of God, but we don't get to make up the truth about who God is and what he expects of us. If that's what you want, it's hard to see why you also still want the name Catholic. My suspicion is that, in another generation, the current sentimental attachment to the Church will simply disappear for anyone with the denominational mentality, as it has in much of Europe.

To be a Catholic means accepting the Catholic Thing, so to speak. What is that Thing? No one has put it better than Hilaire Belloc:

> The essential in our judgment [we of the Faith] is that there stands on earth an Individual to be recognized as we recognize human individuals—by the voice, the gesture, the expression. The chain of reason is complete. Is there a God? Yes. Is He personal? Yes. Has He revealed Himself to men? Yes. Has He done so through a corporation—a thing not a theory? Has He created an organism by which He may continue to be known to mankind for the fulfillment of the great drama of the Incarnation.

Yes. Where shall that organism be found? There is only one body on earth which makes such a claim: it is the Catholic Roman Apostolic Church. That claim we of the Faith accept. The consequences of that acceptation are innumerable, satisfactory and complete. We are at home. No one else of the human race is at home.

This is of far greater moment than the division between Catholic liberals and conservatives. The liberal—say Dorothy Day—who gets this one point, is Catholic to the core no matter how far left her politics and economics. The conservative—even the reactionary like Evelyn Waugh—if he sees this truth, has a heart, whether anyone else can detect it or not.

The great danger, as C. S. Lewis' tempter Screwtape clearly sees, is to regard the Faith as real belief plus something else. Then the devil works little by little to make the something else the greater reality to us until it swallows up everything and becomes our whole life.

All this may seem airy abstraction and a mere distraction when so much is at stake in electoral campaigns. A few thousand votes one way or another may consign millions more unborn children to destruction—or rescue them; which party controls our government may determine whether the Catholic Church is free to be Catholic in this country or will be forced into a ghetto; which economic policies are in place can put tens of millions back to work, or into the streets, as in Greece, protesting unavoidable austerity measures.

A culture of life is inextricably connected to the Catholic Principle, because God is the Lord of Life. All real Catholics know that is not merely an "issue" among a list of others in public debate. It puts a question to us about whether we are Catholic.

Give me the right to life and religious liberty. And I'll be happy to wrestle over the rest with anyone, Catholic or not.

But if Catholics themselves lose a grip on the Catholic Principle, or allow others to take it away from them, it won't take long before we have a different Church. And we'll have a different America as well.

II. Catholica

1. Preparing to Pray

MICHAEL NOVAK

I am not very good at prayer, although I try to be praying all the time, like breathing. (In fact, I have at times asked God—when I am too ill or too tired to think in words—to take my breathing as a prayer.) It is an inner conversation, wordless often, marked just by attentiveness. Every detail of every event is speaking. It comes forth from the creative insight of God.

When I want to ready myself to think about God, I place myself quietly and humbly in His presence. I try to shut out other thoughts, and then quietly think about the most beautiful and ennobling and stunning things I have seen in life—all my favorite things. There are two views in the Alps—in Grindelwald and in Bressanone—that I have especially loved. The peacefulness of an ocean on a quiet day, the blue water barely rippling, never fails to move my heart. And the sunsets—in Iowa, in Wyoming, on the seacoast of Delaware—and that most peculiar green sunset on the plain above Mexico City where the sun drops over the edge of the plain before it disappears behind the earth, so that the light during that interval is eerie and prolonged and unforgettable.

I think then of favorite music of mine, Mozart, Bach, Haydn, Vivaldi, Dvorak's *Stabat Mater*, the most beautiful of all, written after the sudden death of his much loved daughter. I think of favorite paintings from the Pitti and the Uffizi, and the convent walls painted by Fra Angelico. And sculptors. And poets. And philosophers and other writers whose work has thrilled me. (One of my most unforgettable moments as a young man was reading Maritain's *Creative Intuition in Art and Poetry*; it was so beautiful I had to get up and take a long walk down to the lake, almost speechless in silent wonder.) For several years, every Easter I have read one of Dostoevsky's long novels, followed in later years by *War and Peace* and *Anna Karenina*. I think of God as the Creator of all these great minds and artists. I wonder how much greater than they are God's own mind and sense of beauty. I would love to share in contemplation of such works and such persons for all eternity. And all the more so in His beauty.

Then I think of the loves I have known. Close friends, childhood buddies, grandparents, uncles and aunts and cousins, my three brothers and one sister, my dear parents—and then Karen, whose name means what she is, *Clara*, the clear light of my life—and our solid, noble, and strong children and grandchildren. All these loves make me think that God's love is more than the sum of these, of a different order entirely, and yet the source of all of them. "Where there is *caritas* and *amor*," the old hymn goes, "there God is." That is my favorite hymn.

Jesus asks us not only to be just to our enemies, not only to be merciful, not only to forgive. He asks us to resist evil, yes, and to be like steel against unjust aggressors—to defeat them thoroughly—but also, in the end, to be able to see that even our enemies are also children of the one Creator. When all the evil has been drained out of their aggression, we need to be ready to welcome them back into the human community.

The United States and our allies did this rather nicely, I have always thought, in regard to Germany and Japan after World War II. If there is ever to be even a simulacrum of a brotherly world—all right, at least a relatively tranquil world—even one based upon fear of greater power, reaching out in tests of amity and voluntary cooperation is a necessity of human life in our time. Here is one point at which I think Christianity has led the way. It once united all Europe in a common civilization. It has suffused the secular humanism of compassion and solidarity and individual freedom. It is helping to shape one global civilization, with respect for individual liberty, as well as for human solidarity.

If I had to pick out one human experience that for me seems most god-like—the best, the highest that I know—I would choose the experience of choosing to love Karen, and to be loved by her in return. Second would come acts of insight—those little bursts of fire that come when we are puzzling things through. In many ways, these two experiences are related, but saying how that is so would delay us too long right here. Suffice it to say that those are my choices for the best in life—the achievement of mutual love, and the firing off of insight after insight in pursuit of understanding. That *eros* of understanding is almost as powerful (in some ways more so) than the *eros* of love; yet the latter is primary, and is profoundly influential upon understanding. Understanding keeps love from erring badly, but in the dark, love often leads the way for understanding.

2. Saints, Columns of Light

FR. JOHN JAY HUGHES

Saints have long been a favorite subject of Joseph Ratzinger, now Pope Benedict XVI. At a requiem Mass for the then recently deceased Pope John Paul I, Cardinal Ratzinger said: "The saints are the columns of light who show us the way, transforming it into the path of salvation while we pass through the darkness of earth." In 1985 he told an interviewer: "The only really effective case for Christianity comes down to two arguments, namely, the saints the Church has produced, and the art which has grown in her womb." And as pope he told the Roman curia in December 2007: "Each saint who enters into history represents a small portion of Christ's return, a renewal of His entrance into time, showing us His image in a new light and assuring us of His presence."

"How many saints are there?" I get that question often. "God alone knows," I respond. "That's why we celebrate All Saints' Day." Its popularity reflects the awareness of the People of God that those officially declared saints are only the tip of the iceberg—or as they say in Africa, the ears of the hippopotamus.

I have been researching the lives of the saints for a series of talks soon to be available as a recorded book. Such reading is wonderfully uplifting, and deeply moving. Because my mother died when I was only six, the unseen spiritual world—the world of God, the angels, the saints, and of our beloved dead—has always been real to me. I know people who are there: my dear mother first, and now so many other loved ones. Reading about the saints, and writing their stories, deepened my knowledge of that unseen but real world, and of the people in it.

If the saints have one thing in common, it is simply this: they were all, in their own way, in love with God. That is what the Lord wants for every one of us. Is that possible? Is it even realistic? It would be neither, but for one thing. The One Who calls each one of us to love Him with heart, soul, and mind, is already in love with us—passionately, madly, with a totality and intensity that makes the greatest human love seem in comparison like a child's infatuation.

The saints are not remote figures in some stained-glass window. They are real people of flesh and blood. They are our sisters and brothers in the great family of God, into which we were born in Baptism. That is why we pray to them: not as we pray to God, of course, but asking them to pray for us. What could be more natural, what more fitting? God never intended us to be lone rangers. He wants us to support each other. One way we do that is by praying for one another. Priests receive such requests for prayer all the time. "Father, please pray for my little granddaughter," a parishioner said to me only last Sunday. "She is having a difficult operation to preserve her failing eyesight. If it fails, there is nothing more they can do."

If it is right, and natural, to ask our friends here on earth to pray for us, how much more fitting to ask the prayers of our heavenly friends, the saints? Being close to God, their prayers are especially powerful.

When we walk through dark valleys, and clouds seem to shut out the sunshine of God's love, the saints walk with us. When we rejoice at some answered prayer, some great achievement, some unexpected blessing, the saints rejoice with us. When we stumble and fall, and think we can't get up again, because we've been down so often before, the saints are praying for us—starting with Peter, who understands because of his own humiliating fall. When we come to walk the last stretch of life's road, which each of us must walk alone, we'll find that we are not alone. The saints will be with us, starting with Mary, the Mother of the Lord, to whom we have so often addressed the request: "Pray for us sinners, now and at the hour of our death."

Hebrews 11 contains sketches of the Old Testament saints: Abraham, who at God's call, left his homeland and all security and went forth "not knowing where he was going"—but trusting that God knew; Moses, "who endured as seeing him who is invisible"—and many others besides. The opening verses of the following chapter (12) portray these heroes of faith as spectators in an arena, cheering on us who are running the race for which we were entered at baptism, and which they have already completed. The words thrilled me when I first discovered them as a young teenager. They thrill me still.

"Therefore, since we are surrounded by so great a cloud of witnesses, let us also lay aside every weight, and the sin which clings so closely, and let us run with perseverance the race that is set before us, looking to Jesus the pioneer and perfecter of our faith, who for the joy that was set before him endured the cross, despising the shame, and is seated at the right hand of the throne of God." (RSV)

3. The Immaculate Conception

JAMES V. SCHALL, S.J.

Catholicism is an adventuresome religion, not designed for dullards, sissies, or the faint-hearted. Actually, it is not a "religion" at all. Religion is about what obliges men to God insofar as they can figure it out with their reason. Religion is a form of "justice." It differs from justice because we cannot figure out exactly what we "owe" to God.

God does not "need" anything from us. Imagine a "god" that needs us to give it something! Yet the best things are beyond "owing." No one who is given something is complete without acknowledging the gift. We human beings are even given what we are. Our very being is a gift to us. Indeed, we are gifts to one another.

Revelation is what God has informed us about Himself. The only way we know how to relate to God is if God Himself informs us. "I am the way, the truth, and the life." Catholicism is based on a fact. God did inform us about Himself and about ourselves. We do not deal with a human invention, but a divine intervention.

Only when the event of the Incarnation happened can we further try to figure out what it means. And we do try. Faith does seek reason, a reason that is actively reasoning. The doctrine of the Immaculate Conception of Mary, officially defined by Pius IX on December 8, 1854, is part of this seeking understanding.

Pope Mastai-Ferretti wrote 155 years ago that Mary was preserved from original sin through the "merits" of her Son, "Jesus Christ, the Savior of the Human Race." Once we understand what the Incarnation is, this teaching about Mary's beginning makes perfectly good sense. But I doubt if Joachim, at the birth of his daughter, Mary, said to his wife, Anna: "Look, dear, she is without original sin!" Yet one suspects that, from the beginning, both parents knew that something hovered about this child of theirs.

Theology is what we can figure out using our minds about what is revealed. God informed us, as it were, that He was not a mother, but that He had a mother. At first sight, these affirmations will sound confusing if not preposterous. But we are given information that we might think about it. Usually, if we are persistent, we come up with something worthwhile knowing for the good of our very being.

The Church did not first speculate about Mary and then turn

to figure out who this Son of hers was. It began with the Son and worked its intellectual way backward to what His mother was and is. "Hail, Mary, full of grace." Hints about her were found along the way.

In the readings for the Mass of the Immaculate Conception, we find these hints. We recall Eve and the Fall, the promise of redemption. To the Ephesians, Paul says: "Before the world was made, He chose us, chose us in Christ."

In the Gospel, Mary is told "not to be afraid." And she isn't. She has "found favor"; she will "bear a Son who will be called the Son of the Most High." At this point, she tells the angel to hold up. "How can this be?" Gabriel explains. This young woman wants the facts.

Once she understands, Mary replies: "Let it be done to me according to your word." And so it is. Even though she lived in an obscure town, the whole future of the world depended on her response. Whether acknowledged or not, the very being of the human race depended on the response of this young woman. The Incarnation of the Son of God had to come from within our kind. It depended on the free response of this Mary. No wonder she herself was, as they came to say, conceived without original sin.

In the Breviary for the Immaculate Conception, the second reading is from Saint Anselm, the great English bishop: "Blessed Lady, sky and stars, earth and rivers, day and night—everything that is subject to the power or use of man—rejoice that through you they are in some sense restored to their lost beauty and are endowed with inexpressible new grace."

We still find those who maintain that Catholics "worship" Mary and that Trinity means three gods. But we speak precisely. We do not worship Mary. We do not have three gods. Mary is the Mother of God. Her Son is the Word, the Second Person of the Trinity.

The Word, we affirm, was made "flesh" and dwelt amongst us. This is where we find Mary at Christ's birth. When found at Nazareth in the house of Joseph, Gabriel no doubt knew of her own "beginning."

"Blessed Lady," we rejoice that the "lost beauty of things" is restored "through you."

4. Faith's Greatest Threat

WILLIAM E. CARROLL

The secular and materialist understanding of nature and human nature seem to be everywhere and they have come to inform what has been called "a new post-Christian narrative of life." Witness the appearance over the past several years of a strident "new atheism," a kind of "evangelical atheism," evident in the popular books of scientists and philosophers like Richard Dawkins, Daniel Dennett, and Christopher Hitchens. This new atheism claims to be purely rational; it is quite often a kind of scientific idolatry that sees the natural sciences as completely sufficient to explain all that needs to be explained.

But contrary to what appear to many to be the current fundamental challenges to faith, the greatest threat to faith is not unbelief, the "new atheism" (or the older varieties, for that matter), the simplistic philosophical judgment that the world needs no explanation beyond itself and that, as Stephen Hawking once famously remarked, "there is nothing for a creator to do." Rather, the greatest challenge to faith comes from a view often used to defend faith: the view that radically separates and opposes faith and reason and which, at times, maintains that belief is a matter of the heart and not the mind.

In the face of what appear to be challenges from reason and science, believers often retreat to a spiritual citadel, insulate themselves from such challenges, and embrace a kind of "blind faith" that appeals only to the authority of the Bible. We see such appeals in the debates about the great social issues, from abortion and human embryonic stem cell research to same sex marriage. But the wider relationship between faith and reason concerns every element of Christian thought and practice: from the doctrines of the Trinity and the Incarnation to the sacraments and biblical interpretation. The failure to see the essential role of reason in what we believe is one of the great threats to the faith. It is also a threat that is not new.

In the eleventh century, St. Anselm summarized the importance of the fruitful relationship between faith and reason in a famous phrase: *fides quaerens intellectum*—faith seeking understanding. Two centuries later, St. Thomas Aquinas often noted that faith perfects reason. God is the author of all truth, the truth that faith reveals and the truth that reason discovers. Not only is there no contradiction between these paths to truth. When each is properly navigated, there is a proper unity between them. Faith is a divine gift to a human being and a human being is an animal capable of reason.

Faith informs the human mind and will; it does not negate them. Rather it perfects both, by providing new knowledge and helping to orient the human will to virtue. Reason allows us to probe ever more deeply into what is believed, but even the initial act of believing requires the human intellect. Catholics believe, for instance, that the consecrated bread and wine have become the body and blood of Christ, that there is a new reality present. Reason cannot prove it, but through the doctrine of transubstantiation reason helps to make clear what is believed. Christian doctrines are examples of reason in the service of faith.

Mistrust of reason as the sole guide to truth in ethical matters has often meant that ethics has been reduced to religious belief and belief has been identified with mere opinion. Take abortion. When human life begins is not a matter of faith. That it is immoral intentionally to kill an innocent human being is not first of all a matter of faith. Faith perfects what we know about the dignity of each and every human life; that each human being is created in the image and likeness of God and, thus, is sacred. But the moral judgments necessary for a just society are first of all based on reason.

Faith enhances these judgments; it does not contradict them. That abortion is immoral is a conclusion of reason; that it is sinful is a conclusion of faith. This distinction between what is moral and just, on the one hand, and what faith requires, on the other, is also essential for coherent discourse about marriage and all forms of social relations. Without the proper cultivation of rea son, claims about right and wrong based exclusively on faith are not only ineffective in public debate, but ultimately lack intelligibility. Of course, the proper cultivation of reason is not an easy task. Ethics is not geometry. The complexities, however, do not justify a retreat to relativism or the reduction of all moral judgments to matters of faith.

To flee from reason (and science) to the seeming safety of faith alone flies in the face of Catholic teaching and, ultimately, eviscerates faith itself. There can be no faith without reason. This does not mean that faith is subordinate to reason, even though faith presupposes reason. The new atheists are the ones who really have a restricted and distorted notion of reason. They think that there can be reason without God, or, even worse, that to embrace reason one must reject God. But faith helps the believer to see the full amplitude of reason: to see how reason, as well as faith, leads us to God.

5. Guadalupe, a Reset

BRAD MINER

Earlier this year, the American Secretary of State visited Latin America. At the basilica in Mexico City she was shown the image of Mary, Our Lady of Guadalupe, miraculously imprinted on the *tilma* (cloak) of a Chichimeca tribesman in 1531. Hillary Rodham Clinton was wearing a red pantsuit, hardly the proper vestment for the season (she should have been in violet), and, as she admired this most important of all Catholic symbols in the Americas, she asked the priest who accompanied her:

"Who painted it?"

Had she been in Turin and seen the Shroud, she might have asked who faxed it. It was a moment similar to the one a few weeks earlier when Mrs. Clinton presented her Russian counterpart with a mock nuclear button on which was supposed to be written in Cyrillic letters the word "reset," but which was actually the Russian word meaning "overcharged." Somewhere in a cubicle at the State Department there's a translator now nicknamed Reset, and standing there in Mexico City Mrs. Clinton must have been wondering if there's maybe *one* protocol officer—just one!—somewhere at Foggy Bottom who might *actually* explain to her what she should say to people in strange places who speak strange languages, because, you know, cultural sensitivity is part of the Secretary of State's job description.

But . . . she probably still wonders who painted it, because she's not the sort of person who would believe the traditional explanation, discussed in detail in the indispensable new book, *Our Lady of Guadalupe: Mother of the Civilization of Love* by Carl Anderson and Fr. Eduardo Chavez, which is that Mary appeared to a convert, Juan Diego Cuauhtlatoatzin (canonized in 2002), filled his *tilma* with flowers, and the pigments of those blossoms miraculously left her image impressed on the cloth. Although the authors make no mention of Mrs. Clinton, it's clear their intention is to present the story of Our Lady in such a way that skeptics might be awed that such wonders really occur on this earth.

The usual, secular treatment of the Patroness of the Americas is to suggest that she is of significance mostly to Mexican Catholics. Anderson and Chavez will have none of that. True enough that the manifestation of the Virgin to the future saint led to the conversion of the Aztecs and millions of other indigenous peoples throughout Mexico, but there is something in the Guadalupe image that points to the future of all the Americas: Central, South, and North. Her face—and this was all but unthinkable because of social prejudices at the time—is *mestiza*. You have to recall that Europeans had come to Mexico little more than a decade before Our Lady appeared to Juan Diego Cuauhtlatoatzin, and the only *mixed-race* people (*mestizos*) weren't even teenagers yet. But in the emerging social hierarchy they were the lowest of the low. In the sixteenth century, Mary sent her meek Aztec to one of the grand Spanish priests (Juan de Zumárraga) with a message of love. Today, renewed interest in her message is on the rise—just as demographers predict we'll all be *mestizos* soon.

As the authors insist, Mary the evangelist transforms a culture from the bottom up. Most nations became Christian (whether Catholic or later Protestant) because their kings converted, but in the Americas it has been the people, citizens poor and rich, who come to Christ, one by one. Catholicism isn't a political movement, even if politicians and activists of one or another stripe have tried to cover themselves with the mantle of Jesus or Mary. I love it that Mr. Anderson and Fr. Chavez include a quip by Diego Rivera, a communist and artist, but a Mexican: "I don't believe in God. . . . But I do believe in the Virgin of Guadalupe."

It's remarkable—and it's why *Our Lady of Guadalupe: Mother of the Civilization of Love* is so important and needed—that more recent appearances of Mary at Lourdes, Fatima, and even the disputed visitations at Medjugorje are so much more well known to Americans than her visit to our own continent. Is it simply that she came so long ago to a hill in a place called Tepeyac rather than to an Iowa cornfield? Certainly it cannot be because the Aztecs needed her, but we in *El Norte* do not.

In any case, her call to conversion is not so much to nations as to individuals. Our Lady doesn't call America to her Son, she calls you and me. Saint Juan Diego saw Mary and spoke to her and overcame his fear to proclaim her message. It was a miracle, but it's a miracle that began before the meeting on Tepeyac and, like the seemingly incorruptible *tilma* still on display at the Basilica of Our Lady of Guadalupe, it remains with us today. The authors write:

> From Canada to Argentina, all of us who live in the Americas are called, like Juan Diego, to bridge the divides of cultures, religion, and factions of any kind, by presenting to all the message of Our Lady . . . the message of the mother of the civilization of love.

We should proclaim in unity: "*Viva Cristo Rey, viva la Virgen de Guadalupe.*"

6. Lourdes, a Simple Theory

BRAD MINER

It's okay to be skeptical about cures at Lourdes.

According to the Church, St. Bernadette's apparitions and the miracles associated with them are private and not a requirement of Catholic belief. Thoroughgoing secularists cannot accept the idea of miracles, of course, but the corollary of that isn't that devout persons must accept every assertion of a miracle as valid.

Still, millions of pilgrims travel to Lourdes each year, and the site has become a place of devotion, despite the fact that very few cures are actually effected: in 150 years, the Church (through the offices of the Lourdes Medical Bureau) has certified just seventy as possibly miraculous (i.e., scientifically inexplicable)—and that's out of seven thousand alleged healings. Is one percent significant? Probably, since the scientific analysis of each confirmed healing is extremely rigorous. Of course skeptics will say the Lourdes experience simply triggers a mysterious *psycho-biological* response that causes some diseases to remit.

A recent French film by Austrian director Jessica Hausner (starring the hardworking Sylvie Testud: ten movies in the last two years!) looks at Lourdes and—surprise, surprise—does so with sardonic skepticism. One reviewer wrote that the movie winks at the "absurdity of miracle hunting [and] . . . ultimately eschews rigorous religious inquiry to study the mechanics of envy and frustrated desire." (Although it won top prize at the Vienna International Film Festival, *Lourdes* appeared so briefly in New York City that it was gone before film buffs such as I had even heard about it.)

These days, you expect ironic bemusement when it comes to Lourdes. It's hard to swallow the spectacle of something such as LourdesMiracleWater.org, which offers a 1.25-ounce bottle of

Authentic Lourdes Spring Water free with every purchase of perfume, crucifixes, meditation stones, and seashells—holy hardware.

But when actress Loretta Young went to Lourdes in 1956, things were different. She didn't go seeking a cure or shouldering a burden of doubt, but to film several episodes of her popular TV show. The result was the earnest tale of Alice Ward (Miss Young), a dying, agnostic, and angry woman who (by chance?) comes to Lourdes. The closest thing to a cure in her case comes towards the end when she quits smoking. She never does drink or bathe in the water, never kneels to pray, and never has a moment in which she discovers faith, although she does find hope, which is actually what most get from visits to Lourdes.

There are actually four shows on the DVD version: in the others Miss Young plays "Sister Ann," head nurse at a Catholic hospital. These sharply written, black-and-white treasures are as good in their way as the more popular episodes of *The Twilight Zone*, except *The Loretta Young Show* has a moral center that isn't fantasy. By the way, these Young shows were sponsored by the Toni Company—after Procter & Gamble pulled sponsorship because the Lourdes story was judged too religious. Fans of AMC's *Mad Men* will love the Toni ads.

Msgr. Robert Hugh Benson (author of *Lord of the World*, a novel often discussed here) wrote a book called *Lourdes* (1908), a chronicle of a summer journey there—one that also began in skepticism. He'd been Catholic for five years (he was the convert son of the Archbishop of Canterbury) when he made his pilgrimage in a "a long-drawn procession—carts and foot passengers, oxen, horses, dogs, and children—drawing nearer every minute toward that ring of solemn blue hills that barred the view to Spain." He was unimpressed with what he saw, until he said Mass in the Crypt, where daily 4000 came to receive Communion. And at the Grotto spring itself he saw the faces of two thousand pilgrims: "white and drawn with pain, or horribly scarred . . . 'waiting for some man to put them into the water.' I saw men and women of all nations and all ranks attending upon them, carrying them tenderly, fanning their faces, wiping their lips, giving them to drink of the Grotto water."

Of the doctors he met at the Medical Bureau:

> I saw again and again sixty or seventy men, dead silent, staring, listening with all their ears, while some poor uneducated man or woman, smiling radiantly, gave a little history or answered the abrupt kindly questions of the presiding doctor.

Benson saw a number of cures he considered genuinely miraculous (many of which he relates) but about which he cautions that no Bureau confirmation had yet been made. And then he asks the key question, one persistent to this day: "If so many are cured, why are not all?" His answer recognizes that in His life Jesus didn't cure every sick person he met, and that even some witnessing those miracles remained unconvinced. Many won't be convinced of the Truth until the last trumpet blows, and even then: "I believe that some of them, when they have recovered from their first astonishment, will make remarks about aural phenomena."

But for the rest of us . . . who have received the gift of faith, in however small a measure, Lourdes is enough. Christ and His Mother are with us. Jesus Christ is the same yesterday, to-day, and forever. Is not that, after all, the simplest theory?

Entia non sunt multiplicanda praeter necessitatem. That's Occam's razor: *entities must not be multiplied beyond necessity.* Simply put: the simplest theory is best.

7. On Foot to Santiago

Matthew Hanley

My first night as a pilgrim—in the Pyrenees after a long journey from California—was sleepless: a fellow pilgrim was snoring. But I could not have been happier. I was about to walk 500 miles across Spain to the tomb of the Apostle Saint James—the most explicitly religious thing I have ever done.

In the middle ages, pilgrims from all over Europe set out for Santiago de Compostela—in *Finnisterre,* literally the end of the then known world. Getting there was an arduous and chancy proposition. It took well over a year for St. Brigid and her husband to get there and back from Sweden in the 1340s. The snoring stranger I started out with had to stop in Pamplona. Hospitals and bridges, churches and towns sprang up along the *Camino de Santiago* to accommodate the stream of pilgrims headed to one of Christendom's premier pilgrimage sites (with Jerusalem and Rome).

The accumulation of individual acts of this precise Christian observance led, according to Goethe, to the formation of Europe itself—not an insignificant observation today when large swaths of the continent have, unlike Spain under Muslim rule, voluntarily abandoned the Catholic faith. Benedict XVI—deeply committed to a revitalized, Christian Europe—plans to visit in November to mark the Jubilee year which occurs whenever the feast of the Apostle St. James (July 25) falls on a Sunday. John Paul II marked the last one by saying: "Spain and the whole of Europe need to recover the awareness of their identity."

I personally set out on foot to Santiago in order to reconnect with my own Catholic identity. A newfound yet keen awareness of my own need for reconciliation attracted me to the penitential dimension of this pilgrimage. In centuries past, some criminals were given the option to walk to Santiago as penance in lieu of their prison sentence (a practice still "officially" on the books in Belgium today). I was equally motivated by the need to express gratitude for blessings too numerous to count, let alone relate here. In short, I wanted tangibly to immerse myself more deeply into the living heritage of the faith.

At Mass in Roncesvalles (just inside Spain, site of the epic 778 battle that gave us *The Song of Roland*), every pilgrim received a special blessing for the long journey that lay ahead. After the first week, I turned up in the medieval town of Estella with a swollen foot. Every parish in town had, until the 1500s, its own pilgrim's hospital. It happened that an elderly local man frequented the *refugio* (shelters available only to pilgrims for a night) to tend to pilgrims' ailments. Here was a simple man whom I would never see again, yet who believed enough in the worth of my own journey to provide the most precious of commodities for any weary pilgrim: succor and sincere hospitality.

During *siesta* in one already sleepy town, a grandmother who lived next door to the town's gem—a twelfth-century octagonal church—graciously let me in. By the time I had crossed the plains of Castille, I had fallen in love with the simplicity and intimacy of Romanesque architecture—of which I had previously been ignorant. Yet I was simply blown away by the beauty of Leon's Gothic cathedral (even more than that of Burgos, where El Cid is buried), with its expansive stained-glass windows.

Years later, I picked up (non-Catholic) James Michener's 1968 book *Iberia*, and found that he shared that admiration:

> I have seen most of the fine sights of the world. . . . but so far as sheer visual pleasure is concerned, I have seen nothing to excel Leon's cathedral at three in the morning, lit from within, and I say this as a man who likes neither stain glassed windows nor Gothic.

Leon's Romanesque basilica of San Isidro is only a few blocks away. Consecrated in 1063, it contains magnificently preserved frescoes—the "Sistine Chapels of Spanish Romanesque art." Such is the *riqueza* of the Camino.

Another highlight was arriving in the charming Galician town of O Cebreiro—with its ninth-century pre-Romanesque church and Celtic straw-roof dwellings—after walking for hours through dense fog and driving wind. The day's chill was more than offset around the table that evening by a roaring fire, the house's wine, and the company of fellow pilgrims who were by now to be counted as friends.

Upon entering Santiago's cathedral, the pilgrim passes through the *Portico de la* Gloria—the masterpiece of Spanish Romanesque art (completed in 1188)—and encounters a marvelously depicted, smiling Saint James. The impact of such a welcome is hard to describe. I placed my hand in the marble column precisely where the hands of so many other pilgrims over the centuries had left a visibly indented handprint, in gratitude for a safe arrival.

But I did not want it to end. St. Francis had to walk back to Assisi in 1214, I thought wistfully; I was to get on a bus.

Of course, life itself is a pilgrimage. But leading daily life with the spirit of a pilgrim can be more difficult at times than the particular hardships of being on an actual pilgrimage. Pursuing our ultimate destination with perseverance and trust is no small feat when life's pressures are bearing down.

The fact is that the structured yet adventurous act of pilgrimage—walking and praying away from the clutter—focused and freed my easily distracted mind in a way that is unusual, almost singular.

Yet every liturgy reminds me that ours is truly a *pilgrim* Church on earth. Despite my frequent stumbles, that never fails to stir hope.

8. Mythical Thinking

BEVIL BRAMWELL, OMI

Even before the time of Christ, there were philosophers who criticized the thinking going on around them as mythical. By this, they meant that such thought had no reference to reality. It had its own kind of universe that satisfied certain people, allowed them to express their emotions sufficiently, and gave them a sense of power. This phenomenon applied particularly to religious myths, but it was also related to myths about the world in general because the two areas of meaning are tightly interrelated. Some philosophers such as Socrates were even killed because they pointed out problems with mythical thinking.

Yet these myths wove themselves into the fabric of millions of people's lives. It was from them that many people drew meaning: kill this bull; pour oil on that pillar; give a gift at this temple. These actions were a way of participating in the political-religious world of the time. They drew their power from the numbers who believed despite their lack of connection with reality. At the time of Jesus, the Church realized that the critical philosophers were on to something important. In Joseph Ratzinger's words: "The early Church resolutely put aside the whole cosmos of the ancient religions, regarding the whole of it as deceit and illusion." (*Introduction to Christianity*)

A millennium or so later, we come upon another example of mythical thinking, and there are thousands! Consider the widespread medical procedure known as "'bleeding," for example. Over several hundred years in the west, people thought they knew that it was a necessary part of medical treatment to bleed the patient, even though it is now clear that it has no positive effects at all (George Washington likely died from the aggressive use of this misguided therapy). But the myth gave people the illusion of doing something to help the sick. Mythical thinking seems to be a constant feature of human history and it carries a deeply antihuman element within it.

Recently we had—I will not say celebrated—the fiftieth anniversary of the development of the birth-control pill, an antihuman feast day if ever there was one. Bishop Margot Käßmann, at the time the head of Germany's Lutherans, paid the birth control pill deep reverence and tribute. She said that the pill is "God's gift, for it is about the preservation of life, of freedom, which doesn't have to immediately degenerate into pornography, as much as the sexualization of our society is, of course, a problem." This attitude is so bizarre, so oblivious to a reality you have to be blind not to see all around us, that it is difficult to know where to begin in reply. But it's clear that when an intelligent person in a position of responsibility can utter such patent nonsense, something like mythical thinking is in play.

At the most superficial level, we see a blind faith in the myths about the glories of technology, here in the form of the pill. Again, Joseph Ratzinger: "Technological civilization is not in fact religiously and morally neutral, even if it believes it is. It changes people's standards and their attitudes and behavior. It changes the way people interpret the world, from the very bottom up." (*Truth and Tolerance*) So thanks to the technology of the pill, the respect for the deeply human mystery of sexual intercourse—what it means in terms of real human intimacy and permanent human relationships—can simply be swept aside. Those old human things, if you are under the spell of the myth, appear no longer demanded by sexual intercourse as it exists in a brave new world. The myth hides the reality.

Ratzinger went on to explain: "What takes place with increasing frequency . . . is that the Christian faith is shaken off for the sake of people's own authenticity, and in the realm of religion the pagan religions are restored . . . while the element that is . . . magical . . . everything that offers people some power over the world, is preserved and becomes really decisive in people's lives." The authenticity he is referring to here is an imagined one—people imagine that they know more about authentic behavior than the Church does from revelation and natural law. Mythical thinking about birth control is just the start, one example of many that have insinuated themselves into things we have come to take for granted.

There are myths about Catholicism (my Catholicism is valid, but only when I select out the bits that I like); there are myths in politics (there are no spiritual values only material ones); there are myths about economics (profit is all); there are myths about human beings (humans are just another species of animal); and so on. These myths make Christianity's constant, almost pedantic reference to reality (in natural law, in the Scriptures and the teaching of the Church) look strange, so much so that it constitutes an offense against the mythical thinking that is the real oddity in our world.

The Church has always looked strange, but perhaps more so now than ever. The Church and other Christian bodies have themselves been accused in the past of mythical thinking, but—in a sense—Christianity exists precisely to combat mythical thinking. So Catholics who want really to be Catholic today have to accept that they cannot easily just get along with friends, co-workers, the culture as a whole. When delusions rule the public square, we must find ways to refute them, but we must also create truly Catholic spaces where the destructive myths of our confused age can be kept at bay.

9. Lost in Translation

Anthony Esolen

Now that we finally have the *Novus Ordo* translated into English, it's time to look at the other mistranslations that plague us Anglophones in the Church. I'd like to begin with the lectionary.

Apologists for the cardboard-twinkie texts we gnash down every week argue for something called "dynamic equivalence," by which is meant the translation of the general idea of an original text into something that conveys that idea in the receiving language. But the premises here are corrupt at the roots.

To see why, consider the Bauhaus modernist architecture of the twentieth century. Architects like Le Corbusier proclaimed that they were going to create "machines for living," utterly rational—it was supposed—boxes designed for maximum efficiency for our daily needs. But who wants to live in a box? The hideous Pruitt-Igoe apartment complex in Saint Louis, inspired by modernist theories of urban renewal, quickly became a pool of social disintegration and crime.

Human beings are embodied souls. They crave beauty. They like music. They invent poetry. The Italian housewife in the second story of a medieval stone house festoons her balcony with geraniums and eggplants. She keeps pictures of her nieces and nephews in a glass hutch with fancy knobs, next to a statue of Jesus of the Sacred Heart.

Such things are not "extra," no more than food, for a human being, is simply fuel. Animals gobble; human beings celebrate meals. Our very aspirations to the sacred are expressed in earthy, bodily ways, and our humblest bodily needs, like eating and drinking, or caring for the sick, or taking our rest, are most humanly fulfilled when they point to what transcends the human—as when a child kneels down to pray for his sisters and brothers before he goes to sleep.

This is true of our language also. When we speak, we do not simply convey information, as data might be fed into a computer. We express surprise, gratitude, humor, sadness, love. We revel in the physicality of our words. We bring whole scenes of life to mind. We combine and recombine images that we may never have combined before.

So Jesus doesn't say, "The kingdom of God has inauspicious beginnings," but "The kingdom of God is like a mustard seed." He doesn't say, "One should try to cultivate inattention to acts of charity," but "Let not your left hand know what your right hand is doing." It is not simply that his phrasing is better suited for simple people who need to see things to understand them. It is that both his thoughts and his words are essentially poetic, delving into the heart of things by a means inaccessible to the bald abstraction.

We're meant not just to compare the Kingdom of God to a mustard seed and then to toss the seed away once we have "understood" the motive behind the metaphor. We are indeed invited really to see the Kingdom of God *in that seed*, and that is why Christians came up with the charming and deeply human custom of enclosing a mustard seed in a brooch, for girls to wear, as testimony and remembrance.

The reason why we don't always translate word-for-word is not, then, that the particularities of the words are unimportant, but that a mechanical substitution of words in one language for words in another may do violence to the words themselves, or may fail to convey the fullness of the human expression. So the good translator seeks to penetrate *more deeply* into the beauty and the richness of the words and the expressions in the original language. Poetry should be translated as poetry, prayer as prayer, oratory as oratory.

It's nonsense to suppose that some "common language" of the street corner exists, into which the common Greek of the New

Testament should be translated: nonsense, because in both contexts we are dealing with human beings, not data processors, and human beings, especially in the time of Jesus, speak one way when they are ordering their groceries, and another way when they are praying.

They launch into flights of fancy; they rhyme, they alliterate, they build to a climax; they repeat themselves, they reverse direction; they shed light upon a vista of meanings as various as the flowers in a garden, then they shroud all in darkness. Thus it may be rightly said that the problem with a mechanically literal translation is that it is not *literal enough*, that is fails to capture the fullness of meaning suggested by the fascinating bodiliness and spirituality of the speaking human person.

Here is an example. Jesus compares the Kingdom of God to a landowner who left tenants in charge of his farm. Then he sent servants to collect—what? The Greek reads *tous karpous*, literally, *the fruits*, what you pluck from the tree. By that simple word "fruit," a vast field of Scriptural imagery is brought before our eyes. Adam and Eve ate of the forbidden fruit. Abel sacrificed to God the first fruits of his labor. Jesus tells us that a good tree is known by its good fruit. Saint Paul says that Christ is the first fruit of the resurrection.

So what do the lectionary translators do? They build the Bauhaus. They forget the echoes. They muffle the poetry. They disdain the body. Therefore they disdain also the soul. The landowner sends his servants to gather "the produce."

And we lovers of Scripture cry out, like the martyred souls in Revelation, "When, O Lord, when?"

10. Can We Stop Telling God What to Do?

RANDALL SMITH

Plato thought intercessory prayer was ridiculous. If God is all-good, then trying to get Him to change His mind or treat you differently is to ask Him to do something less than fully just, which is contrary to God's nature. Christ, however, instructed us to pray and to ask for what we need. And as much as I admire Plato, I'll side with Christ every time.

By the same token, Plato does have a point. Should we really be telling God what to do? The Bible, too, makes it clear that God knows us better than we know ourselves, and that He knows better than we do what is good for us. Asking for help is one thing; giving advice on the best way for God to help is another thing altogether.

Which is why I'm often made uncomfortable by the current fashion in the intercessory "Prayers of the Faithful" during Mass—when it includes specific instructions on how God should help us. The practice, as you'll probably recognize, goes something like this: "For a resolution of the conflict in the Middle East, *that* God will make all sides recognize that peace is more in their interest than continued fighting." Or: "For the homeless and alienated in society, including those who are alienated due to their sexual orientation, *that* God may help us to realize their infinite dignity and treat them with respect and recognize their rights in society."

Now look, I have absolutely no problem whatsoever praying for either peace in the Middle East or homeless people and gay people. But I'm troubled by the fact that our "that" clauses run on so long, we end up praying for no more than about four or five groups, and usually only those that happen to have shown up in the mainstream media that morning. In my parish, we used to pray for Haiti all the time until countries in the Middle East started rebelling, and now we pray for Libya and Syria. The poor Haitians don't seem to need our prayers any more because they're not on the front page of *The New York Times*, which is odd because I don't think everything is all better there.

I've been to traditional Byzantine-rite liturgies where the intercessions go on for five minutes and where they ask God's blessing on everybody from political leaders to farmers to factory workers to artists to mothers and fathers to children to . . . well, you name it. It's a long list. But they have the time because they don't generally get into the business of telling God what to do. They don't say, for example: "For children, *that* they may come to a better appreciation of the wisdom of their parents." Or: "For members of Congress, *that* they may more faithfully listen to the voices of their constituents." No, they tend to just pray and let God decide what's best.

It's not only that I don't want to be in the theologically awkward position of telling *God* what to do, it's also the case that I don't want to be in the socially awkward (and politically annoying) position of being assaulted in Mass with the latest politically correct fad dressed up as a prayer. Many such intercessions aren't really directed at "God" at all, but at the people in the congregation. When someone prays: "For those who are alienated due to their sexual orientation, *that* we may fully recognize their rights in society," that's not *really* a request to God, it's a political statement. "God" has scarcely anything to do with it.

Notice that such "prayers" rarely involve direct address: "Help us, O Lord, to see your truth and walk in your ways." Rather, they involve talking about God in the third person as though He weren't really present. Then there are intercessions that leave out God altogether: "That we may make a greater use of alternative fuels and lessen our dependence on fossil fuels." Is that a prayer, or a plank in a political platform?

For some intercessions, especially those that come from the congregation, it's hard to know whether I can actually say "Amen" to them. What to do when someone prays "For greater respect among Catholics for sexual freedom?" With regard to all such prayers, I generally just say a silent prayer to this effect: "O Lord, I have no idea what that even *means*, but please help us in the way we need to be helped."

And wouldn't that make more sense? God *does* know us better than we know ourselves, and He *does* know how best to help us. Moral exhortations are best left for the homily and political statements are best left to politicians. And for heaven's sakes (and ours), let's address Him as though He is actually present. But above all, let's remember, there's no need to tell God how best to help. He's been at it for quite a while, after all.

11. The Eucharist and Cannibalism

MICHAEL P. FOLEY

Perhaps the most disconcerting Catholic doctrine is the Real Presence of Jesus Christ in the Blessed Sacrament. Many people today have the same reaction as those disciples who heard Jesus preach it for the first time in Capernaum and were scandalized, "This saying is hard, and who can hear it?" (Jn. 6:61) John says that after, many of His disciples stopped following Him altogether.

What is obviously so "hard" about this saying is that it suggests cannibalism. If Catholics believe the Eucharist really is the body and blood of Christ, then they believe they are eating human flesh and drinking human blood. The Romans accused Christians of cannibalism and that charge has been made against Catholics in various ways ever since.

But while Holy Communion does involve eating human flesh and blood, it is not true that it is cannibalistic. How so?

The Eucharist is life. Cannibals eat what is dead. The Aztecs, the most notorious cannibalistic society in history, ate the beating hearts of victims, but they were still eating something doomed to die, and in the act of eating, it did die. By contrast, Christ is alive. He rose on the third day, and is present in the Eucharist as fully alive (indeed, He is Life itself). Our reception of the Eucharist doesn't destroy or change that in any way.

The Eucharist is the whole body and blood of Jesus Christ. Cannibals only take a part of their victims. But even the smallest particle of the Eucharist contains the entire body and blood of Christ. The familiar characteristics of space and matter don't apply: consuming a larger Host does not mean you get more of Christ's body and blood, nor does consuming a small Host mean you get less. Even receiving from the Precious Cup is unnecessary: by "concomitance," when a communicant receives the Host, he also receives the Precious Blood.

The Eucharist is the glorified body of Jesus Christ. Concomitance is possible because Christ's living and eternal body is forever reunited with His blood; hence, receiving the former entails receiving the latter. Christ's risen body is not a resuscitated corpse like that of Lazarus, but an utterly transformed "spiritual body" (I Cor. 15:44) far different from the spatio-temporal "body of our lowness." (Phil. 3:21) Therefore, when a Catholic receives the Eucharist, he is receiving not just flesh but *glorified* flesh, a resurrected and transfigured "super body" that foreshadows the new reality of a new Heaven and a new earth. Cannibalistic practices don't do that.

The Eucharist contains the soul of Jesus Christ. Some cannibalistic societies eat the flesh or drink the blood of fallen warriors in the hopes of taking on their "life force" or their courage, or of destroying their spirit altogether. Yet precisely because the risen Jesus is alive, His immortal soul is united to His body and blood, and inseparable from them in the Eucharist.

The Eucharist contains the divinity of Jesus Christ. Because Jesus Christ is true God and true man, His divinity and His humanity are also inseparable. Consequently, in partaking of the human "aspects" of Christ (His body, blood, and soul), we also partake of His divine nature. This stands in sharp contrast to cannibals such as the Binderwurs of central India, whose flesh-eating religious rituals tried to bring them closer to the gods, but made them sink lower than most beasts.

Putting all these elements together, we arrive at the Catholic formula: "The Eucharist is the body and blood, soul and divinity, of our Lord Jesus Christ."

The Eucharist is not diminished. If Christ is entirely present in even the tiniest part of the Host, then it follows that the living body and blood of Christ are not diminished by the act of receiving Holy Communion (more communicants does not mean "less Christ" left, and so on).

The Eucharist consumes us. When you eat food, it becomes a part of you. With the Eucharist, however, the opposite happens. We become a part of it, that is, in Holy Communion, we are made a part of the mystical body of Christ. In our Lord's words, those who eat His flesh and drink His blood abide in Him. (Jn. 6.40)

The Eucharist is nonviolent. Catholics understand the Mass as the non-bloody re-presentation of the sacrifice of the Cross. Christ, whose innocent blood was unjustly shed 2,000 years ago, is made available for His disciples under the appearance of bread and wine, but in a peaceful, nonviolent way. Cannibalism is inherently violent and usually predicated on the assumption that the victim is guilty of a crime against a society (usually they are prisoners of war).

All of this suggests that what happens at the Lord's table is fundamentally different than what happens in the dark rites of a depraved tribe. Indeed, from a metaphysical perspective, we can consider all cannibalistic customs (as opposed to those induced by derangement or starvation) as a perverse and even demonic mimicry of our Holy Communion with the risen Lord.

Most anthropologists believe that cannibalism is intrinsically religious in nature. Just as all pagan blood-sacrifices were distorted knock-offs of the one true Sacrifice of Calvary (even if they took place *before* the Crucifixion), so too all ritual acts of cannibalism are a distorted attempt to replace the Bread of Life with the mammon of one's own iniquity.

The disciples scandalized by Jesus' hard saying were right to be horrified by cannibalism but wrong to identify it with what they were hearing. The Eucharist is not another form of cannibalism. On the contrary, it is a holy union with Life itself, which all cannibal acts blindly seek but never obtain.

In this respect Holy Communion is actually the supreme instance of anti-cannibalism, an exposé of all evil impostors for what they are. Jesus made the difference clear enough when He referred to Himself as the "Living Bread." (Jn. 6:41)

So if anyone asks, now you know.

12. More Doctrine, Please

TODD HARTCH

Pope Pius X is often criticized because in 1910 he demanded that all priests take an anti-modernist oath. It's hardly known that in 1905 he ordered all priests around the world to do something else, perhaps even more challenging. Did he call for greater commitment to the glory of Eucharist? Did he demand more emphasis on missions? Or did he rebuke them for their lack of holiness? Although he could have done any of these things, what he actually did was to call them to focus their attention on one simple task: he ordered them to spend an hour every Sunday catechizing the children of their parishes.

He also asked them to offer at least an hour of catechesis for adults on every holy day of obligation and during Lent. Over the course of four or five years they should cover the Apostles' Creed, the Sacraments, the Ten Commandments, the Lord's Prayer, and the Precepts of the Church.

"If faith languishes in our days," he said, "if among large numbers it has almost vanished, the reason is that the duty of catechetical teaching is either fulfilled very superficially or altogether neglected." The great task for priests, therefore, was not complex sermons or new academic books. It was solid teaching of the basic truths of the faith. Children—all Catholics, in fact—needed, and still need, to learn the simple but essential aspects of faith and morals so that they can live Christian lives.

If they didn't learn what was right and true there was almost no possibility that they could live as they should. Christian doctrine, Pius stated, "reveals God and His infinite perfection with far greater clarity than is possible by the human faculties alone." In other words, human beings might imagine that they could figure out what God was like and how they should live simply by thinking or by some sort of intellectual osmosis. But the fact was that they needed to be taught.

Good Christian doctrine was about the best thing a priest could give to his people because, "there is always some hope for a reform of perverse conduct so long as the light of faith is not entirely extinguished; but if lack of faith is added to a depraved morality because of ignorance, the evil hardly admits of remedy, and the road to ruin lies open." Priests who would rather write books and deliver lectures to intellectual audiences than teach the basic truths of the faith had their priorities backwards. It was more worthwhile and more difficult to bring Christian doctrine to the young and uneducated than to the wise and knowledgeable; it took more preparation and more subtlety.

Priests also might be tempted to think that, busy as they were, someone else should take on the duty of catechesis. The Holy Father seems to have envisioned some aid by lay teachers, but he could not have been more clear about who had the main responsibility: "There can be no doubt that this most important duty rests upon all who are pastors of souls." In fact, "For a priest there is no duty more grave or obligation more binding than this."

Obviously, priests are no longer spending an hour every Sunday catechizing the children of their parishes and they are not devoting time on every holy day to adult catechesis. With the priest shortage, they are preaching homilies and celebrating the Mass, often several times, and hearing confessions. It's not as if they're sitting around watching television all day. My pastor, for instance, celebrates Mass five times in three different churches between Saturday evening and Sunday evening. It probably never occurs to him or to most of his brother priests around the world that adding a children's class to this kind of schedule would be a good use of time. Throw in the abuse crisis, which makes priests wary about spending time with children, and the contemporary understanding of the priest's role could hardly be farther from that envisaged by Pius X.

Now, Pius' command to catechize was a matter of discipline that is no longer operative and priests are no longer obliged to teach doctrine every Sunday. The doctrinal part of his encyclical is still applicable, however. At the heart of the priesthood is teaching and preaching. As Vatican II says, priests are "strenuous assertors of the truth, lest the faithful be carried about by every wind of doctrine." Priests today face a difficult and demanding situation, with many worthy claims on their time. Still, Pius X makes clear that the bottom line is this: "It is indeed vain to expect a fulfillment of the duties of a Christian by one who does not even know them." Catholics today, even more than in the day of Pius X, need priests to teach them doctrine.

Finally, some will complain that teaching doctrine, especially to children, would be a waste of time for a priest faced by a world full of poverty and brokenness, but the pope anticipates this objection: "If, assuredly, the alms with which we relieve the needs of the poor are highly praised by the Lord, how much more precious in His eyes, then, will be the zeal and labor expended in teaching and admonishing, by which we provide not for the passing needs of the body but for the eternal profit of the soul! Nothing, surely is more desirable, nothing more acceptable to Jesus Christ, the Saviour of souls, Who testifies of Himself through Isaias: 'To bring good news to the poor he has sent me.'"

13. Advent Resolutions

DAVID WARREN

In yesterday's news: A new microwave technique will kill spores and keep bread mould-free for sixty days. Americans throw out 40 percent of the food they buy, including 33 percent of the bread.

The Eurozone unemployment rate has reached 11.7 percent, a new high. But the inflation rate dropped 0.3 percent in November. The German Bundestag approved a 44-billion Euro bailout for Greece by a vote of 473 to 100 with 11 abstentions. Ice sheet melting has raised world sea levels by between 7.3 and 14.9 millimeters since 1992.

Dominique Strauss-Kahn, age 63, will pay out $6 million to a New York hotel maid, age 33, to settle her civil suit. At least 66 people died from 4 bombings in 3 cities around Iraq.

There's more. The U.S. birth rate fell 8 percent between 2007 and 2010, overall, but 14 percent among foreign-born, and 23 percent among Mexican immigrant women. In 2010, it was 63.2 per 1,000 women of childbearing age. It was 122.7 in 1957.

And that was the BBC. I hadn't got to the news aggregators yet, being distracted. There were urgent emails; my website was under cyber-attack; the phone was ringing. My neighbor's snooze-control works: the alarm goes off at 10-minute intervals, for hours. Is she in Florida, or should I call an ambulance? One email list to which I mistakenly subscribed offered the latest numbers from a "world freedom index."

Gentle reader may perhaps detect *non sequiturs* in the narrative above (*non sequituri?*)—unless my argument is about what happens when one gets up in the morning, in which case everything follows naturally. Yesterday was the Feast of Saint Andrew, and tomorrow will be the first Sunday in Advent. Let us try to make sense.

For the Christian liturgical year is re-starting. Some decades ago, on the analogy of the secular New Year, I took it into my head to make annual resolutions each year on Saint Andrew's. Partly, my reasoning was "Scotch," and practical: better if Advent follows, than the New Year's binge. One's resolutions may have a chance of lasting through the first night.

Like most people, perhaps, I make approximately the same resolutions each year. And this, even though I resolved, around 1992, to make no resolutions about drinking or smoking or eating. Such resolutions are tawdry, I resolved. They play into the culture, in which guilt associated with dieting has replaced guilt associated with sin.

Resolutions should instead be directed towards personal behavior that is morally rather than physically deleterious. That in turn will help focus the mind on objects other than social disapproval. For given a culture like this, who needs social approval?

Sound the gong for a subtlety here. One should, I am persuaded not only by my conscience but by my priest, try to avoid giving scandal. For if one is known to be "a Catholic," one might just possibly have some slight exemplary influence on others reviewing their own denominational status, and should not go out of one's way to give Catholics a bad name.

This alas cuts across my native mischievousness, which likes to leave an impression of scandal even where there is none in fact. (I inherited this from my father, whose indifference to public opinion was heroic.)

So let us consider a resolution inoffensive, yet not prim: "In the next year, I will try to ignore numbers." Some may well prove impossible to ignore, and the perfect may be the enemy of the good. The telephone number to my ancient mama's bedside should be remembered. Bank statements should be occasionally reviewed. The calendar itself contains numbers, and appointments are expressed in times of day.

One needs to specify disregard for the gratuitous numbers that fill one's head from media and Internet: the ungodly "vision of the world" in which truth is statisticized. Through bad habit, one unconsciously buys into this vision of the world, in which death itself is replaced by numbers.

In my line of being, for reasons too boring to relate, it is not really practical to ignore the news entirely. But in the very reading of the news, a resolved, consciously enforced, growing disregard for numbers would be useful.

Quite apart from transferring one's attention from what the media reveal to what they conceal (most even of diurnal reality), there is the moral issue of dependency: that craving for more numbers, numbers, numbers that corrupts the soul. Worse than "likker" or "backy" or saturated fats, it addles reason.

Conversely, where numbers are unavoidable, make them count.

Lauds, Prime, Terce, Sext, None, Vespers, Compline—to say nothing of Matins and the night watches. Somewhere in the monasteries, we believe on fairly good information, the *Liturgia Horarum* is still sung, descending from the Desert Fathers of Egypt.

As an Anglican, years ago, I became intensely aware of these Hours, my imagination captured by the *Preces Privatae* of Lancelot Andrewes. His comprehensive prayer, entitled "The Dial," constructed entirely from Biblical passages and the old Greek *Horologion*, reviews the times of day mentioned in the life of Our Lord. It still wheels through my head. It begins, in the Brightman translation: "Thou who hast put the times and seasons in thine own power: grant that we make our prayer unto Thee in a time convenient and when Thou mayest be found, / and save us."

Most of us do not live in monasteries. Some of us do not even get to Mass every day. Yet, as I found making resolutions many Advents ago, it is possible so to arrange one's daily schedule that the Hours serve as breaks or bookmarks, and are acknowledged if only in one-sentence prayers.

Each year, it seems, I resolve anew to better organize myself around this temporal scheme, by which, even if they are inaudible, the bells from Christendom can still be heard.

14. Mrs. Christ, Teacher of Theology

DAVID BONAGURA

"Mrs. Christ." "The God wife." So ran the headlines after the announcement that Professor Karen King of Harvard Divinity School had discovered a fourth century papyrus written in Egyptian Coptic whose few legible sections quote Jesus referring to his wife. Never mind that we cannot determine the papyrus' authenticity, broader context, author, or even every word on the three-inch page. The public impression has been made: Jesus could well have been married, and why not? He was fully human like us, wasn't he?

Immediately after the announcement reputable scholars rushed to disprove Professor King's hypothesis based on the biblical texts, written by eyewitnesses only a few decades—not centuries—after Jesus. Jesus' earthly father and mother are mentioned by the Evangelists, as are his brothers and sisters (thought to be cousins), but there is no mention of a wife.

When Jesus returned to Nazareth after he began his public ministry, he was rejected by the locals who noted his family members, but do not mention a wife.

When he was crucified, he was accompanied by a number of named women, though no one is identified as his wife.

When he said metaphorically that "the Son of Man has nowhere to lay his head" (Matthew 8:20), that might also have excluded a literal home and a wife.

Based solely on the biblical evidence, the statistical probability that Jesus was married is near zero. But there are also theological reasons that prove Jesus' celibacy, and these underscore not only his divinity, but also his humanity.

From his first recorded words in the Temple at age twelve, to his words in his greatest agony on the cross, to his final words before his ascension into Heaven, Jesus continually expressed his singular focus and mission: to perform the will of the Father. "I seek not my own will but the will of him who sent me." (John 5:30)

What was the Father's will for his Son? "The Son of Man came not to be served, but to serve, and to give his life as a ransom for many." (Mark 10:45)

"Son," Pope Benedict has taught, is a relational term. As the eternal Son made flesh, Jesus did not exist for himself. He is sent *from* God *for* "us men and for our salvation." By becoming man the Son has brought to himself all of humanity, which he has elevated to share in the divine life of the blessed Trinity through grace. Through the Eucharist Jesus has taught that his flesh and blood are not reserved for one person in particular, but for the life of the world.

In exercising his singular mission, therefore, Jesus, the eternal "from and for" of God, indeed has a bride: the Church, the People of God. We form his Mystical Body, having been born "not of blood nor of the will of flesh nor of the will of men, but of God" (John 1:13). In giving himself totally to us, we are able to have life in him.

But the reality of Jesus' celibacy does not just rest on his divinity; it also depends on his humanity and the Catholic understanding of the marital vocation. In marriage, you give yourself completely to a spouse in a unique way until death. The marital covenant is privileged and exclusive; it claims priority in the spouses' lives and regulates all their subsequent relationships, including the love of children and of friends.

This is why Jesus was celibate, and why the Catholic Church requires celibacy of her clergy and religious: their vocation is not to give themselves to one person in particular, but to all people equally. Jesus' mission was to serve the Father by serving all of us, which required him to remain celibate in order to give all of us the gift of himself.

This reality does not undermine marriage; it strengthens it. Marriage and celibacy are not antithetical, but mutually complementary. Both require the complete gift of self. The difference lies in the gift's recipient.

Some have stated that a change in Jesus' marital status would have no bearing on their faith in him. This opinion only holds because the historical and theological evidence clearly disproves the marriage hypothesis. If, however, undisputable proof revealed that Jesus was married, then we would have to reinterpret our entire understanding of him if we truly believe that he is both fully God and fully human.

Jesus' claim that "I and the Father are one" (John 10:30), along with so many other statements, would take on a very different meaning if Jesus were also one with another human being.

Of course, no such reinterpretation is required. As it turns out, the alleged "Mrs. Christ," upon closer examination, has proved a far more effective professor of Christology than not a few theologians who, suspicious of supernatural faith, fabricate portraits of Jesus according to their whim.

She has reiterated for us what Catholics have known for two thousand years: that the only way to understand and interpret Jesus is through the biblical testimony within the context of the faith of the Church. All other theories, and their professors, need not apply.

15. Amateur Night

BEVIL BRAMWELL, OMI

You all know what Amateur Night is. A bar will have an "Open Mike Night" when anyone who wants may go up and sing or otherwise make a fool of himself. Amateur Night also captures the avalanche of theological amateurism after Vatican II. I mean that in the sense of the enthusiastic, though perhaps not the informed amateur.

The Council's first session started in October 1962 and the last one closed in December 1965. Even as the sessions took place there was preemptive talk in the media. Legions of "experts" spoke and wrote about what the Council should do to "bring the Church into the modern world."

In fact, the Council Fathers were as much in the modern world as anyone else and yet, strangely perhaps, they did not simply turn the Church into yet another mirror of modern culture like a cable channel or Disney World.

After the Council, many priests and nuns took the council documents and ran with them. Often their use of texts was not *ecclesial* even though "ecclesial communion is the key to our task of proclaiming the Gospel" and the Church as communion is a basic theme of council teachings. (Benedict XVI)

An inescapable hermeneutical requirement is built into using theological statements: namely, that they should be read ecclesially in the unity of the Scriptures and the documents of the Church as the *only* way even to comprehend them.

This is not eccentricity or authoritarianism. Other complex fields such as medicine or law or engineering, for example, make the same kind of demands. Each field has its own framework of principles and publications. So understanding an article in engineering takes knowledge of pretty much everything else, the technical terms, the mathematics, the logic, previous articles on the subject, etc.

A question for another time is why the rigors of medicine, law, and other disciplines are still accepted in our culture (try being a doctor without being certified!), but taking care with theology is apparently passé or illegitimate.

If unity in communion had been the rule of Catholic mental hygiene after Vatican II, then some people would not imagine that the "conservatives (whoever they are) hijacked the Council" ("Xavier Rynne's" nonsense) or that "logically" those of us who were not at the Council have the insight to correct it.

Fundamentalist Progressives (now there's something new under the sun) would not take one line out of a Council text and make it *the* only key to Christian life (look at most of the "social justice" movement). So much writing and speaking would not jump from a line of teaching to "what I think."

The other day, I came upon someone who misquoted Pope Benedict and then made the misunderstanding the premise for an article. In a different climate of opinion, there would not be the sheer disdain for *reasoned* theological presentation (and for the persons offering them) that demonstrates a substantial grasp of theology by someone who has indeed done his homework.

Most of all, solipsism in theological things loses the beauty of theology and of the *Theos*—God, in the process. Without beauty there is no truth, an insight that is valued in other realms as well. Robert P. Crease noted recently that: "The physicist and cosmologist Subrahmanyan Chandrasekar wrote an entire book on Newton's *Principia*, the book in which Newton proposes his second law of motion, comparing it to Michelangelo's painting on the ceiling of the Sistine Chapel."

Chandrasekar knew the history of his field and was extraordinarily adept within it, winning the 1983 Nobel Prize for Physics. He also knew that even cosmologists can get too blasé and lose the sheer awe at beholding the universe.

Awe comes as well to those who know that they handle sacred things, the Church being one of them. Without the beauty that comes from organic unity of thought (because God and his plan of salvation are an organic unity) there is no love, there is only the vitriol and viciousness of political debate rather than a religious discourse.

For some reason—call it the spirit of the sixties—theology, the most vital, disciplined thought in the world, became a free-for-all. Or even worse, a mere set of planks in the platform of a particular ideological group—the "we want homosexual marriage" group or the "we want ordained women" group or the "we're against authority except our own" group.

Good for you. But in that way of doing theology, theology as such is eviscerated and people use its terms and concepts to mean anything at all.

Bishops became afraid of their clergy ("I can't look too conservative"). Dioceses became doctrinal free-for-alls ("pick a parish that teaches what you like"). Religious orders followed the same script. Universities became anything ("the alternative magisterium").

But the Church is the communion of truth and love that we participate in and subordinate ourselves to. Communion involves both truth *and* love. Amateurism rarely has the tools to deal with such realities.

16. Lent, Monkey Mind, and E-Asceticism

ROBERT ROYAL

Buddhist monks use a lovely image for the usual condition of our thoughts: they call it monkey mind. Picture a monkey scrambling from one branch to another looking for bananas or nuts, or—to mix animal metaphors—just horsing around with the other monkeys. Naturally, the monks seek to detach from monkey mind and to achieve a deep state of contemplation.

Contrary to immediate appearances, monkey mind has its uses, limited though they may be. Very few of us can be full-time monks. And that's a good thing in its way. If we didn't scramble to pay the bills, keep the kids on an even keel, manage all the other things necessary to an ordinary human life, most of us would be making even worse monkeys of ourselves, so to speak, in many practical ways.

The trick—and it's a difficult one—is to find some way, every day, that we can keep the practicalities from eating us alive and get in touch with the deep-down permanent things. Lent is a good season, of course, to reflect on the kinds of obstacles that each of us especially finds most hampers us from that life-giving contact.

Like everyone else, during Lent I need the usual disciplines: fasting, increased prayer. Those in particular are two practices that, we have dominical assurance, are the only way to cast out certain evils.

In recent years, though, I've found that another problem looms larger and larger. It may not be appropriate for the editor of an online publication to say, but I find that the Internet itself is the worst distraction of all. If many of us don't get that version of monkey mind under control, the rest of the spiritual effort may simply get lost.

The Internet has many good uses. Even just casually surfing around can be fine—if you've thought out in advance how much time you should spend and what kind of surfing you're going to do. But there's a tendency, something like drinking that third glass of wine, to reach a kind of point where all bets are off.

So I've started to develop for myself some rules of what I like to think of as e-asceticism. The first thing I do when I'm sitting at my desk is close the email program and the browser, unless work really demands that I stay connected. And I only reopen them at designated times of day and for predetermined stretches unless there's some really pressing reason. The same goes for the smart-phone.

We've gotten used to the idea, young people worst of all, that we should be instantly connected with one another, and somehow with people farther away than the people with whom we're phys-ically present. There's nothing more absurd in the modern world than to see two teenagers walking down the street together each talking on the cell phone—to someone else.

If you try the simple rules above for a few days, you'll find what a strong hold unfocused monkeying around on the Internet now has on your attention. The neuroscientists are starting to look into the ways that this sort of interaction with electronic devices is altering our brain chemistry—and the results are not pretty.

Wandering attention is a common theme in manuals of spiri-tuality. But the classic writers didn't have to deal with the digitized onslaught we do. In one way, it may seem a distraction from tra-ditional wisdom even to bother with this subject. But in another, it may be precisely this form of temptation that most calls for fresh thought—and e-asceticism.

I recently heard a homily by a wise priest who warned about unusual new forms of covetousness: he'd noticed in confession that some people have developed a kind of lust for collecting MP3 music files. And even before you get all the way over to the truly frightening online pornography deluge, there are numerous new digital variations on the old seven deadly sins.

But like almost everything else, our new e-situation can also be turned to great benefit. I've got the liturgy of the hours on my smart phone and, so, now have no excuse for not saying morning and evening prayer wherever I am. Some days get the better of me from the moment I get out of bed, but on the whole I'm doing better than ever at that particular practice.

And if you can keep yourself from spiritual gluttony, you can dip into the Bible, almost all of Augustine, Aquinas, Newman, Chesterton, and many more spiritual masters online and just a couple of clicks away. (And there's always also *The Catholic Thing*, which, of course, you should read daily.)

For certain writers, you need a physical book in hand—one that you can mark up and easily flip back and forth. But in either format, you want to read slow and dive deep. One of the worst mistakes in both the intellectual and spiritual life is to mistake quantity for quality. It's easy to click onto something else. Hard to sit still and meditate on what demands time and personal engagement.

So have a good Lent. And good luck with your e-asceticism.

17. Faith Is Not a Checklist

RANDALL SMITH

A thought-experiment: suppose a student has been told by a friend that a teacher who he had always thought hated him has defended him in front of the principal against other teachers who were eager to have him kicked out of school. What would be involved in "believing" or "accepting the truth" of this story?

First, the student would have to believe that a particular *historical event* had taken place. But that would only be the beginning. The student would also have to believe the teacher did the act out of concern for him, and not merely to be able to continue torturing him in class. And thirdly, the student would have to accept this act of charity in such a way as to let it change him.

And one could believe *that* it had happened and *that* it was done out of charity, but still not be changed by it.

Christianity, in a similar way, means not only believing *that* Christ was crucified for us, but also that he gave his life freely in an infinite act of love (and not merely to increase our feelings of guilt), and then accepting this truth in such a way that it actually *changes* us within our own hearts. Faith that is not born in love and does not bear fruit in love is empty.

Note, however, that in the case of the student, if he refuses to believe or accept what the teacher has done for him, that doesn't mean the teacher ceases caring. The problem is that, in refusing to believe, the student has cut himself off from experiencing the full fruits of that care and concern.

Who has rejected whom here? The teacher who interceded for the student? Or the student who won't believe it?

So too, "not believing" when it comes to God, isn't something that causes God to reject us. Rather, "not believing"—especially when it comes to love and forgiveness—is precisely the way *we* reject *Him*. He continues to love and forgive us. We just won't believe it.

When it comes to faith, I fear we often turn this powerful, life-altering *virtue* (akin to courage, justice, and love) into an intellectual checklist. The question then becomes not whether I've hardened my heart, but merely whether I've got the right "list" or not. Heaven forbid that you should have an entry on *your* item-ized list different from those on *mine*, or that you would have an *extra* item on your list that wasn't there in, say, the fourth century (or third, or second, or after the Council of Trent—take your pick).

And of course then the idea is that, if *your* list isn't the *right* list, then you must not be a good Christian (or Catholic), and you're going to, well, *hell*—as though God somehow had a pop quiz on theology as the entrance exam for heaven. Are we to imagine St. Peter standing at a podium like Alex Trebek on *Jeopardy*: "For the game, now Mr. Smith. Infant baptism: yes or no? *Ooooh*, we're *so sorry*."

How did this happen? How did the grand virtue of "faith"— the virtue the great Patristic and Medieval Doctors hailed as expanding both mind and heart—become nothing more than a question of getting the right checklist? It's always been a danger— human beings love "formalism": it makes the spiritual life so much easier.

But our current problems began, I would suggest, in the seventeenth century, when the scope of "faith" and "reason" each became dramatically narrower. Descartes and his followers insisted that "reason" included only those things with *an absolute mathematical certainty*. Reason had to be based on things that *could in no way be doubted*.

For the earlier Church Fathers, faith and doubt could co-exist, just as one can be sure that he loves his wife or children, and yet still have one of *those* days. After Descartes, no more. If faith was to be a kind of "knowing" (and it is), then it must be ineradicably, unshakably certain.

Quite frankly, not only was this a lot to ask of faith, it was a lot to ask of any kind of knowing. Do you believe your mother loves you? Are you *certain*? Can you *demonstrate it* with scientific rigor and mathematical precision? Hardly.

With the realm of "reason" thus narrowed, "faith"—what had been for St. Thomas that great virtue of the *intellect*— increasingly came to be thought of as something not of the *intellect*, but solely of the *will*. You *accept* these things, you don't *think* about them.

At the same time, divisions among Christians accentuated the importance of the different "creeds": the lists. Not to subscribe to the "right" list became the difference between being *in* and being *out*—not only with regard to central matters like Christ and the

Trinity, but with an equal fervor placed on *all* matters great and small. (Dear *God*, you people baptize *babies?*). And to be *out*, well, we don't even want to talk about where those people are going. Nothing less than one's cosmic destiny was thought to be bound up with the specific contents of one's *list*.

I am far from denying the importance of right *doctrine*, precisely because it makes a difference the sort of things one is committed *to*. You have to believe in some *thing* or some *one*. We are creatures of both will *and* intellect. God both instructs our intellects and assists our will. Faith is a response to God's call, a response *made possible by* God's grace and love.

But what is being called *for* is not mere intellectual *assent* to six or ten or eighteen propositions. What we are being called *to* is a change of heart and a change of life. Faith not born of love that does not bear fruit in love is empty.

18. Catholic Social Teaching—without Fear

JOSEPH WOOD

Since I entered the Church, three words in Scripture have often caught my attention: "Be not afraid." But three other words, deployed by both left and right, still strike fear: "Catholic social teaching."

This teaching comprises a very large body of material, on which I am no expert. But its primary source lies in Scripture.

In the Old and New Testaments, charity towards the poor is important. Christ tells the rich young man that he must sell all he has and come follow if he desires eternal life. But Zacchaeus gains salvation by giving up only 50 percent of his goods.

Does this support high marginal tax rates? This wealth redistribution does not aim at a particular percentage, but to giving out of repentance and conversion of heart, forsaking the shiny things of the world that please the self for the things above.

Taxation to help the disadvantaged, rendering to Caesar his own, is coerced giving to meet the priorities of the state. It corresponds to the prayers of the Pharisee, offered formally and legally. Those on the left forget that Christ told the rich to give to the poor. He did not command that governments be in the middle.

But conservatives must remember that Catholic social teaching seeks to reduce inequality, at least in needs if not in wants. The poor will always be with us—we should not demand absolute equality—but we are obligated to ameliorate their plight out of solidarity. Government can be one means, at times the only means, to achieve ends the Church teaches as right, when government serves citizens rather than itself.

The American left-right divide over Catholic social teaching often the size and scope of government, supported by taxes and debt. This is a debate over means and their consequences, not basic ends. And any means—big government programs, small government constitutions—can become idols if they are confused with the ends they should serve.

Catholic social teaching is practical. It would generally exclude the far reaches of this debate, a government-free libertarianism on one hand, and a total government control of all resources—socialism or communism—on the other. Pope Francis, with his life of direct service to the poor while rejecting Marxist liberation theology, embodies this practical approach.

This middling tendency has its source partly in Aristotle who, as Fr James Schall points out, is highly relevant to American politics today and remains, through St Thomas Aquinas, influential in Catholic social teaching.

To oversimplify, Aristotle provided a scheme of possible governments: rule by the one, the few, or the many. For each type, there is a good variant: monarchy or a good king, aristocracy or a good few, and polity or the many when they rule well. And there are bad variants: tyranny, oligarchy, and democracy.

For Aristotle, the defining characteristic of the good type of government, as opposed to the deviant forms, is that good government rules for the common good rather than the interests of the rulers. "Tyranny" can be applied more generally to any state ruled by the one, few, or many who govern selfishly.

The journal *First Things* has, over the last few months, carried a fine debate over the future of the liberal political philosophy that we associate with the American political system at its founding. Here, liberal means neither leftist nor supportive of large government, but liberal in the original sense of favoring individual rights and duties, and responsible free market economics. Has this liberal philosophy of the Founders yielded tyranny of one form or another?

In the April issue, Professor Robert George of Princeton turns to a later philosopher, John Finnis, to define the common good that distinguishes good government from bad: the common good is "a set of conditions which enables the members of a community to attain for themselves reasonable objectives, or to realize reasonably for themselves the value(s), for the sake of which they have reason to collaborate with each other in a community."

George then argues for limited government as the political means more likely to support the end of the common good. Such government leaves greater room for institutions such as family and local community to take care of responsibilities that, when assumed by government, have the effect of reducing the virtue of the citizenry, speeding the deterioration of representative government into the kind of regime that does not truly serve its people.

I find George's conclusion persuasive. But the choice of whether to turn to government as a means to reach good ends is a matter for prudential decisions in particular circumstances. We can disagree—we can argue about Paul Ryan's latest budget plan—while remaining faithful to Catholic teaching.

The harder question involves the political culture in America today. We know that in the last presidential election, the winner used highly sophisticated internet-based "data analytics" on a massive scale to identify precisely which message would appeal to which households, to get supporters out to vote on the narrowest of self-interests.

This kind of "micro-populism" has little to do with the common good, and everything to do with power. It yields a form of widely enfranchised tyranny that ignores the common good as anything other than the sum of individual preferences.

It appears that we have "progressed" from the imperfect mix of self-interest and larger perspective that obtained in much of the nineteenth and early twentieth centuries, to a rejection of limited government in favor of a state that seeks to meet as many needs *and* wants as it takes to stay in power.

The heart of Catholic (and traditional Protestant) social teaching—a conversion in community to the generosity flowing from the love of God and neighbor—has been replaced with the "forced conversion" of redistribution of goods by the state. Whether this was already present in the American Founders (which I doubt), it's a deep failure to uphold the ends of Catholic social teaching. And it is a failure that is unlikely to be remedied in any political platform. It requires conversion of hearts and culture.

19. The Golden Age Cometh

FR. C. JOHN MCCLOSKEY

My friend, the late Fr. Richard John Neuhaus, was a Lutheran minister from Canada and a great Christian witness who converted to Catholicism. I was privileged to be at his ordination to the priesthood.

Fr. Neuhaus proclaimed in one of his books the advent of a "Catholic Moment" for the United States. As it turns out, he was twenty-five years or so ahead of his time. But perhaps today's "Catholic Moment" is not exactly the kind that he foresaw.

Neuhaus (along with George Weigel and Michael Novak) was generally positive about the American experiment and its "exceptionalism," especially in contrast with decaying and now largely post-Christian Europe.

In 1996, however, responding to the infamous *Planned Parenthood v. Casey* Supreme Court decision, Neuhaus published an essay by Russell Hittinger in *First Things*, which concluded:

"In effect, the Court makes it impossible to have anything other than a procedural common good as a motive or purpose for political activity. There is a real possibility that the moral and religious motivations of some citizens will become not only actionable at public law, through constitutional suits challenging legislation informed by such motives, but also actionable at private law. Unless the elected representatives of the people can compel the Court to refrain from invalidating political activity merely on the basis of the citizens' moral or religious motivation, the task of reform is blocked. Should that continue, the option remaining to right reason is the one traditionally used against despotic rule: civil disobedience."

Fast forward now to 2012. Hittinger appears vindicated, especially following the Supreme Court's recent decision to uphold Obamacare, although the lawsuits against the infamous HHS Mandate and the results of the November 2012 elections still lie before us.

Given the despotic HHS administrative diktat, American Catholics may now find that the right to religious freedom founded in the First Amendment may no longer apply to them and their institutions. In fact, it's possible that even the free practice of the faith may be moving toward de jure or de facto nonexistence.

Like Christians under the rule of Islamic governance or during the Roman Empire before Constantine's edict of toleration, there may come a time when American Catholics become secondhand citizens at best, at risk of imprisonment or worse at the whim of the magistrates. We should continue to pray that such a day won't come. But it is not impossible. Yes: It can happen here!

I should clarify whom I am including when I use the word "Catholic" because, of course, there is much confusion in this area. I believe the best definition—full assent to the Faith—is neatly summarized in the RCIA's *Reception for Baptized Christians into the Church*: "I believe and profess all that the holy Catholic Church believes, teaches, and proclaims to be revealed by God."

Readers may judge from the polls how many among us really qualify as Catholics according to this definition, considering the high number of divorces and remarriages, the dwindling of Catholic births and baptisms, the vertiginous drop in Mass attendance, etc. But there are certainly far fewer than the 70 million or so often quoted, just extrapolating from the percentage of votes by nominal Catholics for candidates with views clearly opposed to Catholic moral teaching (and who presumably live accordingly).

May they all soon return to the Church, as unlikely as that may now seem. Currently, one in every ten Americans is a lapsed Catholic. And each year, for every one convert to the Church, three leave the fold.

But this is precisely where the going gets good for the Church in the United States. Increasingly, the Catholic Church is the only option for serious Christians here. Traditional Protestant denominations are shrinking and Evangelical Christians in many cases are attracted to the sacramental system of the Church and its authoritative teachings. We get their best, and they get our worst, who do not want to live up to the full range of demands on the Christian life.

The seminaries are now generally sound, vocations are on the rise, and the episcopate is mostly made up of men in line with the evangelizing Catholicism of Bl. John Paul and the deep liturgical teachings of Pope Benedict.

Catholic radio is increasingly present almost everywhere. Catholic publishing continues to grow on- and off-line. The Cardinal Newman Society colleges grow each year and with time will replace the apostate former "Catholic" universities, whose now-diluted Catholicism we don't need.

Liturgies in our parishes are now more traditional—in many places the Lord is once again worshiped in a more reverent setting and adored in the centered tabernacle.

Finally, we face life-changing threats to the practice of our Faith, which, paradoxically, has its positive side. That may be our great opportunity to bear witness, as did the first Christians, and to draw converts, even if it means martyrdom.

I say: Bring it on, if it be God's will. Just think of the reward! In any case, it would not be the first time we've had to face and overcome such challenges. The best still lies ahead.

III. Controversies

1. Is Obama Worth a Mass?

RALPH MCINERNY

Now that the abortion president will be honored and feted and listened to at Notre Dame's commencement, the question becomes, who will say the commencement Mass?

The University of Notre Dame has officially and with much self-satisfaction invited President Barack Obama to address its 2009 graduates and to receive an honorary law degree. Not to put too fine a point on it, this is a deliberate thumbing of the collective nose at the Roman Catholic Church to which Notre Dame purports to be faithful. Faithful? Tell it to Julian the Apostate.

That someone who procures or advocates abortion thereby excludes himself from communion with the Church has been clear doctrine all along, and increasingly bishops have found the courage to tell those Catholic politicians who are the great enablers of abortion legislation that they cannot receive Holy Communion. Is it any worse to celebrate such a politician as Barack Obama? So where does that put ND President Father Jenkins? He can hardly say Mass without receiving the body, blood, soul, and divinity of Our Lord Jesus Christ, so doubtless he will recuse himself and have someone else say the Mass. But to whom will he go? All his cohorts must come under the same cloud as he. Perhaps the pastor of the president's erstwhile church in Chicago will be invited to harangue the assembled graduates and parents and faculty—those who can bring themselves to attend commencement this year. Why not?

Perhaps because, having been reminded of the sermons he heard over the years, Barack Obama distanced himself, as they say, from the fiery orator at whose feet he sat for decades. In this, whatever his motives, he has perhaps pointed a way for the Notre Dame administrators to redeem themselves. Perhaps they are unaware of Obama's record on abortion. Perhaps they have not been paying attention to what he has already done as president. On being reminded of all this, and mindful of the parlous position this puts them into vis-a-vis the Church if they thus celebrate the president, perhaps they will as publicly rescind their invitation as they have issued it? Don't count on it.

For one whose fifty-four-year career as a member of the Notre Dame faculty is coming to an end this June, it is a bitter thing to reflect on the 2009 commencement speaker. It is of course convenient to have an excuse to absent oneself from the festivities. Listening to commencement addresses is the penalty that graduates must pay to receive their diplomas. One can count memorable commencement speeches on the cuticle of one finger. They are ceremonial occasions that will be little remembered and less celebrated. One has groaned at previous selections, but the invitation to Barack Obama is far from being the usual effort of the university to get into warm contact with the power figures of the day. It is an unequivocal abandonment of any pretense at being a Catholic university. And it is in sad continuity with decades of waffling that have led with seeming inevitability to it.

No event was more crucial for Catholic universities than the infamous 1967 Land O'Lakes statement in which the assembled presidents of Catholic institutions declared their freedom from the supposedly baleful influence of Catholic orthodoxy. They would continue to call themselves Catholic, but the definition of the term was constantly under construction. And this by institutions whose task is decidedly not to define what Catholicism is. And now we have come to the point where the University of Notre Dame is publicly excluding itself from allegiance to and acceptance of one of the most fundamental of Christian moral truths, mentioned explicitly in the Didache and again and again over the centuries. Abortion is an essentially evil act, both from the viewpoint of natural morality and from the explicit teaching the Church. There is no way in which an individual, a politician or an institution can finesse that fact.

By inviting Barack Obama as commencement speaker, Notre Dame is telling the nation that the teaching of the Catholic Church on this fundamental matter can be ignored. Lip service may be paid to the teaching on abortion, but it is no impediment to upward mobility, to the truly vulgar lust to be welcomed into secular society, whether on the part of individuals or institutions.

Some years ago Archbishop Michael Miller, in his Vatican capacity as overseer of Catholic education, said in an address at Notre Dame that the Holy Father was considering prohibiting the use of the word "Catholic" by institutions whose behavior contradicts that use. By inviting Barack Obama to be the 2009 commencement speaker, Notre Dame has forfeited its right to call itself a Catholic university. It invites an official rebuke. May it come.

2. Politicians, Old Buildings, and Whores

AUSTIN RUSE

Boston Globe columnist Ellen Goodman once called former president of the so-called Catholics for a Free Choice, Frances Kissling, the "philosopher of the pro-choice movement." Well, let's see the Philosopher in action.

A few years ago, pro-life lobbyist Peter Smith ran into Kissling on an escalator at the United Nations. Smith, a jolly Australian with nary a critical word about anyone—even Kissling—gave her a big smile, stuck out his hand, and said, "Hello, Frances." Kissling glared at him and said, "Get away from me or I am calling security."

I had the same experience. A few years ago, I was invited to appear on a session of CNN's "Crossfire" with Kissling. Right before the live show, we were standing next to each other. Though we had met a few years before at a conference in The Hague, we had not spoken since. I stuck out my hand and said, "Hello, Frances." The Philosopher just glared.

Here is Kissling philosophizing about some of her opponents: "The Catholic right is uglier and meaner than anyone on the religious right, worse than the Falwells and Robertsons. The viciousness of the Donohues, the Deal Hudsons, the George Weigels and the Richard John Neuhauses is soul-numbing."

There's no surprise why she was the longtime president of Catholics for a Free Choice, a dissident group dedicated to undermining the teachings of the Church. They are now called Catholics for Choice. Bishops representing the U.S. Conference of Catholic Bishops have twice condemned them. Big foundations pay for her former group—the Ford Foundation, Rockefeller, and others—that wish the Church ill, or at least see the Church as the last bastion against the radical ethos.

Kissling has a long and troubled past. Her enmity toward the Church started, she claims, with how the Church supposedly treated her mother. Kissling claims to have once been a postulant in a religious order. She then went on to run an abortion clinic, and later to head "Catholics" for a Free Choice. As its leader, she famously said that she "searched the whole world for a government to overthrow and found it in the Holy See." Among other things, she ran a campaign to throw the Catholic Church out of the United Nations, an effort that failed miserably and embarrassingly for her and her colleagues.

In recent times, it seems, Kissling has come to believe Goodman's comment that she is some kind of philosopher. She "retired" from Catholics for a Free Choice a few years ago, though she is listed on their 2008 tax return as "former president" with a salary of close to $400,000. In her new role as Philosopher she decamped to the Center for Bioethics at the University of Pennsylvania where she is a "scholar" in residence.

She recently co-hosted a "dialogue" on common ground at

Princeton University in which, behind the scenes, she appears to have bare-knuckled her less experienced pro-life interlocutors into letting her call most of the shots. However, at the conference and afterwards butter wouldn't have melted in her mouth.

Afterward she wrote almost lovingly, "Simply put, one hopes that dialogue between those opposed to and in favor of a woman's right to choose abortion would result in a more realistic public debate; less name-calling and attacking and more reasoned argumentation for each position." She also wrote, "When people who disagree passionately on something important to them take the time to sit down and engage each other, good things happen. At a minimum, they find out the 'other' is a human being, not the devil incarnate." Sounds great.

But just this week, blogging at an Internet site called RH Reality Check, she ripped the Vatican (and me, I am proud to say) for our "brutal" rhetoric. At one and the same time, Kissling can criticize her opponents for calling names and in the same breath call her opponents names.

She is a divided woman. Those of us who have met on the actual field of pro-life battle—at the United Nations and elsewhere—know a very different woman than the one who steps forward at common-ground conferences with the cameras on. On stage, Kissling is funny, articulate, charming, pixyish even. Backstage? Well you have seen what she can be like backstage.

I once held out hope that Kissling was actually changing. Some years ago she began to recognize the humanity of the fetus (though, she does not believe it a child) and its ability to feel pain, and criticized her pro-abortion friends for failing to acknowledge them. It seemed like a good opening. She has not moved at all beyond that point. Maybe she will finally reach the logical conclusion, or maybe she is simply hoping for the kind of status Noah Cross (John Huston) described in the movie *Chinatown*: "Politicians, ugly buildings, and whores all get respectable if they last long enough." For the record, I do not consider Frances a whore. I consider her a true believer in abortion and I actually respect her usual brawling style.

What's more—and Frances knows this—I pray for her by name every single day on the fifth decade of the Rosary. Where there is life, there is hope. I just wish she believed that, too.

3. Scandal Time

ROBERT ROYAL,

The Catholic Church in America suffered another grave scandal this weekend. As was the case in the priestly abuse crisis, it was centered in Boston. If you are a Catholic and did not feel distressed and scandalized watching Senator Kennedy's funeral at Mother of Perpetual Help Church in Boston Saturday, I have to ask in all frankness: why not?

The scandal has nothing to do with his personal sins. I hope he confessed them and was forgiven, as I hope myself to be forgiven. The Church is always generous to sinners who make even the slightest gesture of repentance. In that, she shows that she is not a merely human society bound by certain rules, but the living communion of saints and the presence in this world of the merciful heart of God.

The scandal likewise has nothing to do with partisan politics. If you think it does, as some of the Commenters on Brad Miner's gentlemanly Friday column believe, you should compare Brad with the *New York Times* obituary, which felt obliged to record that Ted's shoulders were "sometimes too narrow" for the task he inherited. And that, contrary to the eulogies, he could be savagely unjust and demagogic, as even some followers admitted (e.g., in the Bork hearings), tarring mere opponents as racists, sexists, and elitists. All such shenanigans are an unfortunate feature of partisan passions, but only of passing importance.

The distress—and the scandal—arise from only one thing: the Church's failure to show the slightest reservation about the man who, more than any Catholic and perhaps more than any American political figure, has led the pro-abortion forces in Washington. Even worse, his longstanding pro-abortion leadership gave political cover to other Catholic politicians and confused simple lay people. That's what scandal (in the theological sense) does: it becomes a stumbling block for the faithful about the very truths of the faith.

The American bishops have been admirably clear that the defense of life is not like their other concerns about the poor and social justice. Defense of life occupies a different level. It is the basis for everything else.

Yet most people watching the Kennedy funeral have never heard a word of our bishops' teachings, except that Catholics are "not single issue voters." They might with justification believe that you can be a notorious pro-abortion Catholic and still be publicly honored by the Catholic Church. No one mentioned the issue, let alone took steps to make it clear that the Church means business about life.

Some have argued that now is not the time to criticize Edward Kennedy. There will be time enough later. But this is not a matter of criticism. This involves a widespread public misperception of Catholicism—or is it a true perception now? Television coverage of the Mass has spread the image of the Church honoring a well-known Catholic, passionately disrespectful of life. The damage may be irreversible.

If you think human respect should govern this moment, *de mortuis* and all that, you have a right to your opinion. But the scandal is not about respect towards Ted Kennedy. It's about the Church's own self-respect. As Benedict XVI recently reminded us, real charity exists where we respect truth. Some Catholics have argued Kennedy should have been denied Christian burial. That is wrong, even though he never publicly recanted a grave public sin. But could the Church have commended him to God in a way that paid respect to the 50 million aborted souls who were not here to watch the spectacle? She could have, and it's a tragedy for the Church and America that she did not.

I sympathize with Cardinal Sean O'Malley, a good and holy man. If he had tried to limit the Kennedy funeral to a private

Mass, he would have had a widespread revolt among both clergy and laity. And the Church would have paid a price at the hands of Massachusetts pols. But maybe the controversy would have been a "teachable" moment as the Catholic professors say.

The Vatican issued very subdued condolences, a signal to those who follow such things, that Rome, for once, was worried how its words would be interpreted. Some also see the small number of bishops and priests at the Mass as an indirect statement of some kind. For the ordinary person, however, the Cardinal was present and Placido Domingo sang *Panis angelicus*, just as if it were a papal Mass. And Cardinal McCarrick, the retired archbishop of Washington (who honored Kennedy a few years ago the very week he helped block aid to D.C. Catholic schools) said the graveside prayers.

During one of the television specials about Kennedy's life, I heard a telling story. A man recounted how the senator arranged for a U. S. Coast Guard cutter to show up in Boston Harbor at his son's birthday party. It's the kind of anecdote often told about the much loved senator, yet another example of his delight in kids and gift for knowing how to make them—and many other people— feel good. These stories touch me deeply, as does this whole unfortunate situation, because growing up in New England I had an equally large-hearted Irish uncle of the older Democratic type, who died not long ago.

But it only takes a moment's thought to realize that the U.S. Coast Guard should not be at anyone's personal disposal, even in a good cause. Any other rich and influential politician using a public service for a private purpose would have been looked at very differently.

Kennedy had a similar relationship with the Church. He didn't have much respect for the Church's proper institutional functions either, but he claimed Catholic privileges when they served his personal projects.

It was an outrage that the Coast Guard allowed itself to be used in this fashion. It is a scandal, one that sadly will have multiple bad consequences, that the Church did the same.

4. The John Jay Report

BRAD MINER

The headline at the United States Conference of Catholic Bishops website:

"John Jay College Reports No Single Cause, Predictor of Clergy Abuse"

So after all the years, money, and study, are we to conclude there is no conclusion?

Maybe it doesn't matter: a paragraph on page eight of *The Causes and Context of Sexual Abuse of Minors by Catholic Priests in the United States, 1950–2010* shows that reports of clerical abuse have fallen off dramatically, and the Church has taken steps to see there'll be no similar "crisis" in the future.

Lead researcher Karen Terry is quoted in the USCCB's press release as saying that "neither celibacy nor homosexuality were causes of the abuse." (About celibacy the report is surely correct.)

The report's Executive Summary offers this summary consideration: Social and cultural changes in the 1960s and 1970s manifested in increased levels of deviant behavior in the general society and also among priests of the Catholic Church in the United States.

This is being called the "Woodstock Defense."

And the Church must be grateful that priests weren't also engaged in the "drug use and crime" that, as the report states, characterized this period of upheaval, although why priests did not in significant numbers succumb to the allure of other crimes of the times is not explained.

And no "specific institutional cause" was discovered. Nothing in seminary admissions; nothing in parish management; nothing in diocesan attitudes. The abusers themselves "were not found, on the basis of their developmental histories or their psychological characteristics, to be *statistically distinguishable* from other priests [emphasis added]," except, of course, that they abused kids and teens but other priests didn't. We learn, though, that those who were ordained in the Sixties and Seventies "engaged in abusive behavior much more quickly after their entrance into ministry" than had their older (or would their younger) colleagues.

Ms. Terry's co-researcher, Margaret L. Smith, suggested last year that the overwhelmingly homosexual nature of the priest abuse cases doesn't prove the priests involved were "gay." She compared the conditions under which priests live to those of men in prison, where sexual encounters are necessarily homosexual: it's *situational*. It's context.

The research team must have faced a serious, albeit familiar, problem: since most of the abuse cases were male-on-male, they were in a pickle as to how they'd deal with the confirming data without demonizing the "gay" subculture. So . . . they barely mention it. Apparently this is fine with many at the USCCB, despite the fact that the bishops, who commissioned the study, ostensibly consider homosexual behavior gravely sinful—and not just for priests. Oscar Wilde was a prophet: it really is the sin that dare not speak its name; not anyway in polite academic and clerical circles; not with a "gay"-friendly media brooking no dissent from its notions of the new normal. The assertion that the abusers weren't "statistically distinguishable" from other priests puts a heavy burden on statistics.

Yet the crisis was self-evidently homosexual in its genesis. This we know from the fact that *eighty-plus percent* of the abuse was same-sex, whereas sexual abuse in the larger culture is overwhelmingly heterosexual. And the John Jay social scientists limited their research and analysis strictly to the abuse of minors, and so don't present (nor did they seek) data on the extent to which priests were engaged sexually with other adult men (or women for that matter).

Not knowing how many homosexuals went into and came out of seminaries during the period, we are missing absolutely critical data. Other studies have sought this information, but the results vary widely, as do their methodologies and reliability. Some estimates suggest the homosexual population in the priesthood has been as high as fifty percent. That seems unlikely. Others have claimed the percentage is less than five percent. But that seems too low.

THE JOHN JAY REPORT

"Individuals who molest children may be heterosexual, homosexual, or bisexual with regard to victim selection," the report states, and this is the only time those descriptors of sexual preference are used, underscoring the report's complete rejection of any association between said preferences and sexual abuse.

But priests are *not* incarcerated criminals, normal heterosexuals do *not* engage in homosexual acts, and anybody who was actually around certain seminaries in the 1970s, as I was, knows that homosexuality—like dissent against Vatican teaching and leadership—*was* rampant. I spent time in two seminaries as I considered entering the priesthood. One was run by faithful priests and impressed me as rather like an Army base: everybody was in uniform and a sense of personal decorum and doctrinal discipline permeated the place. The other seminary resembled a college dormitory crossed with what I suppose a "gay" bathhouse would be like. Nobody wore clerical garb and conversation among seminarians, faculty, and visitors was heretical and profane. I became a Catholic at twenty-six. By the time I was twenty-seven, two young priests had come on to me sexually, which I found both repulsive and discouraging. All this played a role in my decision not to become a priest.

If academics or bishops wish to believe the Church didn't have a homosexual problem, they have their heads firmly inserted into quicksand. Rome's commitment to put things right began with the 2005 directive to weed out "gays" from seminary admissions and was re-emphasized by the Holy Father in *Light of the World*. Cardinal Levada recently wrote a letter outlining new procedures for responding to abuse. The Vatican knows what John Jay won't admit.

The *Causes and Context* report is long (140-plus pages), and deserves more careful scrutiny than I've given it here. But does anybody seriously believe that without so many active homosexuals in the priesthood there'd have been an abuse crisis? A handful of homosexual and heterosexual abuse incidents, no doubt. But nothing on the scale we actually witnessed.

5. A Different Priestly Scandal

Michael Novak

Burning injustices rest on our consciences, and will continue to burn us until we correct them.

I had dinner the other night with a marvelous priest, who started out our dinner by having the little children who were with us recite together (partly in song) the blessing before meals. They loved doing it. Loved the sound of it. Loved the solemnity. Loved the fun.

I did not know until well along in the meal, almost at the very end, that this good priest—so well informed about so many matters of faith, so genial, and so patently good-hearted and faithful—had been falsely accused of sexual molestation eight years ago. He was forced to leave the ministry (an accusation these days is enough to do this—a horrible scandal in itself). His accuser died of a cocaine overdose in his mother's house, but not before exonerating the priest by admitting the falsity of his accusation.

But all that notwithstanding, the bishop in his diocese has not moved—dared?—to reinstate this good man and return him to his proper standing in the priesthood, or even to give a public apology for his unjust treatment. Nor has the press that stirred up the atmosphere of high-tech lynchings revisited his case (and hundreds if not thousands of others) to clear them of this horrible wrong.

Very few raw accusations that have emerged since the priestly abuse crisis erupted were ever subject to due process and full discovery and an open trial.

In America, citizens have a right to their innocence until proven guilty. This good man was never given a hearing. He is still being punished—to the very the core of his being and in his very reason for existence—because of a false accusation and that alone. Further, it is an accusation that has been withdrawn by the accuser, and apologized for by his family: "Billy [name changed] would never have made the accusation if he had been sober."

To have been treated as non-persons, as non-citizens, is an

injustice that cries out to heaven for justice. Yet in addition to the truly evil predators that have been identified and weeded out, this is the fate of a considerable number of innocent Catholic priests in this country today.

I do not understand why the Catholic Church has not fought for a civil process that gives these good men, innocent until proven guilty, fair trials. I do not understand why the American courts do not do this. I do not understand why the American press is not fighting mad about that. I do not understand why the ACLU is not leading this charge—they have a reputation for defending the unpopular victims, the publicly vilified victims.

We all know, of course, that many accused priests have been proven guilty. No doubt, still more deserve to be given their due punishments. The years 1965–1985, give or take, were in clerical dereliction the worst in my memory (including historical memory, going back to the beginning of this Republic). They terribly shamed me and many millions of other Catholics.

But I also know that thousands of the accused have never been given due process. They have been discarded as non-persons. They can hardly comprehend the sudden injustice they have suffered in the Church they love and the country they love. Since birth they have thought themselves safe from that—the kinds of injustices usually thought of as only occurring elsewhere, not in our America. They have been horribly betrayed.

I beg those who have reached the same conclusions I have to act to change the present injustice, to rectify it, to erase it, and to restore to their full standing as human beings, citizens, and men committed to their faith, those who, after due process, are judged not guilty.

They loved that faith in part because of its traditional defense of individual persons from birth to natural death. They loved this country because of its protection of individual rights. They cannot understand how they have been stripped of those basic rights—suddenly, without an outcry on their behalf by the Church, the state, and the public defenders of basic human rights.

Look into it, America. Look into it, Catholic Church.

Examine the facts. Punish the proven guilty. But give the innocent the honor that is due them.

They have suffered so much, for so many years. It is a marvel that some still maintain their morale and their hope. Even if we humans do not fulfill our duty to protect them from mendacious accusations, may God bless them and be faithful to them forever.

6. Tim Russert: The Story Untold

HADLEY ARKES

The death of Tim Russert commanded the news coverage of virtually all of the networks on the day that it happened. And to the surprise even of his friends, it commanded the channels on the next day... and the next, leading to a wake held, of all places, at St. Albans, by the National Cathedral, a Mass at Trinity Church, and a Memorial Service at the Kennedy Center. It was the kind of death and mourning more associated with Presidents, with high figures of state, than with journalists. One could only imagine the scene when Walter Cronkite is called to that Great Newsroom in the Sky. Will he lie in state at the Capitol?

And yet why this out-of-scale display for Tim Russert? One gathers that he was a good guy, down to earth, not pretentious, and far more fair-minded, it was said, than other prominent figures in the media, affecting to be commentators on politics. As H. L. Mencken said of Grover Cleveland, he was a good man in a bad trade. In a profession slanted quite noticeably to the Left, Tim Russert seemed to be willing to ask hard questions of politicians on all sides. But not quite: in the time of Russert's ascendancy on television, the issue of abortion had become the most central, divisive issue in our politics. It was the defining issue in the "culture wars," separating the political parties. And yet, on that matter of abortion, Tim Russert never quite managed to ask questions running very deep, or suggesting even serious reflection. As one blogger managed to show, his pressing questions were reserved for Republicans who were pro-life. His discreet silences here offer clues leading back to the side of the story that remained untold, unsounded, during a week of relentless talk about him.

The part that remained unmentioned became ever more conspicuous in its absence in a week in which Russert was celebrated as a Catholic. His devotion to his family; his education at the hands of the Jesuits; his nurturing by a nun out of central casting, the female equivalent of Barry Fitzgerald—all of this was highlighted. Highlighted, in fact, to such a degree that one savvy observer thought it was one of the rarest weeks in the America media actually celebrating Catholicism. But my own reading is that Russert was not celebrated because he was Catholic; he was celebrated because he was a celebrity.

The sense of "family" and "the faith" celebrated during the week of mourning for Tim Russert was discreetly detached from the substance of any teaching that would define the character of a Catholic family and the Catholicism it professed. The tipoff came at the very beginning of his career. His credential for a high place in the media came through his service as a devoted staffer to Mario Cuomo and Daniel Patrick Moynihan. These two political men managed to navigate their way in the liberal politics of New York by establishing their reluctance to impose, through the laws, the moral teaching of the Church on abortion. They treated that teaching, not as a teaching formed by moral reasoning and the evidence of embryology, but as a matter merely of "beliefs," which they would not claim to be true for anyone but themselves. And indeed, as the wags remarked, Moynihan and Cuomo would not even impose these convictions on themselves. My own surmise was that Tim Russert absorbed these lessons taught by the masters. And it was the surety that he had indeed absorbed them that made him plausible as a figure to direct "Meet the Press," the flagship of all news programs.

Let us suppose, however, that in his heart of hearts Tim Russert did indeed respect, as true, the moral teaching of his Church on the issue that John Paul II and Benedict XVI have regarded as the central moral issue of our day, the issue from which everything else radiates. If so, Russert's discreet silences reflected the tacit bargain for liberal Catholics in the Democratic

Party and the media: they can hold their position only at the price of remaining silent on the moral issue most central to Catholic teaching and to the politics of the day. If my surmise is wrong, it can be tested easily and readily disproved: What understanding did he impart to his own family? Do they understand the issue of abortion in the way that Benedict XVI or Henry Hyde have understood it, or in the way that the Kennedys and Cuomos have taught Catholics now to understand it?

No family has done more to misinstruct American Catholics on the teaching of their own Church than the Kennedys, and their teaching began with this lesson: that one can be pro-choice and effectively pro-abortion and still be a good Catholic. This used to be called "giving scandal": it was gently telling Catholics that the central teaching of their Church could be treated as false, or simply not that important. As my late teacher Leo Strauss once observed, when a wise man preserves his silence on a matter that others regard as important, he leads us to understand that it is not, in the end, all that important. Amidst all of the mourning and celebration for Tim Russert, the most critical thing he imparted as a public man was that the central moral teaching of his Church was not, in the scale of things, all that important or true.

7. Russert II: Every Man His Own Church

HADLEY ARKES

My late leader, the first Mayor Daley of Chicago, once recoiled in anger from a volley of attacks, and remarked that, in holding to his views, "I have been vilified, I have been crucified, I have been . . . criticized!" I well understood that I should brace for some stings of reproach when I sounded a note deeply critical over the memorials, the lessons offered up, over the death of Tim Russert. It must ever be sad to see a man struck down, so comparatively young, when he seemed to be at the top of his game. One must also feel the hurt of the family and friends who would find him missing from their lives.

But that is not all there was. In the effort to draw out the deeper meaning of Russert's life, the public commentary drew a firm connection between his character and his "faith" as a Catholic. And yet, as I argued, the success of Russert's career depended on his willingness, as a commentator, to mute the matter of abortion. But in doing that, he would convey the sense that a matter quite central and preeminent in Catholic teaching, was not, in the scale of things, all that important.

Among the criticisms relayed to me was that Russert was but a "moderator," and on the other hand that he did in fact press certain Democrats to defend their position on abortion. A transcript arrived in which Russert kept challenging Al Gore to state when he thought human life began.

But Gore evaded the question, and Russert showed no doggedness in pursuing it. Besides, Russert never gave any indication that he was willing to treat the answer as anything more than Al Gore's view of the matter. That was quite different from taking matters to the root—as in asking a Mario Cuomo or Pat Moynihan to explain how anyone could be justified in regarded the offspring of *homo sapiens* in the womb as anything less than human, given the findings of embryology and the force of principled reasoning. Were human offspring less human when they were shorter, without arms, not yet gifted with speech? And did one need justifications less compelling to destroy the lives of small humans? I would readily change my estimate of Tim Russert if there was a transcript showing him raising those kinds of questions, truly "running deep," to any Democrat of high standing. A friend I respect deeply, Rich Doerflinger, sent me a transcript of Russert interviewing Howard Dean, but Russert's performance there was even shallower than with Gore, and what it revealed, I'm afraid, is an interviewer who had quite evidently not given, to this matter, any reflection running very deep.

Russert's questioning of Al Gore was enough to undo that curious claim that he had been only a "moderator." Even "moderators" have vast discretion in the issues they raise—and teaching in that way just what they regard as important. I'd propose one simple test: Is there any evidence that Tim Russert ever called in Democrats to see why they were opposing the Born-Alive Infants' Protection Act, the act to preserve the life of the child who *survived* the abortion? It was the strategy finally of the Democrats to let the bill go through, but to avoid any public argument, which could only draw attention to the bill. *The New York Times* fell into line by offering virtually no coverage, and no articles on its op-ed page. Bill O'Reilly did have a segment on his program, expressing outrage that there should be the need for such a bill. Did Russert have any such session? Show us the transcript on that one, and I would gladly revise my judgment—or *rest my case*.

Now it could be that, as a public commentator, Russert was obliged to treat abortion as one issue among many, as though they all stood on the same moral plane: some people want lower interest rates, or mortgage bailouts, others just want to kill innocent babies in the womb for wholly private reasons. But if so that rather confirms the point: celebrating that kind of performance as the work of a serious Catholic offers the most distorted, and false, account of what Catholicism teaches and what it means to be Catholic.

But beyond everything else, the recoil from my piece, with a sharper edge of feeling, came with the view that I had been uncharitable, that there was something gravely wrong in questioning Russert's avowal of his own faith. But if nothing had been said on Russert's faith during the mourning, there would have been no more reason to discuss it than his allegiance to the Buffalo Bills. If the question was, "Do you credit a man's own account of himself," I'm as ready as anyone else to credit Russet's account that he considered himself a Catholic and a fan of the Bills. But the argument was, Who are you to call into question Russert's understanding of his faith? That criticism implied that Russert's understanding of Catholic teaching must be respected because it was *his*. The implication is that any of us would be free to offer our own version of Catholic teaching that fits more comfortably with the state of our own lives and moral shadings. But that could be the case only if there were no Catholic teaching with a coherence and integrity of its own. Evidently there are many Catholics who have made themselves suggestible to these notions. But the truth that has not yet broken in on them is that, as they have backed themselves into this understanding, they have backed themselves out of Catholic teaching and the logic of what it means to be Catholic. With a certain serenity, and without quite realizing it, they have ceased to be Catholic.

8. Catholic Charities: A Two-Fold Challenge

MATTHEW HANLEY

Having funded groups that support abortion and "same sex marriage," and funneled more than $7 million to ACORN over the span of a decade, the Catholic Campaign for Human Development (CCHD) is coming knocking again this weekend at a parish near you amidst calls for reform, The special CCHD Sunday collection, which funds non-Catholic organizations and does not provide direct relief to the poor, arrives at a challenging time for charitable agencies.

Government bodies are increasingly making public funding contingent upon accepting ideological terms and conditions antithetical to the very identity that inspires Catholic social services. But that identity has long been withering from within. Lay people are called to engage vital issues in an indifferent or hostile public square. What recourse is there when their own official charitable agencies fail spectacularly to reflect basic beliefs?

This is all part of a broader trend. African bishops meeting in Rome in October repeatedly denounced the "virulent ideological poisons" being imposed on Africa from the West, precisely what Catholic agencies encounter—and sometimes succumb to—here at home as well. A Ghanaian bishop stated that there is a deliberate campaign being advanced by some NGOs, governments, and international agencies to undermine the family and African cultural values. A South African bishop pointed to the "second wave of colonization" from "liberalism, secularism, and from lob-byists who squat at the United Nations."

It's ironic that our American Caesar, so celebrated on account of his African extraction, champions destructive Western ideologies that African bishops regard as a "subtle and ruthless" form of colonization. Some have argued that, by his actions and rhetoric, he sees himself as more than *merely* an American president—a transnational leader of sorts. Well, he is (as its most powerful and visible proponent) the present face of the culture of death, whose malignancy knows no borders. It is a distinction that, unlike the Nobel Peace Prize, has been earned.

The culture of death knows no borders (or classes) because, as Solzhenitsyn put it in the *Gulag Archipelago*, "the line separating good and evil" cuts first and foremost "through every human heart." He further reflects: In the intoxication of youthful success I had felt myself to be infallible, and I was therefore cruel. In the surfeit of power, I was a murderer, and an oppressor. In my most evil moments, I was convinced that I was doing good, and I was well supplied with systemic arguments.

Perhaps there would be enough in these words to trigger an epiphany within our Caesar's conscience, if he read them, though it is admittedly a stretch to suggest that he has ever been well supplied with arguments for his unrelenting disregard for life (even as C.D.C. data indicate that the number of abortions among African-Americans exceeds their *top seven causes of mortality combined*). He has merely been equipped with what Denver Archbishop Charles J. Chaput calls "great media handlers," and is abetted by an elite culture that has distanced itself from both faith and reason.

Solzhenitsyn stresses that the line separating good and evil within each of us shifts; it "oscillates with the years." This is one reason why *steady witness* to the Gospel—being reminders of what is good and true—is such an indispensable part of Catholic charitable activity.

True, our American Caesar "bullies religion while he claims to respect it." But he does not need to shake down all the kids for lunch money by himself as long as CCHD lends a willing hand. Internal reform of the many Catholic agencies such as CCHD that have gone flagrantly adrift *of their own volition* is a burning priority. The litany of accommodation, in one form or another, is all too familiar: contraception, abortion, condoms, "gay adoption," etc. Underestimating the perils of statism and the value of subsidiarity in large-scale new initiatives like the healthcare debate is another concern.

Reform of our own agencies means nurturing a climate in which committed Catholics can live out their vocations of service even if that means accepting the hazards of being countercultural. At present, such Catholics are unwelcome or marginalized within several Catholic agencies. While that remains the case, reform will stall. This is a matter quite beyond the control of the laity.

Cozy careerism compounds the ideological threats to charitable endeavors, as Theodore Dalrymple attests: "One man's poverty is another man's employment opportunity: as long ago as the sixteenth century, a German bishop remarked that the poor are a gold mine." I once heard Dalrymple address his own lack of belief by saying that the leap of faith has thus far simply eluded him— an honest and even moving admission, which reminded me that faith is a *gift*. It can be asked for, but not procured—even by those who are immensely gifted. This is a *mystery*. It is also a mystery when those granted custody over Catholic charitable agencies sometimes act as if they would rather exchange that gift for the public esteem that comes not from genuinely noble acts, but from what the elite imagine to be their own providential role in society.

We have all squandered the gift of faith. And yet God keeps giving. A renewed gratitude for that gift should animate the reform of our Catholic charitable agencies. That much, at the very least, the bishops *can* control, and CCHD would be a good place to start. Whether or not we are ultimately able to stay afloat on the high, hostile seas of America's Caesar, we can at least leave harbor prepared for the voyage with sturdy vessels and full sails.

9. The Economic Crisis: We're All Responsible

SEAN FIELER

The Archbishop of Birmingham, England, Vincent Nichols, who is widely regarded as the leading candidate to become British primate (Cardinal Archbishop of Westminster), recently said: "A market controlled only by regulation, sooner or later, will succumb to its inherent drive for profit at all costs. Of course the profit motive is crucial, and responsibility to investors is a significant balancing factor in risk taking." This responsibility "to investors," I would argue, should rather be thought of as a responsibility "of investors" more generally. As individual economic actors, we are all responsible, and not just for limiting our particular financial risk. We also have a larger obligation to make sure that our savings are not misused. To this end, the regulations and structure of our modern financial system should, whenever possible, seek to assist rather than hinder us in this effort.

The subprime crisis highlights a critical shortcoming in our financial system when individuals do nothing more than follow rules. In recent years, as mortgage origination became increasingly systematized, loan officers and mortgage brokers were no longer expected to make assessments as to whether borrowers could actually repay their loans. Instead, they were simply asked to help borrowers meet clearly specified requirements. Reduced to putting the borrower's statement of income in the best possible light and obtaining a favorable appraisal value for the house to be financed, mortgage originators focused on and excelled at the task at hand. Rules that were meant to make the origination process more efficient didn't just have the intended effect of limiting the range over which judgment was exercised. They also had the unintended effect of entirely displacing that judgment.

An excess of debt, our overarching economic problem, is to a large extent a result of the same pattern of behavior, rules followed by rule-following without judgment. Banks, which created much of the debt on which we are now collectively choking, are, not coincidentally, among the most regulated private enterprises in our economy. The executives and board members running these organizations, just like individual mortgage originators, over time allowed regulations to displace their judgment. The government-is-the-solution crowd would have us believe that the regulations weren't quite right. They weren't streamlined enough. That this problem is essentially a technical matter, and if we just combine the Office of Thrift Supervision with the Office of the Comptroller of the Currency and allow the Federal Reserve to supervise the largest financial enterprises, this problem won't recur. Better regulation, however, while by definition a good thing, won't prevent future banking crises.

The problem, to be clear, is not that bankers aren't sufficiently risk averse. They are risk averse, but principally to a particular type of risk, namely the risk of making a mistake without sufficient company. Bankers' penchant for uniformity, while ensuring that few competently managed banks have problems during normal times, also ensures an unhealthy level of systemic risk. This willingness to take on unwise risks so long as the risk-taking is done en masse was perfectly captured by Charles Prince just a few months prior to his departure as CEO of Citigroup. "As long as the music is playing, you've got to get up and dance," he said famously in defense of his decision to continue making risky loans to leverage buyout firms, despite his own personal reservations about the solidity of these credits.

Given bankers' conformist bent and regulations' history of exacerbating rather than remedying this tendency, it is naïve of us to think that now regulation will be the solution. Bank regulation, historically speaking, has never been anything more than a thirty-year dam. Without the dam, the waters' periodic rise washes away bankers' imprudent investments, never allowing bankers' imprudence to get very far out of hand. Once built, however, the dam removes the risk of regular flooding and encourages the financing of construction farther and farther out into the floodplain. That the government officially declares all building right up to the dam's edge safe only makes matters worse. Over time, the government's rules and bankers' short-term self-interest win out over prudence, and massive construction occurs right at the dam's edge. When the dam eventually breaks, as it always does, very few banks escape without extensive losses and the banking system as a whole freezes up.

The way forward requires that we confront the structural instability inherent in our banking system instead of simply focusing on building a better dam. Individual savers must reclaim their natural role as responsible economic actors and forego the convenience of risk-free bank accounts that are the root cause of the system's instability. By relieving individual depositors of any financial risk, government-insured bank accounts act as a barrier to moral action, effectively preventing depositors from making responsible inquiries into how a bank is deploying their money. That all financial assets have risk is a reality with which individuals can and must learn to live. The clear alternative to our current system, money market-like accounts that could go down as well as up in value depending on the specific underlying investments, would require savers to know where and how their money is being lent and to make prudential judgments about how their savings ought to be deployed, a responsibility of which we are all capable.

10. The Witness of Pius XII

GEORGE MARLIN

This Friday (October 9) will be the fifty-first anniversary of Pope Pius XII's death. Last year around this time, when Benedict XVI was planning a trip to Israel, the old controversy about Pius erupted once more because a caption at the Yad Vashem memorial, where Benedict was to visit, claimed the earlier pope had done nothing to condemn Nazis and their slaughter of the Jews. Pius is on the track to sainthood—as he should be—and it's worth looking again at these charges.

In October 1939, exactly seventy years ago, one month after the Nazis and the Soviet Union conquered Poland, Pius XII issued his first encyclical *Summi Pontificatus: On the Unity of Human*

Society. Declaring that, as Vicar of Christ, he had "no greater debt to Our office than 'to testify to the truth' with Apostolic firmness," he called on people of good will to unify in opposing world evils, particularly "two pernicious errors": racism and statism.

Pius XII, who served as the Vatican Secretary of State for nine years before his election to the papacy in March 1939, explained to the faithful that the progress of spiritual decay in Europe was due to the "ever increasing host of Christ's enemies" who deify the state. Germany and the Soviet Union were guilty of "the denial and rejection of the universal norm of morality"—the natural law.

All men, said the Pontiff, were "looking with terror into the Abyss" because totalitarian legal positivists had forbidden "every appeal to the principles of natural reason and of Christian conscience" by "elevating the state [as] the supreme criterion of the moral and juridical order."

Since civil sovereignty was created through the will of God, state activities must "converge harmoniously towards the common good" not the collective good promoted by totalitarians, whereas only select groups—Nazi Party members or Aryans—benefit. Pius condemned regimes that abolished "rights peculiar to family" (i.e., education) and insisted that rights of conscience are "sacred and invisible." Taking a shot at the Communists, he stated that it is harmful to the prosperity of nations and their people and "leads to the violation of other rights" if the state is "something ultimate to which everything else should be subordinated and directed."

As for the National Socialists, Pius bluntly stated they had "abandoned Christ's cross for another which brings only death."

On the subject of race (which at the time referred primarily to the anti-Jewish policies of the Nazis), Pius condemns discrimination and emphasizes that all races "have equal rights as children in the House of the Lord." The Church, he proclaims, is open to all people:

The spirit—the teaching and the work of the Church—can never be other than what the Apostle of the Gentiles preached: "putting on the new man, him who is renewed unto knowledge, according to the image of him that created him. Where there is neither Gentile nor Jew, circumcision nor uncircumcision, barbarian nor Scythian, bond nor free. But Christ is all and in all." (Colossians 3: 10–11)

Finally, he expressed his anguish over the war started by the Germans and Russians. He described it as Europe's:

> Hour of Darkness where there reigns in thousands of families death and desolation, lamentation and misery. The blood of countless human beings, even noncombatants, raises a piteous dirge over a nation such as Our dear Poland, which . . . has a right to the generous and brotherly sympathy of the whole world.

The reaction to the encyclical—from both friend and foe—was passionate. In a bold front-page headline, *The New York Times* declared "Pope Condemns Dictators, Treaty Violators, Racism." The *Times* published the entire document and referred to the pope as an Old Testament prophet "speaking words of fire." The London *Daily Telegraph* headline: "Pope Condemns Nazi Theory." And the *American Israelite* praised the pope's "denunciation of Nazism." Records of a November 1939 British Cabinet meeting revealed that the encyclical was considered "in some ways, the most important document the war has yet produced and the wider its circulation the better from all points of view." The French government reproduced *Summi Pontificatus* and air-dropped 80,000 copies on select German cities.

Christ's enemies, however, were not at all happy with the pope's letter to the faithful. Gestapo Chief Heinrich Mueller stated, "This encyclical is directed exclusively against Germany, both in ideology and in regard to the German-Polish dispute; how dangerous it is for our foreign relations as well as our domestic affairs is beyond dispute." SS chief Reinhardt Heydrich said: "this declaration of the pope makes an unequivocal accusation against Germany."

Fearing the political impact the encyclical would have on the conquered Poles, the Nazis distributed an altered version in Poland.

To convince them that the pope supported the actions of the Nazi regime, every reference to Poland was changed to Germany. *Summi Pontificatus* is just one piece of evidence that proves the critics of Pius XII are wrong. It is one of the many reasons why *The New York Times* wrote in a December 1941 editorial:

> The voice of Pius XII is a lonely voice in the silence and darkness enveloping Europe. . . . In calling for a "real new order" based on "liberty, justice and love". . . the pope put himself squarely against Hitlerism. Recognizing that there is no road to open to agreement between belligerents "whose reciprocal war aims and programs seem to be irreconcilable," Pius XII left no doubt that the Nazi aims are also irreconcilable with his own conception of a Christian peace.

It's time for the uninformed voices raised against Pius XII to learn the plain truth—which was obvious to everyone seventy years ago—and to do justice to this much maligned, saintly, and heroic man.

11. Justice and Charity

ROBERTO DE MATTEI

Benedict XVI's *Caritas in Veritate* must be read in light of a debate going on in the Catholic Church for a century. It first arose in the mid–1800s with the social question, and new ideas like liberalism and socialism. *Rerum Novarum*, Leo XIII's encyclical (1891), was considered the Catholic answer to these new challenges. But it was really the result of a wide debate between two different schools of Christian economists and sociologists. One taught that the social question required the primacy of the theological virtue of charity, the other the primacy of the moral virtue of justice.

The primacy of justice leads to an emphasis on the state as administering justice. The primacy of charity, however, underlines the role of the individual. Therefore we have, on the one hand, the regulating state, by nature Socialist; and on the other, the free market, private property, and individual enterprise.

The safest solution, as *Rerum Novarum* pointed out, is a synthesis of justice and charity, with a slight prevalence of the latter. Paul VI's *Populorum Progressio* (1967) reversed this tradition, proclaiming the supremacy of justice over charity, and a negative view of liberal capitalism and free trade. It called for Programs and Planning, envisaging limitations on private property and the redistribution of income, while encouraging the cult of progress, work, and international solidarity.

Benedict now brings back traditional doctrine in new terms, by developing paragraphs 26–31 of his own *Deus Caritas Est*, which were focused precisely on the relation between charity and justice.

Caritas in Veritate declares that "Charity in truth is the principal driving force behind the authentic development of every person and of all humanity" and constitutes "the heart of the Church's social doctrine." It is in fact "the principle not only of micro-relationships (with friends, family members, or in small groups) but also of macro-relationships (social, economic, and political ones)."

Populorum Progressio called for the liberation of all peoples from hunger, poverty, endemic disease, and ignorance. Post-Conciliar enthusiasts believed it possible to provide peace and well-being to all. "Justice and Peace" were the key words Paul VI employed for achieving "man's complete development and the development of all mankind."

Benedict roots Charity in truth: "A Christianity of charity without truth would be more or less interchangeable with a pool of good sentiments, helpful for social cohesion, but of little relevance." The social doctrine of the Church is therefore "*caritas in veritate in re sociali*: the proclamation of the truth of Christ's love in society." Without truth, "charity degenerates into sentimentality. Love becomes an empty shell, to be filled in an arbitrary way. In a culture without truth, this is the fatal risk facing love. It falls prey to contingent subjective emotions and opinions, the word 'love' is abused and distorted, to the point where it comes to mean the opposite."

Justice has its place: "Not only is justice not extraneous to charity, not only is it not an alternative or parallel path to charity: justice is inseparable from charity." Nevertheless, "Charity goes beyond justice, because to love is to give, to offer what is 'mine' to the other; but it never lacks justice, which prompts us to give the other what is 'his,' what is due to him by reason of his being or his acting." Charity is linked to gift: "Charity is love received and given."

Benedict XVI takes a stance towards Paul VI similar to the one he took towards the Second Vatican Council: it should re-interpreted in the light of Tradition. The pope emphasizes that *Populorum Progressio* is still relevant, if "situated within the great current of Tradition." But to fully comprehend development in Paul VI, we need "the Tradition of the apostolic faith, a patrimony both ancient and new, outside of which *Populorum Progressio* would be a document without roots—and issues concerning development would be reduced to merely sociological data."

Following the neo-Malthusianism of the 1960s, Paul speaks openly of responsible limitation of births. Benedict XVI notes instead Paul's *Humanae Vitae* (1968): "This is not a question of purely individual morality: *Humanae Vitae* indicates the strong links between life ethics and social ethics."

Benedict knows that demographic growth does not produce poverty, but wealth: "Morally responsible openness to life represents a rich social and economic resource" and it is "at the heart of all real development." In view of this, states are "called to enact policies promoting the centrality and the integrity of the family founded on marriage between a man and a woman, the primary vital cell of society."

Benedict XVI sees positive value in free markets and enterprise, if grounded in ethical principles: "Admittedly, the market can be a negative force, not because it is so by nature, but because a certain ideology can make it so." The market is merely an instrument and "it is man's darkened reason that produces these consequences, not the instrument per se. Therefore it is not the instrument that must be called to account, but individuals, their moral conscience and their personal and social responsibility."

Many believe economic freedom means freedom from the moral sphere. For instance, "liberals" often favor drug decriminalization, abortion, and bio-ethical experimentation. Benedict counters: "the social question has become a radically anthropological question, in the sense that it concerns not just how life is conceived but also how it is manipulated, as bio-technology and a pro-euthanasia mindset places it increasingly under man's control."

Finally, a far-reaching assertion: "God has to have a place in the public realm, specifically in regard to its cultural, social, economic, and particularly its political dimensions." In fact, "without God man neither knows which way to go, nor even understands who he is." This is the heart of the document, and possibly of the whole Magisterium of Benedict XVI.

12. Excommunicate Pelosi

BRAD MINER

It's an election year: time for some provocative thoughts about faith and politics.

Two Februarys past, Nancy Pelosi met with Benedict XVI in Rome. No press attended the meeting; there was no photo op. Afterwards, Mrs. Pelosi praised the "Church's leadership in fighting poverty, hunger and global warming, as well as the Holy Father's dedication to religious freedom . . ." This was somewhat at odds with the Vatican's version of the papal-politico confab:

> His Holiness took the opportunity to speak of the requirements of the natural moral law and the Church's consistent teaching on the dignity of human life from conception to natural death which enjoins all Catholics, and especially legislators . . . in creating a just system of

laws capable of protecting human life at all stages of its development.

Mrs. Pelosi has been cautioned, lectured to, and scolded by any number of priests, bishops, and cardinals since then, but she proceeds blithely along as before.

"I feel what I was raised to believe is consistent with what I profess," she told *Newsweek* in December, "and that we are all endowed with a free will and a responsibility to answer for our actions. And that women should have the opportunity to exercise their free will."

This led San Francisco's archbishop, George H. Niederauer, to once again undertake some remedial instruction. To wit: free will does not excuse sin.

In May of this year, the Speaker addressed a meeting of something called the Catholic Community Conference and said:

> My favorite word is the Word, is the Word. And that is everything. It says it all for us. And you know the biblical reference; you know the Gospel reference of the Word. And that Word is, we have to give voice to what that means in terms of public policy that would be in keeping with the values of the Word.

As some exasperated Catholic wags quipped at the time, this suggests a new bumper sticker: *WWJA* ("Who Would Jesus Abort?").

Now, nobody expects Mrs. Pelosi—mother of five and grand-mother of seven—to be a politician *and* a theologian (moral or otherwise). Her stepping into the middle of such things has been foolhardy. Remember 2008 when she tried to instruct the American bishops on the theology of St. Augustine, which was only slightly sillier than Joe Biden attempting to instruct them about Aquinas? Her political position and profession of Catholicism in private and public require something more than wrist-slapping and finger-wagging so that American Catholics will see that what she is pushing is not Catholicism.

It's time somebody finds the gumption to excommunicate her.

She is all but certainly excommunicated already, *latae senten-tiae* (literally, "given sentence," meaning her loss of union is inherent in her actions), but where is the public value of that? Her continued misstatements about the faith and her unrepentant support of abortion rights (where she most obviously stands outside the faith) amount to textbook case of scandal, the sort that begs for formal redress.

One of America's leading canon lawyers, Edward N. Peters, has written: "If her prolonged public conduct does *not* qualify as obstinate perseverance in manifest grave sin, then, in all sincerity, I must admit to not knowing what *would* constitute obstinate perseverance in manifest grave sin." His point of reference is to a passage in Canon 915: "Those upon whom the penalty of excommunication or interdict has been imposed or declared, *and others who obstinately persist in manifest grave sin*, are not to be admitted to Holy Communion." [Emphasis added. And, N.B., I must qualify the opinion of Edward Peters. At his website (*In the Light of the Law*) he pointed out in response to this column that he has never called for Mrs. Pelosi's excommunication—only that she be denied Communion. It's an important distinction and one I'm sorry I hadn't grasped right away.]

And here's the rub: *How is a priest* (in Washington, D.C. where Mrs. Pelosi works or back in her California district or, for that matter, at St. Peter's in Rome) *to certainly know that she should not be allowed to receive the Host unless he has been directed to refuse her by ecclesial authority?* (I ask this even though a priest may be required by 915 to refuse Communion even without a bishop's formal declaration.) How are Catholics to judge the distinction between her position on abortion and that of a pro-life candidate who may be her opponent? (In fact, opponent John Dennis is not a pro-lifer, but a libertarian Republican who opposes government funding of abortion.)

Why haven't bishops in Washington, San Francisco, and Rome stepped in to make clear that Mrs. Pelosi should be refused at the rail? Recall the 2007 statement of Archbishop Raymond Burke: if "the lack of right disposition is serious and public, and the person, nevertheless, approaches to receive the Sacrament, then he is to be admonished and denied Holy Communion." Admonished and denied, he means, *by the individual priest*—without the necessity of a bishop's direction.

But with all due respect, isn't that kicking the can down the road? Isn't that like the Joint Chiefs giving platoon leaders ad hoc responsibility for rules of engagement? There's bound to be a priest out there who'd like nothing better than to be the one to say "No!" to Nancy (and then get three minutes on "The O'Reilly Factor"). But the faithful will only be left wondering if the priest hasn't "acted alone." Archbishop Burke's wiggle-waggle will be confusing, given his strong summary statement:

> No matter how often a Bishop or priest repeats the teaching of the Church regarding procured abortion, if he stands by and does nothing to discipline a Catholic who publicly supports legislation permitting the gravest of injustices and, at the same time, presents himself to receive Holy Communion, then his teaching rings hollow.

Donald William Wuerl, George Hugh Niederauer, Raymond Leo Burke, allow me to introduce Nancy Patricia D'Alesandro Pelosi. She gives unending scandal to the Church, and she is about to be re-elected with a majority of the Catholic vote in California's 8th Congressional District—unless, that is, one of you says what needs to be said.

As you know, Mrs. Pelosi's salvation may also be at stake. Correct her—for her own sake.

13. The Seamless Garment Revisited

PETER BROWN

In the early 1980s, Chicago's Cardinal Joseph Bernardin made some provocative remarks about abortion. He argued that abortion was one of a "seamless garment" of life issues. He was careful to state that all life issues were not equal and that abortion was chief among them. His idea was to provide the intellectual framework to integrate the new Catholic activism on abortion with existing Catholic social activism driven by concern for the poor.

Still, his approach was widely panned by movement pro-lifers. Broadening the scope to a "seamless garment" of life issues, they thought, rather than keeping a laser like focus on abortion, would only lend oxygen to liberal Catholics who were indifferent (or worse) to *Roe v. Wade*. And it would only sow discord in the right-to-life coalition itself, which was deadlocked over other "life issues" like capital punishment and nuclear arms.

But the "seamless garment" problem foreshadowed how difficult it would be over time to prevent many pro-life Catholics from striking Faustian bargains with pro-choice Democrats, who promised to deliver on the rest of the "seamless garment," while the GOP's progress against abortion seemed stalled both in Congress and the courts. A number of these Catholics disagreed with nearly every plank in the GOP platform but the one on abortion. The effect of the "seamless garment" is that Democrats have not paid quite as dearly for their support for abortion as they ought to have among Catholic voters.

This is why, when it comes to the politics of abortion, pro-lifers tend to be a pretty pessimistic bunch. And why not? After decades of ink being spilled, pixels and band-width being consumed, hours spent lobbying the government, praying at clinics and in churches, legal abortion seems as firmly entrenched as at any time since 1973. Indeed according to Gallup, the number of Americans supporting first-trimester abortions is essentially unchanged from the mid–1970s. Yes, there is a small upswing in disapproval of abortion among Americans under thirty. Yet given the fact that this same cohort overwhelmingly supports gay marriage and Barack Obama, it is hard to shake the feeling that their pro-life trend is a statistical mirage.

But one thing that is not a statistical mirage is the fact that abortion is declining and has been declining rather steadily—something that neither Bernardin nor partisans on either side of the issue had predicted. Indeed data from the Centers for Disease Control show that the number of abortions declined every year from 1990–2005 (the last year available). The Guttmacher Institute, whose methodology is even more rigorous, reports figures even more striking. Not only have abortions declined 25 percent since 1990, but the abortion rate is now down around its 1974 level, one year after *Roe*—a whopping 33 percent decline from its peak in 1980.

Neither side in the abortion debate knows quite what to make of this. The most readily offered explanation for the decline—the increased use of contraceptives—is not terribly convincing. The effects of the birth control revolution on U.S. fertility rates have been fully felt since 1975 when the birth rate plummeted from the height of the baby-boom in 1957 to just over half that level. Post-*Roe* birth rates have actually fluctuated. After peaking in 1990, then falling slightly until the mid–1990s, rates inched upwards until 2007, a year which saw the largest number of U.S. births ever recorded—*all while abortion rates were declining*. Contraception alone cannot account for this. Even accounting for exogenous factors such as the higher rates of twin births, it is evident that, regardless of how they vote or what they tell pollsters, American women are rejecting abortion in increasing numbers. Even people who call themselves philosophically "pro-choice" are far more likely than not to be functionally "pro-life."

Is it then time for the pro-life movement to declare victory? Certainly not. For one thing, lacking better legal protections for the unborn, there is nothing to stop the abortion rate from surging upwards again. Even if the abortion rate falls below pre-*Roe* levels, there would still be around a million abortions a year—a truly horrifying statistic that will keep right-to-lifers awake at night.

Legal abortion itself will remain galvanizing. Laws are an expression of the moral health of society. Abolitionists were not satisfied with Lincoln's original plan that slavery remain protected while put on a path to eventual extinction. Neither will most pro-lifers be satisfied with a world in which abortion remains perfectly legal, even where fewer people actually choose it.

And this leads to the real reason why pro-lifers are not noticeably happier today than, say, in 1980, when there were many more abortions. Even with fewer abortions, society as a whole is not visibly more "pro-life." The basic cultural norms and assumptions that undergirded the surge in abortion in the 1970s seem as firmly entrenched as ever. Indeed, the achievement of fewer abortions has mostly come at the cost of a much higher illegitimacy rate—Murphy Brown's revenge, one might say.

The abortion fight has always been at least in part a proxy for the broader struggle for a more just, life-affirming society and a more family-oriented culture. Stopping abortion is, in other words, part of a "seamless garment." Framing the abortion debate this way, as Bernardin did, was politically naïve and tactically stupid. But as things look now, it is increasingly clear that the good cardinal had a point.

14. "Catholic Identity"

JOHN W. CARLSON

College and university administrators welcome this time: a week of pomp and celebration with graduating students and their families, culminating in commencement, followed by a period of relative calm in which they can reflect on the academic year and develop future plans. Very likely, in 2010 no administrator looks forward to this period of calm more than the Rev. Robert A. Wild, S.J., president of Marquette University.

Two weeks ago, Father Wild rescinded an offer made to Dr. Jodi O'Brien to become dean of Marquette's College of Arts and Sciences. Currently chair of the Sociology department at Seattle University, O'Brien had been recommended by a dean search committee. As a university press release candidly acknowledged, the committee had mentioned potential "issues" concerning her candidacy, but senior administrators initially did not give those issues the scrutiny they deserved. It became clear that—since the Arts and Sciences dean must be able "to represent [Marquette's] Catholic identity"—the decision to hire O'Brien had been premature and needed to be reversed for the good of all concerned.

O'Brien is a self-described "out" lesbian with a long-term partner. The focus of her scholarly work is gay and lesbian sexuality and its interrelations with other social phenomena—in particular, religion and civil society. In a *New York Times* interview the day after rescinding the deanship offer, Father Wild emphasized that O'Brien's sexual orientation was not a major factor in his decision. Rather, he said, it had been discovered that her writings included "strongly negative statements concerning marriage and the family." Wild presumably was alluding, *inter alia*, to a 2004 article titled "Seeking Normal? Considering Same Sex Marriage." In the present writer's judgment, this article is well crafted but manifestly at odds with Church teaching on sexuality—as well as with the underlying philosophical realism that characterizes the Catholic intellectual tradition. It assumes throughout that institutions such as marriage and the family are "socially constructed," i.e., that they have no independent reality or significance. In this perspective, debate about "defining" these institutions reduces to competing discourses and political wills.

Unsurprisingly, the decision to rescind the offer set off a firestorm. The dean search process and outcome were condemned by Marquette's Faculty Senate. The administration's actions, said the faculty body, sullied the reputation of the university and gave cause to wonder whether Marquette was genuinely committed to academic freedom and diversity. Speculation was rife that the president had responded to pressure from wealthy donors, and/or the Milwaukee ordinary. (Archbishop Jerome Listecki later confirmed that he had expressed concerns about the appointment, but added that he recognized the decision was the university's responsibility.) Groups of students at both Marquette and Seattle U.—

also sponsored by the Society of Jesus—protested the decision. The *Shepherd Express*, a Milwaukee newsweekly, asked why, if being a supporter of gay and lesbian causes did not disqualify a person from serving on the faculty of a Catholic school, it should disqualify her from becoming dean.

Readers of *TCT* may wonder how such an unedifying scenario could have been allowed to unfold. Academics familiar with the internal workings of most Catholic colleges and universities are more likely to marvel that this is the exception rather than the rule. For, while no topic is more spoken about at our institutions (including Jesuit institutions) than "Catholic identity," truly crunchy issues are rarely addressed. And while search committees are given copies of college and university mission statements, they almost never are instructed about their implications for the committees' work. In fairness, such instruction is difficult to articulate. Moreover, given the variety of circumstances that may arise during a search, no formula could substitute for the prudential judgment of the individuals involved. However, certain implications of Catholic identity surely can be proposed for discussion.

To do this, of course, is to invite a war on most campuses. But it is a war that is needed—and one far better to have in advance than in the midst of cleaning up messes after the fact. The debate might well go differently at different institutions, given varied perceptions among stakeholders, including local Catholic ordinaries.

Let me propose the following:

> 1) Quite apart from legal and public funding concerns, a Catholic institution simply should not make faculty hiring decisions based solely on sexual orientation (or any of the other enumerated categories). However, it can happen that, in the judgment of appropriate officials (in particular, the dean), a prospective faculty member would use his or her position to promote—in the classroom and/or in publications—ideas contrary to Catholic faith. In such a case, a refusal to hire would not constitute unjust discrimination.

2) Respect for academic freedom entails that, once hired, faculty members may pursue their scholarly activity as they see fit. This does not imply a right to promotion and tenure. By the same token, a probationary faculty member whose scholarship is proving to be unacceptable, on grounds of incompatibility with Catholic identity or any other grounds, deserves to be warned of this fact as early as possible by his or her dean and department chair.

3) Because of their overall leadership positions and their roles in faculty hiring and evaluation, deans typically shape academic cultures and students' educational experiences. Accordingly, dean candidates at Catholic institutions must realize that the content of their published ideas is proper matter for scrutiny. If these ideas are at odds with basic teachings of the Catholic *magisterium*, or with the Catholic intellectual tradition more generally, the institutions in question have not only a right, but a duty, to reject their candidacies. More appropriate individuals will present themselves.

Now shall we talk?

15. Pornography and Marriage

PATRICK FAGAN

It's not exactly news that marriage is in crisis. Marriage rates are dropping, which means the next generations will be weaker because children won't have the benefit of the love of both parents. Nations will be poorer, less healthy, and less happy also. We know all this from sound social science.

Pornography is likely one of the key ingredients in this evisceration of society. Consider its documented effects on family life:

• Married men involved in pornography feel less satisfied with their conjugal relations and less emotionally attached to their wives. Wives notice and are very upset, even clinically traumatized.

• Among couples affected by one spouse's addiction, two-thirds experience a loss of interest in sexual intercourse.

• Both spouses perceive pornography viewing as tantamount to infidelity.

• Pornography is frequently a major factor in infidelity and divorce.

• Pornography viewing leads to a loss of interest in good family relations.

• The effects on individuals compound these problems.

• Pornography is addictive, and neuroscientists are beginning to map its biological substrate.

• Users tend to become desensitized to the type of pornography they use, and then seek more perverse forms of pornographic stimulation.

• Men who view pornography regularly have a higher tolerance for abnormal sexuality, including rape, sexual aggression, and sexual promiscuity.

• Prolonged consumption of pornography by men produces stronger notions of women as commodities or as "sex objects."

• Pornography engenders greater sexual permissiveness, which in turn leads to a greater risk of out-of-wedlock births and STDs.

• Child-sex offenders are more likely to view pornography regularly or to be involved in its distribution.

These are just some of the tragic effects from habitually viewing pornography but the most deleterious lie in the heart, and in family life the heart counts most.

Most men, including doctors, have not the foggiest notion that the wives develop deep psychological wounds, commonly reporting feelings of betrayal, loss, mistrust, devastation, and anger at the discovery of their husbands' use of pornography, especially Internet use.

Many wives also begin to feel unattractive or sexually inadequate, and many become depressed, even severely depressed, so badly that they need treatment for trauma, not just for depression. Many pornography-viewing husbands lose their emotional capacity for marital relations, and this, in turn, causes both husbands and wives to be less interested in the marriage bed. (Viagra sales are soaring while Internet viewing of pornography continues to rise steadily.) Not only is there a loss in sexual intercourse, but even distaste for the affection of a spouse and a cynicism about love can replace the affection that used to be present between them.

It is not surprising then that pornography users increasingly see the institution of marriage as sexually confining, doubt the importance of faithfulness, question the value of marriage as an essential social institution, and are skeptical about its future.

One study of "cybersex"—sexually explicit interaction made possible in the last decade and a half by the Internet—suggests that it leads to a fourfold increase in procurement of prostitution.

When the use of pornography rises to the level of addiction, as many as 40 percent of these addicts lose their spouses, and close to 60 percent suffer considerable financial losses. About a third lose their jobs.

Given all this, it is not surprising that pornography addiction is a major contributor to separation and divorce: In the only study to date of the relationship, 68 percent of divorces reviewed involved one party meeting a new paramour over the Internet, 56 percent involved "one party having an obsessive interest in pornographic websites," 47 percent involved "spending excessive time on the computer," and 33 percent involved spending excessive time in chat rooms (a commonly sexualized forum). This particular study is far from satisfactory from a strictly social scientific point of view, but it suggests a potent threat to social stability.

The effects on children are grievous: finding pornographic

material a parent has stored away, overhearing a parent engaged in "phone sex," experiencing stress and conflict in the home caused by online sexual activities of the parent, exposure to the treatment of women as "sex objects," and living in a home where this has already happened to their mother.

Where are the studies from the National Institutes of Mental Health on this matter? This phenomenon is big, nasty, and devastating, and likely robs more children of their fathers and families than smoking does, to say nothing of the debilitating effects on their mothers. Among the tools of the culture of death, pornography likely ranks in third place, after abortion and contraception.

It would be wonderful if a massive class-action suit could be brought by wives and children against the pornographers who made their money by addicting and warping their husbands and fathers. If massive multi-billion dollar damages have been procured from tobacco companies, why not from pornographers who also do demonstrable damage to our society? Where are those class-action attorneys when we really need them for something worthwhile?

16. AIDS and "Risk Reduction"

MATTHEW HANLEY

Hall of Fame quarterback Troy Aikman sustained at least seven concussions over a twelve-year NFL career. He brings a perspective few can to the long-term effects of head injuries on players. Aikman proposes a surprising remedy: "For years, I've said the best way to eliminate head injuries is to take away helmets. Players would be a lot less willing to jump in and stick their heads in if their noggins weren't protected. I used to say that tongue-in-cheek. But I'm starting to believe that's a pretty good idea."

In other words, the helmet is a device that *enables* greater risk-taking on the football field, even as it provides a measure of protection from any given highlight-reel collision between players bigger, stronger, and faster than ever before. Such hits would be exceedingly rare were it not for helmets. The net result is that there is, paradoxically, a greater level of head injuries in today's game *with* helmets. Indeed, other commentators note that the rates of concussions are lower in the rough and tumble sport of rugby— whose players wear no helmet—than in American football.

If those claims are true, it lends further credence to the concept known in public health circles as "risk compensation" or "disinhibition," which suggests that people respond to technical advances by exposing themselves to greater risk than they ordinarily would.

A similar dynamic stymies progress in containing the STD and HIV/AIDS epidemics that afflict us today. The World Bank's AIDS experts acknowledge that greater risk taking occurs not only in response to preventive measures such as condoms, but also to advances in treatment such as antiretroviral therapy. The *British Medical Journal* called risk compensation the Achilles heel of HIV prevention. The pope (among others), however, is often rebuked when he expresses concern that condoms too often convey a false sense of security.

The mere hint of this phenomenon (which can at times be difficult to measure) typically threatens the public health establishment because it is so thoroughly invested in the *philosophy* of risk reduction—a defeatist philosophy that insists that the best we can do is to minimize harm from behavior that will supposedly take place no matter what.

Deeper still, it is mostly a repackaged expression of modern cultural (rather than scientific) conviction, which denies and relativizes moral truth, and which prizes absolute sexual freedom above all else. Modern culture desperately needs a technical remedy for STD epidemics in order to validate its preferences. If the undesirable side effects of sexual license can be eliminated, then on what grounds could objections to such license be sustained? If, on the other hand, "risk reduction" actually results in more harm than good, it would be a crushing blow to prevailing aspirations for complete sexual autonomy.

This is not to say that all measures that have the ability to reduce risk are to be categorically rejected. The problem is that we make little to no effort to situate technical innovation in an ethical framework, which should always complement a person's innate dignity and never rob a person of hope.

I was reminded of the importance of hope from an unexpected source over the Christmas break watching Dickens' *A Christmas Carol* on TV. The transformational moment in Ebenezer Scrooge's life comes after his regrets are intensified (and his joys refreshed) by the Spirits of the Past and Present. He is confronted with his own mortality. Terrified by the sight of his own grave and the waste that has defined his life, he pleads in exasperation with the Spirit of the Future: "Why show me this, if I am past all hope? . . . Assure me that I yet may change these shadows you have shown me, by an altered life?"

Hope for an altered life is simply indispensable—and precisely what risk-reduction measures generally fail to cultivate. Is it far-fetched to imagine that Mr. Scrooge would today be treated for a mood disorder, or provided with potent sleeping pills, should he be troubled by restless nights? Such measures would simply hold in abeyance the truth that stings, but ultimately sets him free.

What most STD risk-reduction measures ultimately say about the human person is false; people are capable of more; they deserve better. That is the good news. And in modern western cultures, where faith has atrophied and the moral sense has been obscured (as John Paul II noted in *Veritatis Splendor*), it is literally the Good News that desperately needs to be made known. It is the antidote to the radical individualism and relativism that deceive and destroy. Those bankrupt ideas constitute the feeble foundation that props up the failing cause of STD-control by risk reduction.

The Center for Disease Control in Atlanta has in successive years released depressing reports on the extent and persistence of our national STD epidemics. Those with power and influence seem disinclined to change priorities, but what is really needed is something fresh—something Tennyson clamored for in his 1883 poem, *Ring Out, Wild Bells*: "Ring out the false, ring in the true;. . . . Ring out a slowly dying cause; . . . . Ring in the love of truth and right; . . . . Ring in the nobler modes of life. . . ."

There is an appealing alternative to confirming untold millions in various forms of misery. Why not ring it in?

17. Beyond the Dictatorship of Relativism

ROBERT ROYAL

Almost everyone who pays attention to religion and public affairs knows of Joseph Ratzinger's famous homily shortly before he was elected pope denouncing the modern "dictatorship of relativism." The future Benedict XVI rightly drew the connection between, on the one hand, the alleged tolerance and openness professed by many people opposed to the old faith and morals, and, on the other hand, the highhanded public means by which they now force their views on everyone else.

All quite true and profound. But it's become quite clear that what now most threatens traditional religious belief and behavior is not exactly relativism. Or openness. Or tolerance. Not by a long shot. It's a substantial set of alternative beliefs and teachings. And claiming that this new faith is fairness or neutrality simply won't survive a moment's thought.

Take the gay marriage measures passed in New York State. The ground had been prepared for this and a whole host of other public policy shifts by claiming, for instance, that for all of us sexuality is fluid and "socially constructed." A kind of relativism, if you will.

Except, it seems, in the case of gay men and women, who are "born that way," or the product of a "gay gene." If you have homoerotic feelings, in this perspective, nature—and perhaps God—have apparently hard-wired you. And that's *what you are*. Even gays who are unhappy and want to change their orientation are encouraged to believe that they have only "internalized homophobia."

This is the kind of simple assertion of nature or biology that we've been taught to think of as crude and naïve—even slightly fascist—when used to support heterosexuality as the norm. Or notions like marriage, family, and two opposite-sex parents as ideal for children. No appeal to biology or stubborn fact is allowed in these areas.

The inconsistency here is a clue that we're not dealing with a scientific or rational truth, but an ideology, indeed a kind of alternative faith. Though there's no solid scientific evidence for gay genes, and plenty of evidence about the disaster for children and adults that results from our cavalier treatment of marriage, it's become something of a blind faith and a moral crusade for a certain segment of our population to pretend otherwise.

Our social radicals deplore moral crusades in principle when Christians and others are merely standing up for the accumulated wisdom and social practice of every human society in every age, not some groundless experiment in social tolerance. The radicals claim that society ought to be open and neutral, not dominated by divisive public moral rules.

But moral passions do not go away just because we change their objects. If you come to believe that gay marriage is a fundamental human right—as is now happening here and in some international forums—you are saying that anyone who believes differently is morally repugnant and a threat, even prior to actually doing anything, to the kind of civic attitudes all decent people should have. This is why traditional Christians, Jews, Muslims, Buddhists, etc. are—absurdly—accused of promoting "hate" as a family value. And though the radicals are careful not to make the point too clear—to avoid political problems—they've essentially declared traditional religious morality bigotry.

So we have the equally absurd situation in which the vast majority of the human race is regarded as morally perverse by a small slice of the populace in a few wealthy countries. Meanwhile, the history of the twentieth century is marked by a series of ill-advised social theories that seemed humane and scientific at the time, somehow got control of the levers of power, and littered the landscape with victims of various kinds.

The sexual revolution has already produced an illegitimacy

crisis—and a tsunami of problems over the concrete reality of being *related*—that seemed all but impossible prior to our time. As usual, the poor and marginalized are the ones who suffer most. By any measure, for instance, racism is much reduced from what it was fifty years ago. But illegitimacy is roughly 80 percent among blacks, about *five times what it was in 1960.*

There's no mystery here: sexual revolution plus government programs that substituted for fathers produced similar increases, though lower in absolute percentages, for all races with the usual social pathologies and psychological turmoil added. Meanwhile, there's a mountain of social research that shows living in a stable family and worshipping regularly produce enormous advantages in health and human happiness.

This is the point in the argument where the other team calls a time out and says: look, you heteros have done a demolition job on marriage already. What possible harm can the small percentage of gays who will decide to marry—and those few out of a mere 1–2 percent of the population—do anyway?

There's a simple answer. Family breakdown is a fact, but a fact that doesn't deny the crucial role of family in principle. The legalization of gay marriage simply obliterates the most important prepolitical union—the intricate web of reproduction, affection, and the education and formation of new generations that has been recognized in every society as something unique and indispensable—by equating it with whatever two, or more, people may claim is marriage.

In the 1970s, President Carter tried to hold a "White House Conference on the Family," which radicals even then forced him to alter to rename "on Families," in recognition of the several forms of families. That might have been justified, properly done, but the definition of family adopted in the proceedings applied equally, as one wag observed, "to the traditional family and two winos sharing a boxcar."

Just wait until we get our first Family Czar. You'll see things you won't believe. And they won't be advanced under the banner of relativism, but of a different and quite militant faith.

18. With Backs Unbowed

FR. PHILIP DE VOUS

T. S. Eliot once quipped, "paganism holds all the most valuable advertising space." This, I think, is a significant reason why the pro-life cause continues to suffer setbacks or is sidelined, even as a majority of Americans, if polls are to be believed, identify themselves as pro-life. Eliot's quip, uttered over a half century ago, reminds us that conglomeration of forces that constitute the "culture of death" are in fact what are informing citizens' actual decisions, if not always their personal beliefs—a serious and difficult problem.

Often, because of the cultural deformation many of our citizens have undergone, the culture of death makes advances great and small under the guise of "equality," "individual choice," and even "liberty." On the surface, these easy and empty slogans seem appealing and even correct to many.

We must, however, never forget that liberty unmoored from truth invites disaster and destruction on a vast scale, the bitter fruits of which we are already seeing. The truth of the inalienable right to life for all is a moral red line that cannot be crossed without leaving behind civilization itself, and which must be defended anew in every generation.

In the wake of recent setbacks to the pro-life cause, there are many ill-advised calls for Christians to retreat from the public square and to retire to little, self-constructed islands of moral sanity. This, of course, may be a special vocation for some people. But if adopted on a wide scale, it would be to ignore the Gospel commission to "go out" into the world with the message of the Good News of Christ's redemption, and of the dignity and worth of every human life, made in the image and likeness of God.

It's precisely because our culture is becoming more self-centered, more materialistic, more hedonistic, and more uninterested in making the commitments and sacrifices the gift of life entails, that it has become even more imperative that Christians and all people of sound reason and good will continue the necessary fight to create, build, and sustain a culture of life.

Now is not the time to withdraw but to advance even more vigorously. A nation founded on the principles of the preservation of life, liberty, and the pursuit of happiness cannot long survive if two of the most fundamental human tasks—the begetting of life and caring for life—are ridiculed in the culture and dismissed from the public square without voices of protest. As Blessed John Paul II said: "For religious believers, our times offer a daunting yet exhilarating challenge. I would go so far to say that their task is to save democracy from self-destruction."

Let's be clear: the work will be hard, to be sure, and we will not always be liked, loved, and popular in standing strong for truth in a culture that makes an idol of emotions, propagates lies, and even mandates mendacity.

Much of our thinking, strategizing, and messaging on behalf of the culture of life and the Gospel in the present hostile environment will have to be done while "on the fly." The allies and acolytes of the culture of death do not rest. We must learn and pray for the spiritual gift of being contemplatives in action, day in and day out.

As Dietrich Bonhoeffer once noted, there is no authentic Christianity without the Cross. So we in the pro-life movement will have to carry the Cross—a Cross that has likely gotten even heavier in recent weeks—in order to witness and remain faithful to the sanctity of life.

Participation in the Cross always requires us to accept some portion of loss, rejection, and ridicule as we hold high the standard of Gospel truth in our part of the battle. That is the only thing that leads us to the victory of Jesus Christ, our Life, over death and death's allies.

The continued ascendancy of the culture of death in our nation, among us, and within us *is not inevitable*. We, who defend the sanctity of life as the primary foundation of our republic, must take the long view as we seek to change and convert the country to the cause of life. The Rev. Martin Luther King, Jr., offered this insight decades ago on another front in battle for the dignity of every human life: "Change does not roll in on the wheels of inevitability, but comes through continuous struggle. And we must straighten our backs and work for our freedom. A man can't ride you unless your back is bent."

It's good for us to remember that advice today. Surveying the land as it is, with all its present troubles and likely tribulations, with our task and goal always in mind, let us not be afraid to stand erect and hold our heads high—for our redemption is drawing near. (cf. Luke 21:28)

19. The Bioethics Gang

HADLEY ARKES

Our late friend Henry Hyde at once lovable and savvy, was willing to go along with us out of affection, but he really couldn't understand what we would gain by enacting a law so very modest: a law that would protect the child who *survived* an abortion. That was the bill that came to be known as the Born-Alive Infants' Protection Act (2002). Henry and some other pro-lifers were surprised on the day the hearings opened when the National Abortion Rights Action League actually came out in opposition to this move to protect a child born alive.

The melancholy truth revealed at that moment was that the opposition understood our bill better than many of our friends, for they understood the principle that lay at the heart of the thing. They understood that, if they conceded that simple premise to us, we would be able to raise the kinds of questions that could unravel their position: What was so different about that child five minutes earlier—but then five hours, five weeks, five months before it was born?

The hard fact was that the partisans of abortion could not really explain the grounds on which they could actually support such a bill. For none of the main arguments for abortion would be affected or negated by the fact that an unwanted child had now been born.

At the urging of sober counsel, the radical feminists held back from their vocal opposition and did not put the Democrats in the embarrassing position of voting against this bill to protect a child born alive. But now the question is being tested anew as to whether it is really embarrassing any longer for the party of the Left to come out openly for the killing of children born alive.

Apparently the editors of a supposedly reputable print and online periodical, the *Journal of Medical Ethics,* thought it was a perfectly plausible "academic" argument for two professors to make that pitch openly. Alberto Giubilini of the University of Milan and Francesca Minerva of the University of Melbourne hoisted the flag in a piece called "After-birth abortion: why should the baby live?"

Just why controversy should flare over this article may be a puzzle, since the argument was quite straightforward, drawn from the familiar logic of the argument for abortion: If a child in the womb is afflicted with conditions such as Down syndrome or other "deformities," conditions that the authors think would justify aborting the child in the womb, why should it make a difference that the child has been born? The child may still not have a "life worth living."

And besides that, the child could strain the health—that is, the mental health—of the parents, who come to the judgment that it is just too much for them and their families to bear. As the writers quickly acknowledged, the same reasoning could apply to babies quite healthy if they would strain the mental health of the mother.

Well why not put the baby, through adoption, in the hands of people who are willing and eager to nurture the child? Answer: it may be easier for a woman to kill an embryo or a born child rather than give away what is distinctly *hers.* In other words, the right to an abortion is the right to an "effective abortion" or a dead child. That was the critical premise that the Born-Alive Act meant to reject.

But with the prospect of Obamacare the horizon is extended: The choice may not fall solely to the pregnant woman as to whether the child is an "unbearable burden." That decision may now come within the authority of the "society as a whole, when the state economically provides for [the birth and care of children]." The State, rationing funds in medicine, may decide that it will not fund post-natal care for certain children even when the parents may want the child. But why call these killings "after-birth abortions?" Why not homicides? The authors reply that these are not yet real persons who are killed, for they are aware of no life plan, no "aims" yet of their own. Neither of course are young children, and if the test is an awareness of "aims" in life, there may be many youngsters in college who are candidates for an "after-abortion."

It may be the mark of a moral sensibility not entirely extinguished that the news of this article caused an uproar, with death threats against the authors. The editors thought the threats were extreme, and why was that? Because death would be visited on innocent human beings? Because someone actually threatened to do, in two cases, what the writers had been willing to license and justify for large numbers of innocent beings?

The man who introduced the Born-Alive Act in the Senate was Rick Santorum. For strategic reasons he has not said much about that Act during his campaigning for president. The accent has been on Obamacare, as a policy that will alter the rest of our lives—and deepen the hold of the party of abortion. If Santorum does get the Republican nomination, he will be running against the only national Democrat who opposed the Born-Alive Act. And if the public reaction over the last two weeks is a test, there is a public need to be served—and a political gain to be made—in making the argument yet again.

20. Six Things the Bishops Must Do

MICHAEL UHLMANN

President Obama's proposed revisions to an HHS regulation requiring health insurance plans to cover contraception, abortifacient, and sterilization procedures has met none of the objections of Catholic, Evangelical, Jewish, and Muslim leaders, and in some respects even made matters worse. A committee of Catholic bishops (headed by Cardinal Timothy Dolan) responded with a strongly worded critique. Meanwhile, over 170 bishops publicly decried the HHS rule, and a coalition of Catholics and Evangelicals has issued a joint call for protection of religious liberty.

The administration underestimated the breadth of this reaction. The palpably superficial, even presumptuous character of their proposed revisions merely underscored their deep commitment to regulation by administrative fiat. The HHS rule, clearly, was not an aberration by bumbling bureaucrats. It is the cutting edge of a wide-ranging agenda that seeks to empower politically unaccountable, self-styled "experts." The recently enacted health care law is only the most sweeping and potent expression of this disposition.

When it comes to women's health, the president's agenda is essentially one with Planned Parenthood's, backed by government force. In Obamaspeak, "health" means the full array of new-found women's "reproductive rights," including mandatory insurance coverage. HHS Secretary Sebelius is the most visible official advancing this agenda, but she has the support of many other senior White House and agency officials, including the EEOC, which says that employers who fail to provide insurance coverage for morally objectionable services may be violating their employees' civil rights.

This reproductive rights program dovetails with a broader political strategy that seeks to narrow the scope of religious activity in the public square, qualified by this distinction: religious opinion that supports the president's programs is to be encouraged; but religion that takes exception to his policies is intrusive. If the recent HHS controversy did nothing else, it should have alerted Catholic bishops to the full extent and gravity of the administration's efforts to silence religious opposition. Even if the bishops succeed in whittling back the HHS rule (an unlikely event), they should not delude themselves that the battle is over. In truth, it has only begun.

What, then, should the bishops do in the weeks and months ahead? Six things:

(1) They must make every effort to control the terms of debate. The president will continue to say, disingenuously, that HHS is only trying to protect the right to use contraceptives. The public reacted favorably when the bishops focused instead on the threat of government coercion, but that favor will quickly evaporate unless the bishops deploy their strongest weapon, which is, and always has been, the people in the pews. Most Catholics will side with the president on contraceptive use, but if the bishops cannot rally them to oppose Obama's brazen assault against religious liberty, the HHS rule will be the least of their worries.

(2) The people in the pews, however, will remain passive if all they have are formal statements or church bulletin inserts. They must be instructed and exhorted to act, not merely as Catholics, but as Americans who take their First Amendment liberties seriously. Many bishops today have no experience in fighting battles of this sort, and some will refuse to do so. But those who are willing can learn. Virtually every diocese has hundreds, if not thousands, of laypeople experienced in the political arts, who can render useful advice. The bishops need not, and should not, do all the heavy lifting; but they can, and should, instruct, inspire, and lead.

(3) The USCCB leadership should be wary about getting drawn into extended negotiations over the administration's proposed revisions. They need to move the argument beyond obtaining an exemption for church-related institutions, which may end up being so narrowly defined as to be useless. Besides, an exemption strategy may prove counter-productive in the long run by conceding that the government is constitutionally empowered to grant or withhold religious privileges. The only safe negotiating position is to make clear from the get-go that the HHS rule must be withdrawn. Only then can good-faith negotiations begin.

(4) The bishops also need to distance themselves from the "seamless garment" rationale that has animated many Catholics since the 1970s. The principal effect of that rationale has been to give Catholic politicians a free ride when they support

pro-abortion measures. It is beyond scandal that so many promi-nent office-holders have been allowed to avert their gaze from the rights of unborn children. Just how many politicians like John Kerry, Nancy Pelosi, Joe Biden, and Kathleen Sebelius do the bish-ops wish to tolerate? It is time to say good-bye to all that, and deep-sixing the "seamless garment" argument is the place to start.

(5) More broadly, the bishops need to re-address their long-standing support for "universal" health care. Many well-meaning prelates seem not to understand that once universal coverage is mandated, the government is necessarily empowered to decide what services are covered, for whom, and how. Unless they rethink health care reform from top to bottom, the bishops will be fighting morally obnoxious regulations for the rest of time, with little prospect of success. Alternative reform proposals (there are many) deserve the bishops' most serious *moral* consideration. It is time, in short, for the bishops to move beyond feel-good slo-gans.

(6) Finally, the bishops should not rely solely on the courts. Litigation is essential, but this battle must be, and in any event will be, fought in the political arena. It is not a battle of the bishops' choosing, but they're in it nevertheless. The Obama administra-tion seems to believe that its religious opponents lack the courage or the resources to resist.

It is time for the bishops to prove them wrong.

IV. Catholicism and Culture

1. Gray's Anatomy

ROBERT ROYAL

A common refrain in American popular culture tells us that it's a Bad Thing to view moral questions as black and white. The better sort of people know they are mostly shades of gray. This judgment—sharp moral distinctions are wrong and fuzzy ones are right—is, of course, self-refuting, like many other lapses in simple logic that seem to have taken up permanent residence in our culture. You can't even make the argument without black and white categories. And anyway, the very same people profess moral absolutes about a woman's right to choose, homophobia, and a host of other matters. But in this they get things precisely backwards: moral principles are always simple and clear (black and white if you will); their applications are less certain and complex (and gray if you also will), especially about the things people who think of themselves as sophisticated are most certain.

I started reflecting on this phenomenon the other day while I was riding a train back to Washington and reading—I wish I could say *The Critique of Practical Reason* or even the good gray *Times*, but in truth it was *The New York Post*. If you've never had the pleasure of perusing this fine publication, which it is the most scurrilous slander to call a tabloid, let me say that in its immediate effect, it's much closer to the world you and I live in. If you read the good gray paper, for example, you may be tempted to think that crime and lurid human dramas are to be viewed from a safe penthouse altitude, preferably through statistics put out by some government agency. The *Post* is there every morning to remind you that original sin is not merely something theologians cooked up to keep the laity in line. It's right outside, and often enough inside, the front door.

I was especially taken on this particular morning with the *Post*'s profile (the *mot juste*) of Ashley Dupre, the young, high-priced prostitute whose engagements with former New York Governor Elliot Spitzer led to his downfall. Prostitution, we are often told, is a "victimless crime," one of those practices sophisticated people do not exactly approve of, but that is essentially harmless, consenting adults and all that. A gray area. And in truth, Ms. Dupre protested that she never meant any harm to anyone and was deeply distressed by the pained expression of Spitzer's wife, Silda, at the press conference where he announced his resignation. But beyond these professions of sympathy, my antennae started to vibrate at her explanation of how she got into her profession: she ran away from home, was chronically short of money, and one day it occurred to her that having paid sex with men was "not that different from hooking up" with someone you just met.

Now, rationalization has been with us since the Garden of Eden, but it's rare to come across rationalization like this that does not merely confuse the issue but actually illuminates something. Lots of us have been saying for years that all those trashy episodes of *Sex and the City* and other television shows that paint sex in a purely recreational mode have been giving people, especially young people, a false idea of the world. In that never-never land, there are no serious consequences of bad behavior, no pregnancies (at least none that cannot be conveniently done away with), no messed-up lives and careers, no sexually transmitted disease, not even much effect on the psyches of people who seem to go through life with no real attachments to other persons of any kind. It's not a stretch to say this kind of attitude also prepared the way for the acceptance of homosexuality in the West as just another instance of a form of sex "not that much different" from other relationships we now routinely accept.

It's too bad for Elliott Spitzer that no one thought to bring in his fellow Democrats Nancy Pelosi and Joe Biden as theological consultants after his lurid tale broke. They could no doubt have usefully reminded us that Thomas Aquinas thought prostitution too difficult to stamp out and that it might have to be tolerated to some degree, which if you think about it, is not that much different from calling it a gray area. St. Thomas was a very sophisticated thinker and with a little work up—he's got a lot of "on the one hand" and "on the other hand" in every one of those articles in the *Summa Theologiae*—no doubt he too could be put to good use in gray areas. He was always debating things, and his views are a lot more subtle than he's usually given credit for.

Come to think of it, all those medieval theologians and philosophers seemed to do almost nothing but dispute questions. There's a great resource to be tapped here. As a Catholic, Vice President Biden could do a great service to the nation if he made it a high priority in the first months of his tenure in office to encourage us all to go back and study St. Thomas and his contemporaries, and save us from those terrible simplifiers who, in their narrowness of mind, have parceled out our complex world into black and white.

2. A Dark Knight of the Soul

RICHARD DOERFLINGER

Director Christopher Nolan's second Batman movie, *The Dark Knight*, has now been in theaters long enough for comment using "spoilers" that give away the end of the film. If you still have not seen it, you may want to read no farther. Go. It will be quite an experience. Then come back and read this.

Many critics have called this a powerful film, transcending the "comic book" genre even more than its predecessor, *Batman*

Begins. But I believe this is also one of the most powerful Christian movies of 2008. Let me explain.

It involves the usual primordial battle between good and evil—with the complication that the writers know the truth articulated by Aleksandr Solzhenitsyn that "the line separating good and evil passes not through states, nor between classes, nor between political parties either, but right through every human heart, and through all human hearts."

Evil in pure form is represented by the Joker. He not only does evil, but lives to seduce seemingly decent people into doing evil—so that they will see their goodness, and goodness in general, as an illusion. He even kills other criminals, his wickedness being so far beyond theirs that even they are relatively innocent victims. He is the ultimate utilitarian, inviting people to kill or disgrace others on the pretext that they will save more people by doing so. The scene in which he encourages each of two boatloads of people to blow up the other boat, to save themselves, is especially harrowing. The reality is that if they save themselves by doing evil, they lose, and the Joker wins. The denouement suggests, however, that maybe Gotham's people are worth saving after all.

The Joker is an embodiment of evil so convincing, so enigmatic, so thoroughly creepy, that it's easy to believe that playing the role factored into Heath Ledger's death by drug overdose. He has no known identity, no background, but infinite ingenuity and resources. At one point we think there's a childhood cause for his mania and facial scars—but later he gives a completely different explanation, and we realize he is merely playing with our expectations of a rational cause. He is, as is said at one point, an "agent of chaos." For all intents and purposes, he is Satan. (Roger Ebert says Mephistopheles—I won't argue demons with him.)

The forces of good capable of fighting this seemingly unstoppable force are conflicted and complicated. And here we are forced to meditate on what it means to be a hero.

Batman is the conventional action hero—he swoops in and punches out evil. He has great physical courage, and little regard for law if it hampers justice.

A second kind of hero is district attorney Harvey Dent, the "white knight" the city needs to feel good about itself. Incorruptible, he fights within the system, aggressively prosecuting evildoers. At one point, Batman realizes that such heroes for a more civilized world may soon render him unnecessary. He is not entirely unhappy about this.

So two kinds of heroism emerge within a secular framework: The heroism of action and of moral agency. (Those of classical mind may picture the Spartans in the movie *300*, or the equally noble heroism of Cicero speaking against dictatorship.)

Okay, here come the spoilers. I warned you.

So how does the Joker confront these two heroisms? He mocks both, repeatedly defeats or eludes Batman, and drives Harvey Dent into despair, disfiguration, and "the dark side." The Joker even boasts that Batman cannot kill him because of his moral decency, and the Joker cannot kill Batman because he sees him as the opponent who "completes" him. The two kinds of heroism have produced a stalemate. So what's left?

A third and unexpected heroism—the hero who offers hope by accepting exile and disgrace. Gotham has been battered and demoralized. The knowledge that its "white knight," Harvey Dent, joined the Joker and became an insane murderer in his last days, would be the last straw—the city would "lose its soul," as one character observes. In effect, though temporarily incarcerated, the Joker has won after all. And so Batman, already widely suspected of being an outlaw, saves the city's soul—by framing himself for Dent's murders.

The police, mostly tolerant of Batman earlier, henceforth will hunt him down, thinking he has murdered policemen. He is branded a villain, abandoned by his former friends. The bat signal on the roof of police headquarters is smashed, and the city can take out all its rage and frustration on him.

As Batman flees the police in one of the final scenes, his only friend in the police knows the truth. The friend's young son asks: Why is Batman running away? He's done nothing wrong. No, agrees his father—he's done nothing wrong. That's why he has to run.

The man without sin, who takes on himself the sins of the people?

Okay, people have long been finding Christ figures in the movies. I think this one holds up, whether explicitly intended by the scriptwriter and director or not. One thing is clear: This is the only kind of heroism that the Joker, the embodiment of evil and chaos, can't touch. He can't do anything to someone who, for the sake of others, is willing to let others unjustly think him wicked. This form of heroic virtue transcends earthly definitions of heroism.

The title *The Dark Knight* obviously refers to Batman as a greater hero than the "white knight" Gotham had trusted. But in his self-imposed exile and loneliness, Batman must now experience a Dark Night of the soul. We'll have to wait and see whether the third movie in the series believes in resurrection.

3. Empty Cradle, Empty Gallery

MARY EBERSTADT

Deep in the hypermodern heart of downtown Berlin lurks an unexpected classical jewel worth meditating upon in these days of post-Christian Europe: the museum of painting, or Gemaeldegalerie. Opened in 1998 following the reunification of some 1500 artistic masterpieces that had been dispersed East and West after World War II, it is one of the finest collections available of thirteenth to eighteenth century paintings—which is to say, one of the finest collections of paintings on earth.

So why—as several visits in balmy June demonstrated—is this airy, practically new, 72-room gallery that's stuffed with masterworks so inexplicably empty? Unlike the Louvre, the Prado, the Uffizi, or the Vatican galleries, the Gemaeldegalerie is practically free of human traffic. No noisy tour groups mar your enjoyment of Jan van Eyck's famously exquisite *Madonna in the Church*, say, or your contemplation of Hieronymus Bosch's astounding *St. John on Patmos*. About the only humans in possible oversupply are the museum guards, who in some rooms outnumber the paying public. (Perhaps as a consequence of their ubiquity, the gallery is not only as empty as most European churches, but also even quieter.)

This curious lack of curious humanity is not due to an absence of amenities. Housed in a building that like most modern oddities is far better experienced inside than out, the gallery is impeccably lit and even air conditioned, with comfortable benches placed thoughtfully throughout. Its tony cafeteria, also (inexplicably) nearly empty, is both tasty and tastefully done. Even the gallery's price tag beats the local competition. At eight euros per non-student head, it is two thirds the price of visiting the Checkpoint Charlie museum, slightly less than a visit to the top of the needle in Alexanderplatz, and considerably less than admission to Berlin's gorgeous Zoo. And its location in the heart of downtown—right near the Philharmonic and the Sony Center, with its movies and outdoor restaurants and IMAX screens—could hardly be improved.

For these reasons and more, the Gemaeldegalerie appears if anything to be one of the most user-friendly artistic sites in Europe. So why—unlike other museums in cutting-edge Berlin—isn't it crawling with culture vultures?

It's hard to avoid the obvious here: given the centuries in question, the gallery's collection is inevitably, ineradicably, inescapably Christian. Such is true not only of the majority of paintings, whose subjects are overtly Biblical or otherwise religious, but of many "non-religious" pieces too. Even the Dutch masterpieces by Steen, Brueghel, and others portraying "ordinary life," for example, are often hortatory comments on the gaps between Christian morality and Christian practice. Similarly, one of the collection's most outrageous signature pieces—Caravaggio's *Amor Victorious*—does not so much overturn the known (Christian) universe as poke fun at people for thinking themselves in charge of it.

Might the overall Christian character of these artworks somehow account for the seeming lack of public interest? Earlier this year, also surveying contemporary Berlin, George Weigel reflected that, "Europe's collapse of faith in the God of the Bible may have made evocative public monuments impossible" (his reference is to the city's frankly hideous "monument" to the murdered Jews of Europe). And surely that same growing religious illiteracy might help to explain something of the Gemaeldegalerie's relative emptiness, too.

But I wonder if another, perhaps less obvious factor—the simultaneous disappearance of something known as the human family in the lives of many Europeans—may turn out to explain a lot, too. That's one disappearing act at which the Germans, even more than any of their neighbors, have excelled. Almost a third of the German women born in 1960 have had no children. Only half as many children were born last year in Germany as in 1964—and that's even throwing in the Turks. And this empty cradle may be just the human backdrop against which the empty Gemaeldegalerie makes best if perverse sense.

After all: how do you explain the sublimity of Raphael's *Madonna with the Infant Jesus* to someone who's never held a baby? Or what's so perfect about Botticelli's adolescents in *The Virgin and Child with Singing Angels* to people who haven't seen real teenagers up close for decades? How to convey what is throat-tightening about Grien's *Mourning of Christ* to a fit, childless man or woman of any age who has never seen death?

In cutting-edge Germany as elsewhere in Western Europe, increasing numbers of people can no longer be assumed to have hands-on experience of any of these things. This familial illiteracy may yet turn out to be more connected to religious illiteracy than we've so far understood.

4. Cormac McCarthy's *The Road*

JOAN FRAWLEY DESMOND

Last week, while my family gorged on turkey and pumpkin pie, I feasted on Cormac McCarthy's post-apocalyptic bestseller, *The*

Road, followed by the newly released film adaptation of the novel. The film is true to the spirit of the novel, but doesn't stir the soul like the author's stark lyricism.

Let others be merry and bright, I relished my journey through McCarthy's bleak, dangerous America, gutted by an unexplained disaster and sparsely populated with survivors who trap and eat people, and showing as much perturbation in the process as we might experience shopping for groceries at Safeway.

Yet *The Road* may be the most weirdly inspirational story of modern American fiction—unlike *No Country for Old Men,* McCarthy's last dark tale, which concludes with the depressing implication that evil men often outlast and outsmart the law. In *The Road,* McCarthy shifts the context: civilization has been extinguished. Guess who fills the breach?

The story follows the struggles and musings of a dying father and his young son, possibly the last "good guys" in the land. Fear and hunger fuel their urgent journey, past the wilderness of brittle falling trees and empty towns stripped by scavengers. The reader joins their erratic pilgrimage to the warmer environs of the Gulf Coast, a destination that offers only the faintest hope of survival.

In Genesis, the intermingled fate of creation and of man is confirmed and blessed. But if you ever wondered how that primeval story might read if Yahweh suddenly hit the rewind button, then *The Road* will leave you spellbound. The earth is stuck in a perpetual nuclear winter. The remains of men and animals scatter the burnt fields and the grey air is thick with dust, marking "the onset of some cold glaucoma dimming away the world." Still, the father retains a deeply human fascination with creation's origins: "Perhaps in the world's destruction it would be possible at last to see how it was made. Oceans, mountains. The ponderous counterspectacle of things ceasing to be. The sweeping waste, hydroptic and coldly secular. The silence."

Initially, the reader assumes that a primal instinct for survival prevents the father from adopting his wife's desperate solution to their plight: soon after her son is born, she commits suicide, deeming it a gentler fate than the more likely prospect of a violent, brutal end. She wants to take her son with her, but the father refuses and embarks on a seemingly impossible path. "My job is to take care of you. I was appointed to do that by God. I will kill anyone who touches you," he tells the boy.

Bereft of the gratuitous beauty of nature and the consolations of its ordered rituals, the father struggles to believe in his paternal mission, let alone God. Indeed, despite the awful loneliness, strangers are feared, not welcomed. The standards of decency are drastically lowered: "Do you eat children?" asks the boy, warily assessing the true intentions of a man on the road. The death rattle of the world fulfills Old Testament warnings: "There is no prophet in the earth's long chronicle who is not honored here today."

But as their pilgrimage rolls forward, as they care for each other and speak of ultimate things—of sin, death, love, and sacrifice, their community of two adopts the grace-filled elements of a sacrament.

Starving, filthy and desperate, the father and son take part in "some ancient anointing. So be it. Evoke the forms. Where you've nothing else construct ceremonies out of the air and breathe upon them." He strokes the boy's head and thinks: "Golden chalice, good to house a god." The son's purity of soul provides a balm for the father's broken heart. The boy leads him to the wellspring of love and bids him to drink. Contemplating his son, he thinks, "if he is not the word of God, God never spoke."

What does it mean to believe in love? And if you do believe in love, are you halfway to believing in God, the source of all love?

When I was in my twenties, newly reconciled with the Church, I was given a book, *I Believe in Love: A Personal Retreat Based on the Teaching of St. Therese of Lisieux.* The title puzzled me, as if the notion was self-evident and didn't require further explanation. But more than two decades later, reflecting on the missteps of my own life and witnessing the normalization of selfishness in the culture at large, I find St. Therese's statement of faith both radical and urgent.

Most book and film reviewers sift through *The Road* to try to identify the source of the environmental disaster that shrouds the land in ash. It is far more difficult to speak of the ravages of sin that remain hidden, but no less destructive. Why does this beautiful and terrible story inspire? It testifies to a love stronger than death. Evil will not have the final word.

"You have my whole heart," the father tells his son at the end. Still, the boy remains fearful of what might come at the next bend in the road, what darkness of purpose might lurk in the heart of a stranger—or even within his own heart.

"But who will find him if he's lost? Who will find the little boy?" he asks his father, in a reference to a grim vision that has plagued his whole childhood.

"Goodness will find the little boy. It always has. It will again."

5. Teachers as Witnesses

AARON URBANCZYCK

"Contemporary man listens more willingly to witnesses than to teachers, or if he listens to teachers, he does so because they are witnesses." John Paul II and Benedict XVI have quoted these remarkable words of Paul VI. As Paul's successors, they know wisdom when they see it. The Church is, of course, no stranger to education. The Catholic intellectual tradition is rich with insights into the nature of learning, but we should expect no less of the very institution that gave us the university.

I am a college professor and I would like to reflect upon the powerful words of Paul VI from that perspective. It is hard to think of contemporary college professors as "witnesses," especially when so many of them are reticent to "profess" anything (so why do they merit the term "professor?"). One plague of the modern university is the bizarre notion that the teacher ought not to impose his beliefs upon his students. No, indeed! The professor ought rather to be a sophisticated master chef preparing the sumptuous banquet of neutral information.

With prejudice towards no idea, a kind disposition towards all, and grave objectivity, the professor merely comments upon the relative strengths and weaknesses of each factual morsel comprising the feast of knowledge. Under this model, the uninitiated student, whose tastes are unformed, is left to his appetites—he gravitates towards what he personally finds interesting and meaningful. College thus becomes a type of four-year buffet where the student, safeguarded by the scrupulous "objectivity" of his instructors, makes knowledge and meaning for himself, without fear of interference from those serving him the banquet.

Such an educational model rejects outright the notion of teacher as witness. Yet in an odd way Paul VI does have advocates in university circles. The intellectually honest among the professoriate know that the notion of the "purely objective" teacher is nonsense. Those who probe into the nature of education quickly conclude that it is simply impossible to "teach from nowhere," as if the positions and perspectives of the teacher could simply be suspended in a weightless vacuum of objectivity. Further, this notion of pure objectivity in pedagogy treats neither the teacher nor the student with anything resembling the seriousness befitting human persons.

Among the candid advocates for the notion of teacher as witness we find one of modern America's most influential philosophers, the late Richard Rorty. Rorty is often classified as a postmodernist, but in a strange way, he sounded his own hearty amen to the words of Paul VI. Rorty understood that the teacher must passionately commit himself to what he believes to be true and must do all in his power to form his students according to these truths. Rorty's witness as teacher lies in his own particular brand of liberal democracy, and he saw the teacher as pivotal in preparing young people for full citizenship in a democratic society.

He lamented the fact that some students are raised by what he calls "racist or fundamentalist" parents (the yoking of these two categories is telling, but must be a subject for another day). Taking Socrates as an example, Rorty insisted that the teacher must inculcate truth and rescue students from error, which for him means actively forming students only in ways beneficial to a democratic polity. And he confesses what he and his colleagues must then profess: "We [professors] are going to go right on trying to discredit you [parents] in the eyes of your children, trying to strip your fundamentalist religious community of dignity, trying to make your views seem silly rather than discussable."

Professor Rorty understood the notion of "teacher as witness" quite clearly. In principle, his passion was admirable (though in application misguided). He hardly considered himself, as teacher, an objective purveyor of ideas. Rorty's successors are eager, indeed quite eager, to play the role of witnessing teachers. Yet, tragically, such teachers seem only to allow witnessing as authentic when it forms people to fit into their version of "the earthly city."

If Rorty's passion is admirable, it is because education by its very nature presupposes eternity. The university is only coherent insofar as each distinct discipline is understood to be a lens through which the human person can perceive truth and reality. All those disciplines, pursued with the curiosity and passion for truth proper to full persons, lead to ultimate questions about the nature of humanity, creation, and God Himself. It is an unwelcome truth for some scholars, but facts have never interpreted themselves. If the information discovered through a particular discipline "means" something, someone must witness to its significance in the cosmic scheme. And these witnesses who stand before the mystery of existence and speak it we call teachers.

Perhaps this is why Augustine so beautifully notes that all who teach are mere shadows of the one great teacher and witness, our Lord himself. In *De Magistro*, Augustine insists: "We listen to Truth which presides over our minds within us, though of course we may be bidden to listen by someone using words. Our real Teacher is . . . Christ . . . the unchangeable power and eternal wisdom of God." Paul VI stood in that tradition and reminded us that the teacher is simply "someone using words" who witnesses to the Word Himself, who is finally The Teacher. And such teachers must always be compelling.

6. Are Catholics Creationists?

GEORGE SIM JOHNSTON

Today, the Pope Pius V University in Rome will be the setting for a day-long conference with the arresting title, "The Scientific Impossibility of Evolution." The sponsors of the event are known crusaders against Darwin. But they go further than most Darwin dissenters and postulate a "young earth" chronology based on a literal reading of Scripture. Needless to say, the Catholics among them are not comfortable with what the ordinary Magisterium has to say on the subject. Both John Paul II and Benedict XVI have affirmed that the Book of Genesis is not meant to teach science and that theories of evolution are permissible so long as God is not excluded from the big picture.

F. Scott Fitzgerald famously remarked that the test of a first-rate mind is to hold two apparently contradictory ideas and still be able to function. In the debate over evolution, a Catholic must allow both revelation and science their due authority, reconciling the apparent contradictions between Genesis and modern research. Catholics also have to be skeptical about the claims of materialist ideologies disguised as science, while being open to the genuine findings of geneticists and paleontologists.

In 1986, John Paul II gave a series of general audiences on the subject of Creation. In them, he laid down a principle of Biblical exegesis that has been around since the Church Fathers: The Book of Genesis is not meant to teach science. Genesis tells *what* God did, not *how* he did it. "Indeed," writes John Paul, "the theory of natural evolution, understood in a sense that does not exclude divine causality, is not in principle opposed to the truth about creation. . . .as presented in the Book of Genesis. . . . It must, however, be added that this hypothesis proposes only a probability, not a scientific certainty . . . . [But] it is possible that the human body, following the order impressed by the Creator on the energies of life, could have been gradually prepared in the forms of antecedent living beings."

In an address to Italian clergy on July 24, 2007, Pope Benedict

XVI also recognized evolution as a legitimate scientific theory. At the same time, he expressed impatience with the false polarities of "creationism" and "evolutionism." The doctrine of creation and the theory of evolution, he said, are not "mutually exclusive alternatives." The world need not be divided between fideists who cram scientific data into a Biblical template never meant to receive them and materialists who think that soothing phrases like "random fluctuation in the quantum void" dispense with the need for a Creator.

While allowing for the possibility of evolution, neither pope has issued a free pass to evolutionary materialism. The Church has nothing to fear from legitimate science, but is wary of materialist philosophies tricked up as science—which is what Darwinism often amounts to. In *Truth and Tolerance*, Benedict complains that evolutionists often trespass their legitimate bounds by making sweeping metaphysical claims. As a result, the educated public has the vague impression that "evolution" explains everything. Why, it even explains Darwinists whose purpose in life is to explain that the universe has no purpose.

Benedict reminds us that there are fundamental questions that science *in principle* cannot answer. Such as: Why is there something rather than nothing? As G. K. Chesterton, an astute observer of the evolution wars, remarked: "Nobody can imagine how nothing could turn into something. Nobody can get an inch nearer to it by explaining how something could turn into something else."

Apart from the origin of the universe, there are two other ontological leaps that elude scientific explanation. First, the origin of life: Life only seems to come from life. Second, the human person: How could a purely "natural" process produce a creature so unlike anything else in nature? Mankind did not need the ability to write *Hamlet* or compose *Don Giovanni* in order to compete with the apes.

While aspects of evolutionary theory are certainly open to criticism, I don't think a conference of Christian scholars who read Genesis as a textbook in geology is very helpful. One could argue that there is not a single scientific datum anywhere in Scripture—for the simple reason that the sacred writers had no notion of science in the modern sense. Whenever I encounter a creationist, I like to ask how we can see the Milky Way if the universe is only a few thousand years old. The response, needless to say, is wonderfully baroque.

The Big Bang is a perfectly reasonable model—as is the common descent of species, since all animals share genetic coding and homologous structures like wings and limbs. Still, we know very little about the origin of species. Darwinists have not satisfactorily explained how bacteria, which appeared over three billion years ago, gradually morphed into everything from trilobites to *Homo sapiens*. Paleontologists like Steven Stanley and Niles Eldredge tell us that the fossils do not show gradual Darwinian evolution. Geneticists never observe the systematic mutations they deem necessary for major evolutionary changes. Breeding experiments show species stubbornly clinging to their blueprints: Dogs remain dogs, fruit flies remain fruit flies. All Darwinists can show are small adjustments within species (e.g., the famous beak of the finch) from which they extrapolate macro-evolutionary changes which occur off-stage, as it were.

Catholics should take their cue from the Magisterium: Welcome the genuine discoveries of modern science while casting a skeptical eye on evolutionary "science" that for philosophical reasons dispenses with a Creator and treats man as a thing. At the same time, Christians who insist on explaining the universe in terms of ancient Hebrew cosmology are going to have a difficult time engaging the modern world.

7. Two, Three, Many Charlotte Simonses

MARY EBERSTADT

In a few weeks, millions of idealistic and enthusiastic teenagers will embark on or continue a time-honored and familiar American ritual: losing their religion. Granted, the rest of us don't usually put the passage in such blunt terms. We commonly call it "going off to college." But the facts whistle past our euphemisms.

It is true that American colleges and universities remain the envy of the world, true too that many American students will find in academia a happiness and satisfaction known nowhere else. But many, even at religious colleges, will also find the campus to be a graveyard for their morals and faith—one whose internment there will leave permanent scars, even if the owner does manage to exhume it some years or perhaps decades later. Many others, of course, will not.

Why do so many students "lose their faith," as the going polite phrase has it, when they hit the quad? The common answer today is the secularist one: because college is where young adults learn to reject their foolish childhood ways, religion most emphatically.

Like many other exercises in self-deception, of course, this one gets the actual causality of the thing perfectly backward. Most college students do not ditch God after giving Him a good long mature think, only later to realize—*mirabile dictu!*—that doing so will free them up for some pretty exciting things. No, like any other people who have no problem with faith until it gets in the way of something they really, really want, most students typically run that sequence in reverse: wanting those pretty exciting things, which are available in spades on most campuses today, they go for them by first jettisoning God.

It is important to get these facts of the matter straight, I think, because many of us who are supposed to be the adults in charge today have particular reasons for wanting to deny them. Consider, for example, the provocative fact that Tom Wolfe's masterpiece *I am Charlotte Simmons*—by far the most searing and true meditation out there on contemporary campus decadence—fell both critically and commercially short of the two novels preceding it. Why? Surely not for want of literary merit; the same technical brilliance, uncanny ear, and moral fearlessness are displayed there as in Wolfe's better-received *Bonfire of the Vanities* and *A Man in Full.*

No, the same public that devoured Wolfe's other novels resisted *Charlotte* for another reason: because middle-aged readers, many of them parents, found the books truth-telling about what their daughters and sons on campus are really up to simply unbearable. They're not alone. "Every Saturday night," confided a friend whose daughter was a freshman last year, "I'd think of her and worry about what she might be doing at college—and then I'd purposefully put the whole thing out of my head." She—and a few million other mothers and fathers, too.

Yet face facts we should, because the nihilism tattooed permanently into some of those students settles not just in classrooms dedicated to the orthodoxies of post-modernism, but in the dorm rooms and common rooms where those teachings get played out up close and personal. Yes, promiscuity and binge drinking on campus are nothing new. Yes, perhaps even the hook-up culture—so critically exposed in *Unprotected* by campus doctor Miriam Grossman—is arguably just the old one-night stand on steroids. But what is new is that the adults in charge, on campus and off, are so passive about it all—the more so because, unlike the parents of the Baby Boomers, today's mothers and fathers cannot claim ignorance.

Kids will be kids. Let them have their fun. I was pretty wild then, too. Who am I to say they're wrong? And so we justify, bit by bit, our sitting this one out on the sidelines. That's a shame, because campus is one place where much could be done, even by those not there. As Robert George among others has forcefully observed, students need alternatives to the anything-goes sexual gobbledygook—the LGBT centers and indoctrination sessions and prurient workshops in "sexual health," etc., etc., etc.

Groups active in campus ministry—Newman Centers, local parishes, and the rest—need real help in bringing alternative speakers, publications, and ideas to campus life. As philanthropists big or small, we can also help by sending individual students or traditional-minded groups alternative literature of a different sort, such as gift subscriptions to magazines or books that deliver apologetics without apologizing. Or just send the students you know links to fellow-travelling websites, including this one.

These aren't just shots in the dark, after all. Plenty of students, too, have misgivings about what for many is a four-year bacchanal bizarrely regarded as sacrosanct. Consider as emblematic this fact: the Anscombe Society, founded years ago at Princeton—Princeton!—has not only thrived on that campus, but inspired groups like it on other campuses too. Today these counter-cultural platoons draw on each other for mutual support (and an annual conference) under the umbrella of the Love and Fidelity network—another outstanding worthy cause, by the way.

These and other forms of student resistance go to show that the moral gig on campus is not up. It's just underfunded and undermanned compared to the other side. In sum, there are plenty of lifelines to throw students who do not want to become the next Charlotte Simmons. But first we must lose what so many of us, perhaps out of our own self-deception and self-exculpation, seem to have acquired as a stumbling block: the despairing notion, masquerading as worldly wisdom, that Charlotte's fate is simply inevitable. It isn't—so let's not allow our passivity to make it so.

8. Sin—and Pet Lions

BRAD MINER

In T. S. Eliot's play, *The Cocktail Party,* Celia Copelstone tells a psychiatrist, Sir Henry Harcourt-Reilly, of her symptoms, which are two. For one, she has an "awareness of solitude," which we gather Sir Henry considers uncommon though not rare. But that second symptom? CELIA: "That's stranger still./ It sounds ridiculous—but the only word for it/ That I can find is a sense of sin." REILLY: "You suffer from a sense of sin, Miss Coplestone?/ This is most unusual."

Eliot's play had its premiere at the 1949 Edinburgh Festival (with Irene Worth as Celia and Alec Guinness as Reilly), and half-a-century on a sense of sin is no less unusual. Who am I kidding? It's about as rare as the Pinta Island tortoise.

It was not always so. Sin was once a concept at the center of religious attention. Early American children used to recite: "In Adam's fall, we sinned all." Not even kids were permitted to savor life without tasting bitter fruit. But that was then. Newfangled science and old-fashioned selfishness—sometimes masquerading as social science—have joined to give cover to behavior that once carried the peril of Hell.

Many consider this an existential upgrade: there are no sins, just disorders; there are no sinners, just victims. Sin, like witchcraft and other superstitions, has been overtaken by a more progressive dispensation. Well, witchcraft has actually been making a comeback, but many people, including progressive Catholics, see sins as so many strangled snakes lying lifeless around the crib of our Heraclean age. A sense of sin is no longer, as Eliot believed, a sign of an awakened spirit, but a symptom of a disordered psyche to be treated with therapy not penance.

In 1973, Karl Menninger published a well-received book, *Whatever Became of Sin?*, the thesis of which was this: "The very word 'sin,' which seems to have disappeared, was a proud word. It was once a strong word, an ominous and serious word." With the demise of a belief in sin comes a new, politically correct ban on sin-talk. According to Dr. Menninger, the last mention of sin made by an American public figure was in 1953 by Dwight Eisenhower on the occasion of the second National Day of Prayer. Few have spoken of it since.

But wait. The good doctor, not making a religious argument, wasn't really concerned with sin as an offense against God—which is what it is after all—but with challenges to normative morality by certain behaviors and ideas arising out of the swamp of the Swinging Sixties. Menninger used the word "sin," as he put it, broadly enough to "meet the needs of both believers and non-believers."

He was a shrink, not a confessor. He wanted to see Americans recover feelings of shame and believed that whereas common, secular ethics were derived from Judeo-Christian religion, which is to say from God's law, religion itself was on the wane and secularism on the rise. And he thought it necessary to fight a kind of rearguard action against aberrance with the only tool at hand: science—an often powerful bludgeon to be sure. In this case, however, science was and is an ineffective weapon.

I'm struck by how emblematic of our time Dr. Menninger's book still is. It appropriates the potent language of a great truth, but by dismissing the truth itself, weakens not only its own position but, for some, the truth itself. Everybody loses. This reminds me of the way a professor once described to me the life of the philosopher Nietzsche: He was the world's most influential atheist, who saw the implications of unbelief and went nuts. In Menninger's case, he was driven to hectoring about responsibility.

It is, of course, right to hope for healthy, responsible men and women, but healthiness just won't work as an even swap for holiness. For half a century, lots of people have been preaching therapy rather than repentance, and where has it got us? Sin recast as psycho-social disorder rends the garment of faith and leaves us naked. If all folks need is treatment, they don't need Salvation, and about that we know they are wrong. "If we say we have no sin," John writes in his First Epistle, "we deceive ourselves, and there is no truth in us."

Just recently, Benedict XVI said: "These days, the correct formation of believers' consciences is without a doubt one of the pastoral priorities because, unfortunately, as I have reaffirmed on other occasions, to the extent that the sense of sin is lost, feelings of guilt increase which people seek to eliminate by recourse to inadequate palliative remedies."

So, as to the question, whatever became of sin? The answer is that it's still wild and roaring looking for souls to devour, but too many people are treating the lion like a domesticated tabby, an arrangement that won't end well.

9. Of Doubtful Humility

ROBERT ROYAL

I've been noticing lately that some prominent public figures have started to make an odd case for the virtues of doubt. According to this new dispensation, certainty leads to intolerance, doubt to tolerance. This does not square with my own experience, nor does it explain the lives of, say, Mother Teresa as opposed to, say, Richard ("parents teaching religion is child abuse") Dawkins. But there's something in the air that gives this sophism an initial plausibility—and needs to be carefully watched.

Pope John Paul II lamented some years ago that there are many among us now who think that relativism is the only possible basis of democracy. So much for self-evident truths. But the new professors of doubt have a more subtle approach. A Certain Person who appeared at A Certain Catholic University recently— enough said about that already—remarked, not entirely in passing: "remember too that the ultimate irony of faith is that it necessarily admits doubt. . . .This doubt should not push us away from our faith. But it should humble us. It should temper our passions, and cause us to be wary of self-righteousness."

To ask an indelicate, pre-modern question: is this true? I don't like unruly passions or self-righteousness any more than A Certain Person, but I myself doubt that this doubt will work as advertised. People just as often let loose their passions when in doubt, and get self-righteous over not being self-righteous. Sadly, that's the way we're made.

And besides, the sort of person who typically recommends doubt to others is not saying, "You know, I really shouldn't hold so much to my own convictions. I should be more open to you." He's actually saying, "You shouldn't be so sure of your positions. You should be more open to me." It's a clever undermining of someone else masquerading as an open-minded plea for humility—on your part.

Doubt is also often confused with questioning, which is a very different kettle of fish. The great Cardinal Newman is famous for:

"Ten thousand difficulties do not make one doubt." Newman, the great expositor of the development of doctrine, knew that we progress in truth not by doubting, but by wondering about the truth. How can Jesus be God or how is it that bread and wine on the altar can become Christ's Body and Blood? Great thinkers like Augustine or Aquinas were not foolish enough to try to prove such mysteries, just to address rational difficulties.

Even in more mundane matters, doubt does not get us far. I may doubt whether one of my children is telling me the truth, but the important thing is the truth and the truthfulness. In certain matters, doubt is decadent. If someone had asked the Reverend Martin Luther King, Jr., "aren't you being a little too sure of yourself about this 'all men are created equal'?," King would have rightly said "get thee behind me," the proper place for the Spirit that Denies. There are truths about which doubt doesn't make the slightest bit of sense, nor is it a mark of sophistication and humility.

This is eminently true about killing babies in the womb. That the child in the womb is a "person" deserving of full rights may not allow of proof beyond all doubt. Many things cannot be proved: that a spouse or parent loves you, that no one ever played the piano like Beethoven, that someone is bald though he has a few hairs on his head. Things are unprovable in various ways that do not affect the fact that they are true.

But those very unprovable things may still make large moral claims on us. To kill someone with the claim that you weren't sure he was alive would not go far with a jury. A few people celebrate abortion as a kind of sacrament, but they are not part of the serious dialogue. The people we want to talk with are still sane enough not to believe that because someone has raised a doubt, we are free to do what we want. A Certain Person seemed very certain that women who get abortions agonize over it morally and spiritually. Perhaps that's sometimes so, but opening the door to doubt has also had the effect of reducing and in some cases eliminating the moral struggle. There may yet be enough moral sanity at large to make this clear. A majority of the country for the first time since Roe seems to have been convinced.

The doubt gambit is aimed at undermining the effort. It's curious how Christians have been publicly chastised lately for being too self-assured. Whatever happened to the old stereotype of Christians as forever guilt-ridden, obsessed with sins and faults, unable to live a confident, normal life in the world? The answer, I believe, is that the new stereotype serves a specific purpose, as the old one did. Early modern secularists and naturalists used the old one to show how "unnatural" Christianity was. It gets you divided within yourself, questioning what you know and do.

The new stereotype wants to do something similar, though to opposite effect: now that even nature is too moral for us, Christians who found a voice about crucial public issues like gay marriage over the last quarter century can only be silenced by telling them they're forgetting the essential Christian virtue: humility.

Humility is always something to strive for, never something we possess. But we keep a grip on it not by doubting—and certainly not by feeling superior in doubting. We grow humble by knowing the truth. The truly humble people I've been lucky to know in my life were not humble because they practiced intellectual doubt, but because they had come to understand that they are sinners. Not were. Are. The truth.

10. A Defense of "Organized" Religion

HOWARD KAINZ

We frequently hear people criticizing "organized" religions and boasting about not belonging to one. What exactly do they have in mind? They aren't hankering after disorganized, disunited, or anarchic religion. The discontent seems to be something like the following:

Some are for religion, but against *organized* religion. For example, those who pride themselves on being "spiritual," but completely free from any creed or conventional religious practices. (Although some "spiritual" persons who are against organized religion, organize with others to combat organized religion!). In this same category are people who see religion as something essentially and completely spontaneous. Individuals might decide to get together once in a while to receive and share inspirations, and even pray, but without any established rituals.

But there are also others who are for organization of all kinds, as long as it isn't a *religious* sort of organization—for example, the "New Atheists," who portray attempts to transmit religious teachings or practices as a kind of pernicious mind-control and threat to human freedom. (Paradoxically, materialism can't really allow freedom; in a materialist perspective, all "free" actions are mere determinations produced by the brain and nervous system reacting to physiological or environmental influences.) Also included in this category are practical materialists (not card-carrying materialists) who have never had the least thought about anything besides their everyday pursuits (which are organized in various ways in the search for their own satisfaction).

When I hear the first type, who give lip service to the importance, or at least usefulness, of religion, I begin to think, "Are they serious"? Religion without organization?

I am perhaps overly influenced by Aristotle, who declares that we are instinctively socio-political beings. He goes on to say that a completely unsocial "loner" would have to be either a beast or a god. The animalized type would be someone living on the level of the lower animals, purely sensualized, unable to enter into normal human interactions. (Aristotle was unfamiliar with physical or mental handicaps or diseases that can make individuals appear animal-like.) For the god type, it is not clear that Aristotle had any specific person in mind. There may have been ancient Grecian mystical equivalents of the Hindu Yogis who retreat from society for constant contemplation on a mountain top; or, as a Christian equivalent, St. Simon Stylites in the fifth century, who ascended a pillar to remain in constant contemplation and prayer for twenty-seven years. Apparently he did not come down even to go to church.

But any religion that is between these two extremes, and

compatible with human nature, would have to be organized—maybe even supremely organized, if it was large and wanted to remain unified. Jean-Jacques Rousseau and Auguste Comte, who scarcely had a religious bone in their respective bodies, looked to the Catholic Church as a model to implement their utopian ideals for civic-secular unity. And mainstream Protestant churches, even when they try to avoid looking "hierarchical" like the Catholic Church, develop more decentralized, but still highly organized, administrative and jurisdictional schemes. Even the Quakers, who are against not only ecclesial organization but also Baptism and other sacraments, at least get together systematically in meetings to allow the Spirit to inspire them.

Anyone serious about becoming "spiritual" ought to note the elaborate and painstaking ascetic rituals and gradations of meditation techniques that some Hindus and Buddhists adopt, who wish to attain the status of spiritual proficients.

For a Catholic, Jesus Himself (Matt. 16: 13–19) gives the original organizational impetus, while he and his disciples were standing next to a massive rocky cliff, dotted with niches containing statues of pagan gods—a rock on which the city of Caesarea Philippi was built. On this occasion, as God had changed Abram's name to Abraham, Jesus changed the Apostle Simon's name to Peter, and promised that his Church, analogously to Caesarea Philippi, will be established on a rock (*Cephas*), the rock of Peter (*Petrus* as the masculine form of the Greek translation of *Cephas*). He also entrusts the very specific and non-reproducible keys to the Kingdom of Heaven to Peter.

Contemporary Protestant commentators tend to interpret Jesus' words choosing Peter as the authority in his Church as inauthentic, inserted in the Gospel by Matthew to indicate the prevailing understanding of ecclesiastical authority in his time; or else, interpolating actual words spoken *after* Jesus' Resurrection into a narrative concerning a particular event during Jesus' ministry on earth.

The *Interpreters One-Volume Commentary* on the Bible works this vein hard:

- "The designation of Peter as 'the rock' does not view him as the first bishop of Rome and the founder of the Roman hierarchy, but as the first witness of the Resurrection and therefore as the prime apostolic witness that God raised Jesus from the dead."
- "The word translated **church** (in Greek *ekklesia*) refers to the community of faith, not to an ecclesiastical organization as the church later of necessity came to be."
- "The exercise of authority to **bind** and **loose** has to do with the regulation of the inner life of the community."

In other words, in a Protestant construal, some necessary, but definitely non-hierarchical, organization is necessary to coordinate the development of the ecclesiastical community, preserving its unity and identity. But the "rock" is not Peter, just the "faith" of Peter.

This leads to all sorts of difficulties. Building up the church on the basis of faith as a subjective state, involving private interpretation of the Bible, has resulted in multiple divisions and denominations among non-Catholics (often accompanied by dissenting "Catholic" theologians and Scripture scholars), and their continuing disagreements regarding fundamental Christian doctrines and/or morals. The rock of Peter is buffeted by these swirling challenges, but has remained—for those not sitting on that ecclesial Gibraltar—irritatingly unmoved.

11. The Nation with the Soul of a Church

JOHN KIENKER

If it is not heresy, then perhaps it is just bad manners to say on a website called *The Catholic Thing* that I find G.K. Chesterton to be better quoted than read. Some years ago when I was seeking to deepen my knowledge of the Church, Chesterton's name came up again and again among the great modern apologists considered must-reads. When I found him quoted by other authors, I was charmed by his amusing, clever insights. So finally I dove into his book *Orthodoxy* . . . and had to abandon it after fifteen pages or so. Chesterton's leisurely, rotund prose was too much for my American impatience, and after that, as far as he was concerned, I made do with what I could learn about the Catholic mind from his Father Brown mysteries (which, as it turns out, is a lot).

So, it was with some hesitation that I sought out his essay "What is America?" after being struck by his famous reply contained therein—"a nation with the soul of a church." The essay begins, after the usual paragraph or three of throat-clearing, with Chesterton having a great deal of fun with the form he had to fill out at the American consulate for his trip abroad. For example, one question asked "Are you in favor of subverting the government of the United States by force?" to which Chesterton suggests he ought to have written: "I prefer to answer that question at the end of my tour and not the beginning."

Laughing at others' peculiarities is good fun, says Chesterton, but what is unfamiliar ought to make us think as well as laugh. For him, the incident was a way "to get some ultimate idea of what America is." And what makes the United States unique, Chesterton argues, is that it is "the only nation in the world that is founded on a creed."

That creed has at its heart an understanding of human equality, which is "set forth with dogmatic and even theological lucidity in the Declaration of Independence; perhaps the only piece of practical politics that is also theoretical politics and also great literature."

"Now a creed is at once the broadest and the narrowest thing in the world," Chesterton continues. America's creed is universal in its implications, recognizing knowable truths applicable to all men at all times. And in that sense, the country's essence, he concludes, is "religious because it is not racial" in the way that "England is English as France is French or Ireland is Irish; the great mass of men taking certain national traditions for granted."

At the same time, America's creed is limiting because the creed itself defines what it is to be an American; it is the truths we hold. As Chesterton puts it, even when American pluralism is compared to a melting pot, "that metaphor implies that the pot itself is of a certain shape and a certain substance; a pretty solid substance. The melting-pot must not melt." That solid substance—that creed—he writes, is "traced on the lines of Jeffersonian democracy."

What Chesterton has struck upon is that for all his seeming hostility to authority, Thomas Jefferson was not opposed to orthodoxy. He was the proud father of the University of Virginia precisely because it was to be a school of republican orthodoxy, educating citizens to understand and perpetuate good government. As he wrote to James Madison, with whom he planned the curriculum, the school would be "our seminary," in which the "vestal flame is to be kept alive." Before devoting himself to this endeavor in his retirement, Jefferson, along with almost every other prominent American founder, had called for a national university dedicated to the same purpose.

Chesterton recognizes that America's is "a creed, if not about divine, at least about human things." Some Catholics fault America's founding principles as owing too much to the Enlightenment liberalism of John Locke, for presenting a truncated view of human nature defined exclusively by rights, and for fostering a pursuit of private happiness however one chooses to define it. But the moral order in the Declaration is in keeping with a broad natural law tradition that includes Saint Thomas's "five ways." The Declaration does not preach Christ crucified because that mystery is beyond the limits of human reason and therefore, rightfully, beyond the limits of politics.

Catholic critics of the American founding overlook the character of its creed and how much it has in common not only with *a* church but with *the* Church. Such a statement may have shocked Jefferson's decidedly nonsectarian sensibilities, but not nearly as much as the modern invention of an amoral pursuit of whatever you like, which is wholly at odds with the founders' public philosophy. In asserting their liberty, Americans remained, as Jefferson put it, "inherently independent of all but the moral law."

In his essay, Chesterton asserted that America will retain its original shape "until it becomes shapeless." Today, the only truth many Americans hold to be self-evident anymore is that there is no moral truth such as Jefferson spoke of. But without moral order, there is no American creed, no shape to America, and so, in a sense, the most powerful nation on earth may have gained the world only to lose its soul.

Though ideas such as truth, virtue, and natural law may now be passé in American politics, they still retain vitality in the Catholic Church, where they were preserved and nurtured for many centuries. It falls, then, first of all to American Catholics, enlightened by their faith as G.K. Chesterton was, to understand the creed we celebrate this Independence Day, and to convert their fellow citizens to the self-evident truths we are called to affirm by the laws of nature and of nature's God.

12. The Power of the Third Commandment

PATRICK FAGAN

It's little known to the public or to elite commentators in the national discourse. But an amazing phenomenon has been uncovered in the social sciences: the more frequently Americans worship the better they do on every observable outcome measured to date. This holds for rates of smoking, getting drunk, use of hard drugs, being charged by the police, theft, shoplifting, adultery, running away from home, watching x-rated movies, homosexual conduct, cohabitation, or the number of sexual partners that teenage girls have.

Most U.S. federal surveys track weaknesses more than strengths, but occasionally positive outcomes are measured. Grade point averages for U.S. high school children is one such factor, and there too religious attendance is beneficial. The federal government's "No Child Left Behind" initiative, which has cost taxpayers billions of dollars, would be ecstatic to report such outcomes as these. Yet the beneficial effects of religious practice cost the taxpayer nothing. The documented relationship of religious practice to other goods include: children's positive social development, the quality of parent-child relationships, levels of happiness—including marital happiness—participation in charitable services, and pride in work.

Most of the Commandments are in the negative form: "Thou shalt not. . . ." And contrary to popular opinion, God's negatives are a net plus for us. In addition, the third commandment, "Keep holy the Sabbath day" is in the positive. And what benefits flow from it It is foundational not only for the individual but for society as a whole. Our founders were well aware of that as George Washington made clear in his Farewell Address: "Of all the dispositions and habits which lead to political prosperity, religion and morality are indispensable supports."

Public commentators such as Christopher Hitchens and Richard Dawkins, enemies of God but friends of science, are here presented with a scientific dilemma: How can something they call anti-human be so good for human beings? If their theories were correct, the more people worship God, the worse off they should be. Instead, the more we worship God the better off we are, and society is too. Can the cultured despisers of religion explain why something so "dysfunctional" gives rise to such highly functional people?

Leaving Hitchens and Dawkins aside, there are a few lessons the social sciences drive home. For statesmen, that they should have the courage to defend religious practice, for it is good and necessary for all men and for the prosperity of our United States.

For the ordinary lay believer, the social sciences should give every one of us confidence to do what we already know we should before the studies appear: speak out and confront those aggressively trying to wipe religion from our way of life. Why can we not teach these benefits of religion in our public schools? Why can we not show this basic route to the thriving of man and woman? This in not teaching religion, this is teaching common sense (or common sense confirmed by carefully arrived at numbers).

For Catholics, the social sciences can give a little additional pat on the back to one of our central and differentiating beliefs: infallibility in matters of faith and morals. There is nothing that the

Church teaches should be held by all (the universal moral law) that is contradicted by the data assembled in the social sciences. Indeed, we can see that what the Church teaches about morality is strongly confirmed empirically. Social science is not infallible and has nothing to say about the tenets of faith. But anyone looking at the accepted data with an open mind today would have to marvel at how the old, unscientific Church got so much exactly right.

Philip Rieff, a major social theorist whose critique of modernity, especially its most admired proponents, Nietzsche, Freud and Joyce—all bent on upending the sacred order of society embodied in the honoring of the divine commands—dedicated his last years to elucidating the fundamental relationship of the Ten Commandments to the good of mankind, especially in their salutary clarity on what is forbidden.

John Paul II made the same arguments in briefer and clearer form in *Veritatis Splendor*: "[The commandments] are the *first necessary step on the journey towards freedom,* its starting-point." "The beginning of freedom," Saint Augustine writes, "is to be free from crimes . . . such as murder, adultery, fornication, theft, fraud, sacrilege, and so forth. When once one is without these crimes (and every Christian should be without them), one begins to lift up one's head towards freedom. But this is only the beginning of freedom, not perfect freedom."

In our time, it helps to have the social sciences in the service of such a journey. Such is their chief splendor, though not too many practitioners see it this way—yet.

13. Mother of the Unborn

GREG PFUNDSTEIN

The Chiaroscuro Foundation recently released New York City abortion data by zip code in the form of a map. Since it took us a while to have the map developed, we have actually had the data for some time. As we thought about it and discussed it, it occurred to us that the zip codes with particularly low abortion rates were perhaps even more interesting than the zip codes with particularly high rates. We wondered why some zip codes, such as 11219 in Brooklyn, came in substantially lower than many other parts of the city. We decided to see if we could find anything interesting in some of these places.

So I searched for a Catholic church in 11219 and found Regina Pacis. I contacted the pastor, Msgr. Marino, and asked to meet. When I arrived the following Monday morning, I drove around the neighborhood a bit before going to the church. It isn't a terrible neighborhood, but it isn't a well-to-do neighborhood either. With such a low abortion rate, I had expected it to be somewhat more upscale. As I arrived at the church, I was even more curious than before about what Msgr. Marino might think of the low rate of abortion in his neighborhood.

And then I saw it: the Chapel of Mary Mother of the Unborn.

It all started in 1989, when Msgr. Marino was parochial vicar at Regina Pacis. He went to have dinner with a cousin upstate who had married a Jewish woman. The conversation turned to abortion, and things got so heated between Fr. Marino and his cousin's wife that she asked him to leave. On his way home, he was heartbroken to think that he, a Catholic priest, was unable to defend the Church's teaching on abortion adequately, even among family. He thought and prayed about it for days, and eventually came up with the idea of developing a response that would not be anti-abortion, but pro-life: a devotion to the Blessed Virgin, Mother of the Unborn.

After being treated a bit dismissively by his pastor and his bishop, Msgr. Marino got official recognition for the title of Mary Mother of the Unborn from Rome. He wrote a prayer and had it approved by his bishop, found a statue, and converted the old baptistery at Regina Pacis into the chapel of Mary Mother of the Unborn. And so it began.

Next to the statue, which is perched atop the baptismal font, is the Book of Life: prayers written for women who are expecting; couples who are having a hard time conceiving; couples mourning the loss of an unborn child through miscarriage; women mourning their abortions; parents wrestling with the anguish of an adverse prenatal diagnosis; mothers, fathers, grandmothers giving thanks for safe delivery. Nearly seventy large books have been filled with handwritten prayers since 1989. The walls are adorned with pictures of babies born in answer to prayer to Mary Mother of the Unborn. Every year, on the Feast of the Annunciation, Msgr. Marino brings the statue up to the church and blesses all the pregnant women of the parish, all the newborns, and all those mourning the loss of a child.

Occasionally women considering abortion come to Msgr. Marino, and he gives them his best counsel. When he senses that he has done all he can, he often takes the woman to the chapel and leaves her there. He tells the story of a couple who discovered by ultrasound that their child had not developed any arms at all and who were considering aborting him for that reason. He feared he had been unable to persuade them to carry the child to term and left them at the chapel, dejected. Several months later, they returned to present to him a child—born with two fully developed arms.

There she was, Mary Mother of the Unborn, right in the middle of a zip code with one of the lowest abortion rates in the city, in the middle of a cluster of zip codes with relatively low abortion rates. After two years working in the pro-life movement in New York City, I had never even heard of her. I hope some of you have and that many more will. Perhaps it is a devotion for our time, certainly for this city. Mary, Mother of the Unborn, pray for us:

O Mary, Mother of the Unborn,
protect the gift of human life which your
Divine Son has allowed to be given.

Give strength and joy to all parents as
they await the birth of the precious
child they have conceived.

Give courage to those who are fearful,
calm those who are anxious and guide

all of us, with your motherly care, to
treasure and protect the miraculous gift
of human life.

We ask this through your Son,
Jesus Christ our Lord. Amen.

14. A Callus on the Soul

ANTHONY ESOLEN

A young man in fourth-century Rome, not yet a Christian but of
extraordinary sensitivity, was teased by his friends for refusing to
attend the gladiatorial games. He gave in, but determined to
cover his eyes during the fighting. Suddenly he heard a great cry
rise up. Perhaps it was the moment when the fallen fighter would
appeal for mercy to the spectators, and, if they were in a foul
mood, they would shout, "*Jugula, jugula!*"—"Give it to him in
the throat!" Whatever it was, Alypius looked. And was
fascinated and caught. He took others to the games. People
crave company in their vices.

Alypius was the friend and protégé of another young man,
Augustine, who was caught in the grip of a different sin, lust. His
Confessions, which tell of Alypius, spare us most of the ugly
details (not all: he kept an assignation in a church). He finally
determined to fence his lust within marriage, not because he
desired married love, but because he believed he could not do
without the pleasure. He dismissed his long-time mistress, the
mother of his beloved son Adeodatus, got engaged to a girl not yet
of age (she was ten), and picked up another mistress to tide him
over. Alypius began to wonder whether he was missing out. After
all, if a man as brilliant as Augustine set so much store by sexual
pleasure, it must be something glorious indeed.

I believe that each of these sins sheds light upon the other.
Now, of course, we are too enlightened to take pleasure in human
slaughter as a game, and too benighted to feel disgust at regarding
the marital act as mutual rubbing and scratching. But there is a

lust for blood, and cruelty in lust. Both sins involve an *apparent* susceptibility to something genuinely bold and fascinating: a man's desperate attempt to fight the terror of death, or the naked human body in all its vulnerability and potency.

What really happens, though, is that the prurient sin raises a callus on the soul. It would not do for the sophisticated Romans merely to set one man with a sword against another. That ceased to be interesting, because the *lives* at stake ceased to be interesting. Instead they had to invent new and clever twists on the cruelty: for instance, setting a nude "Neptune" with net and trident against a man armed with plate, shield, and sword.

In the same way, mere fornication has ceased to be interesting. It must be spiced now, with ever more inventive and perverse pornography, unnatural peculiarities, or acrobatic performances—the observers as harsh and unforgiving as spectators in a blood sport tend to be.

The poets knew this. Catullus wrote that he hated the adulterous woman he loved: *odi et amo.* Shakespeare wrote that "The expense of spirit in a waste of shame / Is lust in action." He gives us not a single portrayal of a fornicator that is pleasant or admirable. Typical is Lucio in *Measure for Measure,* who fathers a child on a whore and then ignores both. Why not, when sex is appetite? "One full meal," says Lucio, "will set me to't."

In Scripture, we read that after Amnon raped his sister Tamar, he turned away from her in disgust. "Such love is hate," says the poet Spenser. His figure of Lust, in the parade of the seven deadly sins at the House of Pride, cruelly deceives women and tosses them aside. His very body is a sign of that deception: beneath his handsome exterior he is riddled with the disease "that rots the marrow, and consumes the brain."

Why have we forgotten this? My brother-in-law overheard a conversation in a drug store. "Why are you buying those?" Reply: "The (vulgarity) I'm (obscenity) won't take the pill."

We play the card "We're in Love," but we know it's not true. We are caught in an irrational passion. We are lonely, bored, wanting excitement—someone who will take care of that particular need—a sexual butler or chambermaid. We are more or less pleased by the person's general attitude, and without any question of love, which always gestures towards eternity, we settle into an agreement, like a mutually profitable business deal.

The trouble is that the act itself, to be "successful," must at least mimic genuine passion, and is oriented towards the eternal, whether we acknowledge it or not. It is the act that brings new life into being. The Romans would have turned away in boredom if one gladiator had faced another and said, "This life is a lie. Here, kill me now." So, too, fornicators could not keep up the pretense if one said to the other, "I know that what I'm doing is not love."

We hate the people we deceive. It is one of the perversities of our fallen nature. If a life of fornication necessarily involves deception, we should see the hate creeping in, numbing the soul. When he saw his first arena killing, Alypius was doubtless overcome with the horror and pity of a lost human life. But the evil, once pursued, brings contempt; a man bleeding his life out onto the sand brings a shrug, and a glance at the card to see what's next.

The same goes for fornication. It does not make men and women more careful of one another's welfare. It raises a callus on the soul. It makes them contemptuous of one another. Even in their acts of lust there is hectic willfulness, frank savagery, or, worse, blankness. "When I was twenty-six, I met my wife," I said to a twenty-six year old fellow the other day. He smiled sadly, picked up his video game, and said: "I guess I've already had three wives."

I don't like writing about evils, but somebody has to be honest about them.

15. Why Catholics Are Right

Michael Coren

When I first told friends and colleagues about my new book *Why Catholics Are Right*, they were intrigued by the proposed content but disturbed by the title: "Sounds a little proud"; "Is that sufficiently conciliatory for these progressive and pluralistic days?"; and "You ought to be careful because it might offend people."

Which is odd. When I suggested to them titles for other books by other people such as *Why Liberals Are Right*, *Why Conservatives Are Right*, even *Why Muslims Are Right*, and especially *Why Atheists Are Right*, they thought them entirely reasonable and unlikely to cause any problems at all.

To believe something is, self-evidently, not to believe something that is its contrary. So obvious is this that it is not questioned and seems a taken-for-granted truth about most subjects. It is, after all, just common sense. But to claim that being an authentic Roman Catholic necessitates believing that Roman Catholicism is correct positively terrifies many modern men and women, as though a Catholic claiming to be right was some terrible sin. Not that many of these people believe in sin of course.

The implication—that being Catholic means, well, being Catholic and leads to the persecution or killing of others who are not Catholic—is naturally insulting. But as we know—and I think the critics really do as well—being Catholic means nothing of the sort. Still, it usually takes only a few moments during a disagreement for someone to bring up the days when Catholics did indeed give their opponents a hard time, as though in all of history only Catholics have ever got that wrong or even just acted like most people in earlier ages.

So I kept the title for a specific reason: to oblige and demand a certain clarity from readers. I'm a Catholic and believe in Catholicism. And thus I believe that people who disagree with my beliefs are wrong. I do not dislike them—or at least don't dislike all of them—nor do I wish to hurt them, even those who wish to hurt me and will probably wish to hurt me even more after they read this book, pretend to read it, or read nasty reviews of it.

I do, however, want these readers to consider what I have to say and not to abuse my beliefs in a manner and with a harshness that they would not dream of using against almost any other creed or religion. It might be a romantic hope, but hope is a theological virtue, one of those Catholic qualities we like to think of as important and helpful.

Having said this, there are degrees of wrongness. Some people are only slightly wrong, others wrong most of the time and to a shocking degree. Non-Catholic Christians and in particular serious Evangelicals and Eastern Orthodox believers are examples of the former. Many of them could teach Catholics a great deal about love, charity, and devotion to God.

Alleged Christians who want to edit rather than follow Christ, professional atheists who flood the Internet with their obsessions, and part-time Catholic-bashers are in the latter camp.

Which brings me to the anti-Catholicism that has become the last acceptable prejudice in what passes for polite society and has become so obvious and so pronounced that even to point out the fact seems almost banal. We have all heard comments about Catholics that, applied to almost any other group, would simply not be tolerated. It's bad enough when this is street conversation and pointless gossip, far worse when it passes for informed comment in allegedly serious newspapers.

British historian and biographer Christopher Hibbert put it well when he said that historically the pope had been thought of as, "an unseen, ghost-like enemy, lurking behind clouds of wicked incense in a Satanic southern city called Rome." In much of contemporary Anglo-Saxon culture, as well as the greater modern world, this perverse caricature has found a second wind.

As you can see, my book was written out of experience as well as research. My experience has taught me that attacks usually begin with the history, then with a misunderstanding of what the Church believes and teaches, then with angry comments about why the Church is so "obsessed" with the life issues and then a whole bunch of criticisms. These days, tragically, the Catholic clergy abuse scandal is thrown in somewhere. It has to be discussed—but honestly and accurately.

The rest of the punches thrown at the Catholic body? The Church was nasty to Galileo; the Church tried to convert Muslims, and the Crusades were horrible; Hitler was a Catholic and the pope was a Nazi; the Inquisition slaughtered millions of people; the Church is rich and does nothing for the poor; children were abused and the Vatican knew about it all and did nothing; celibacy leads to perversion; Catholics worship statues; Catholics believe the pope is infallible and can never do anything wrong; and so on and so on and so on.

It's all nonsense. Yet nonsense that is given a veneer of credibility by thinking people who shape opinion. All this makes the Church unique in the twenty-first century as a victim institution. In almost every other area, we've matured as a people and a culture to the point where such crass generalizations and fundamentally flawed opinions would not make it past the alehouse door.

I am often driven to say to the mass of uninformed critics: think and agree, think and disagree, think whatever you like. But in the name of God and the Church He left us, please think!

16. *Les Miserables* as Via Crucis

KAREN GOODWIN

In his homily for the opening Mass of his pontificate, Benedict XVI said: "There is nothing more beautiful than to be surprised by the Gospel, by the encounter with Christ. There is nothing more beautiful than to know Him, and to speak to others of our friendship with Him."

Many know the surprising joy of meeting the Gospel in *Les Misérables*: Victor Hugo's nineteenth-century novel, in the dozen film adaptations, and in the musical theater phenomenon. (My production company was one of the partners in the London and Broadway version of *Les Mis*.) I believe many more will be surprised to enter the modern day *Via Crucis* of director Tom Hooper's new film adaptation of the musical, which opens on Christmas Day.

There is no Hollywood sacrilege here. Protagonist Jean Valjean's journey in the story is a living witness to the Way of the Cross.

Writing about the novels of William Faulkner, Thomas Merton observed that: "a writer can be profoundly biblical in his work without being a churchgoer or a conventional believer, and. . , in our time it is often the isolated and lonely artist, facing the problems of life without the routine consolations of conventional religion, who really experiences in their depth the existential dimensions of the those problems."

This is certainly true of Victor Hugo (1802 1885), the author of *Les Misérables*, but it's true too of the many collaborators, investors, and producers of what has become the most beloved musical of all time—true whether or not they acknowledge it. Some artistic expressions—in literature, theatre, film, fine arts, dance, music, television, and in so-called New Media—intuitively show us dimensions of redemptive longing, and they are the ones that touch the depths of the soul. And often surprise cynics in New York and Hollywood.

These are the avenues of *inculturation* that Blessed Pope John Paul II urged us to pursue in proclaiming the Good News: "The inherent missionary nature of the Church means testifying essentially to the fact that the task of inculturation, as an integral dissemination of the Gospel and its consequent translation into thought and life, continues today, and represents the heart, the means, and the goal of the new evangelization."

Critics, of course, often resist such works, even as the general public embraces them. It was true in 1862 when Hugo's novel was published. Critics skewered the book; readers made it an international bestseller. It was true in 1985 when the Royal Shakespeare Company premiered the musical adaptation of *Les Misérables* in London, which met with tepid critical acclaim at best. One critic wrote: "There is a string of impressive sights over the three-and-a-quarter hours, but little to grip the ear and still less to trouble the mind."

I can testify that all involved in the show were puzzled by such comments after the New York opening. Were the critics really deaf to the show's soaring score? To songs such as "I Dreamed a Dream," "A Heart Full of Love," and "Bring Him Home"?

What is it about the interior journey we take when we enter this story that makes some critics lambaste it but audiences love it? I think it's because, despite his own moral lapses and spiritual doubts, Victor Hugo gave us a story that reflects the Gospel of Jesus Christ. As the boy Gavroche sings on the barricades in the musical, "I never read the Bible but I know that it's true."

Christopher West has said there is no other theatrical production that has so awakened his yearning for heaven or given him such him hope of its fulfillment, because the show "explores the hidden realms of our hearts and beautifully affirms what we long for *(desire)*, what we're created for *(design)*, and what we're headed for *(destiny)*."

> It's as Chesterton put it in *The House of Christmas*:
> To an open house in the evening
> Home shall all men come.
> To an older place than Eden
> And a taller town than Rome.
> To the end of the way of the Wandering Star,
> To the things that cannot be and that are,
> To the place where God was homeless and all men are at home.

Victor Hugo's own words were a harbinger of the musical theatre adaptation of his masterpiece: "Music expresses that which cannot be put into words but about which it is impossible to remain silent." The critics' laments seem to suggest that such themes as forgiveness, justice, self-sacrifice, and love are unworthy if they are redemptive.

Hugo wrote his novel when the moral and political crises of nineteenth century France had consigned so many to unrelieved suffering. Today the creators of the stage version, and now the film adaptation, present their interpretation at a time when we endure our own set of cultural and political crises that can render us broken-hearted, but can also raise hope and inspire us to become agents of transformation.

We may be a "creative minority," as Pope Benedict XVI describes us, but all of us hear echoes of something primordial when we hear true, good, and beautiful music and lyrics in our own day. If we act on these inspirations, in ways great and small, we can each contribute to the flourishing of a civilization of love.

17. Should Catholics Have to Pay for Anti-Catholic Bigotry?

FR. VAL J. PETERS

Last year, the FX cable network debuted a new series by Ryan Murphy (*Glee*, *Nip/Tuck*, *The New Normal*) called *American Horror Story*, conceived as a number of season-long, self-contained mini-series.

The first season, which focused on a married couple who move into a "haunted house," was marked by explicit sexual content, often tinged with violence.

The second season, "Asylum," is set in the year 1964 in an institution for the criminally insane run by the Catholic Church. It contains some of the most bigoted, offensive, and depraved content you can imagine—all squarely aimed at the Catholic Church, its beliefs, and its institutions. And if you are Catholic and a cable subscriber, you helped make this content possible.

From the opening sequence—in which creepy music, graphic surgery, and copulation are interspersed with images of the Virgin Mary—*American Horror Story: Asylum* is virulent anti-Catholic propaganda from beginning to end.

Among the program's catalogue of anti-Catholic canards are:

• **Nuns are abusive and sadistic.** Sister Jude brutally canes a serial killer known as "Bloodyface," allows him to be attacked by other inmates, then orders the asylum's orderlies to beat him. The episode ends with Jude strapping another character to a table and threatening her with torture.

• **Catholic clergy are motivated solely by ambition.** Monsignor Howard rhapsodizes at length about how success in running the asylum will cause him to be promoted to cardinal, and eventually "the first Anglo-American Pope!" He offers to share his power with Jude, whom "thousands of sisters will call 'Reverend Mother!'" Admittedly, this does take place in Sister Jude's fantasy. But this is only natural, since...

• **Catholic clergy are sexual perverts and hypocrites.** Before dinner with Monsignor Howard, Sister Jude is shown fondling her cleavage and donning lacy red lingerie as religious music soars. Her fantasy concludes with the nun stripping off her habit and straddling the priest's crotch.

• **Catholic piety is phony, and Catholics are secretly bigots.** Sister Jude is shown praying the "Hail Mary"—after which, she proceeds to abuse her patients and Sister Mary Eunice. Instead of leading to compassion, Sister Jude's prayers are shown only to engender a shrill hatred of everyone and everything that does not meet her limited worldview, and actually cause her to exhibit only brutality and sadism toward others. Sister Jude is also a bigot; while taunting "Bloodyface" (who killed his African-American wife), she sneers, "Did her dark meat slide off the bone any easier than your other victims?"

• **Catholics are ignorant and substitute irrational dogma for science.** Sister Jude snarls that one inmate was committed by a doctor who "compared her to a wood nymph." "You mean nymphomania?," Lana asks. "Just more nonsense from the charlatans," Jude replies. "That young woman is a victim of her own lust! Mental illness is the fashionable explanation for SIN!" Sister Jude also persistently criticizes Dr. Arden's treatment of the patients. That a nun with such beliefs would have been put in charge of a mental institution in the pro-science, pro-psychology Vatican II era of 1964 Catholicism is ridiculous.

• **Catholics use their influence solely to oppress others.** In addition to her blatant abuse of the charges under her keeping, Sister Jude wrongfully imprisons Lana—a woman she knows to be sane—then bullies Lana's lesbian lover Wendy into signing commitment papers by threatening to expose their liaison, which in 1964 would result in Wendy's disgrace and dismissal from her job as a schoolteacher.

There is an audience, apparently, for this kind of anti-Catholic invective. At least three million viewers tuned in for the second season premiere. But that also means another 87 million cable subscribers who chose not to watch, presumably including many faithful Catholics and non-Catholics who are offended by this content, paid for this program to come into their homes, whether they wanted it or not.

Murphy may have his reasons for disliking the Catholic Church, and he is entitled to his opinion; but it is unconscionable that every cable and satellite subscriber in America (including many Roman Catholics, who comprise the single largest religious denomination in the country) is forced by the entertainment industry to subsidize Murphy's bigoted attacks on their faith.

The reverse is also true, by the way. Is it fair to make a committed atheist pay for religious programming? Is it fair to make a childless bachelor pay for children's programming, or a person with no interest in sports pay for ESPN?

According to a recent survey, 92 percent of respondents said they would prefer to pay for cable channels à la carte. *Variety* reports that: "U.S. consumers would overwhelmingly prefer to pay for just 19 TV channels at $1.50 a pop than their current multichannel packages."

Unbundling cable channels is only fair, and it is the only way to set right a distorted market that forces people to subsidize content that assaults their deepest beliefs and attacks their very faith.

18. The French Debate on Gay "Marriage"

Jean Duchesne

Much is being heard in France these days about gay marriage. Does this mean a genuine debate is developing? Not at all. Critics of the government's bill on "marriage for all" put forward all kinds of excellent reasons to reject it, and no one replies.

Government ministers say they are happy to allow everyone to make their points. But the advocates of families with two daddies or two mommies simply don't bother to argue back. They apparently believe that a self-evident right does not need to be justified. It ought to be acknowledged, they say, not discussed.

This is why no official or defender of the bill has stooped to comment on the elaborate case made against it by cardinals, bishops, imams, rabbis, and also non-religious individuals and organizations. The media generally find such rational analysis too sophisticated. It cannot be reduced to bold headlines. The general public would get bored.

By contrast, the notion that anyone should be able to marry anyone else is based on simplistic ideals that any honorable person allegedly will grasp and adopt at once. Shying away from actual dialogue first rests on the principle that any form of discrimination is bad. Denying gays and lesbians access to marriage if they feel like it then amounts to refusing to consider them as human beings. It is therefore morally unacceptable, a form of "homophobia," which has been declared a hideous crime that toddlers are now warned against in kindergarten.

It is also argued that several American states and some European countries have already opened marriage to gays and lesbians, and that France must catch up in order remain among the world's most advanced countries. (We are, of course, supposed to be the exemplary standard bearer of equality and justice.)

Another excuse for declining to deal seriously with objections is that gay marriage was part of candidate François Hollande's platform. Since he was elected president, the conclusion is that a majority approved this idea, and that it is undemocratic to challenge it now.

Opponents (and especially Catholics) are now beginning to stage mass demonstrations. Because rational debates have proved impossible, yet another form of indirect rebuff is taking shape. Mass popular political pressure is branded as unnatural, because marching down boulevards chanting slogans belongs to progressives and defenders of the oppressed, not conservatives and reactionaries.

All this is highly paradoxical indeed. It would be rather unusual for a leftist government to have to yield to protesters peacefully invading the streets. There has been a precedent, though. In 1984, after a million people demonstrated in Paris, another socialist president whose first name was François (Mitterand) was forced to fire his prime minister and entire cabinet and to give up his party's plan to nationalize all private schools, most of which are Catholic.

Hollande is by no means sure to do better than Mitterrand. His promise to legalize "mercy killing" has already been postponed—the official explanation is that he wants to give a panel of experts time to investigate the matter in depth and to write a comprehensive scientific report whose conclusions no one will dare disagree with.

The supporters of euthanasia are obviously more patient than the champions of gay marriage. The latter's blind determination is another paradox. At a time when marriage is no longer very popular, with boys and girls marrying later or not at all, even if they have children, and divorced more often, it is ironic to see the avant-garde claiming the right to take advantage of such an old-fashioned institution.

There's more: no unanimity exists on the left, and even among gay and lesbian groups. Their traditional bisexual and transsexual allies obviously have different priorities, so the LGBT lobby is falling apart. Meanwhile the socialist rank and file, who have higher priorities on their agenda, are perplexed and divided. And to be honest, a few voices in favor of gay rights have also made themselves heard in the Gaullist opposition party.

It appears that a small "enlightened" elite have persuaded themselves (and a handful of politicians who would be ashamed of being left behind) that same-sex unions are the inevitable next step in the modernization of social life and the growth of civil liberties, a logical continuation of universal suffrage, the abolition of slavery, the repudiation of racism and sexism, divorce, and birth control.

Because it is rooted in the illusory faith in "Progress," this belief is impervious to reasoned objections and resorts to caricatures and contradictory arguments to impose itself without ever deigning to disclose its real motivations or to examine likely consequences.

In the present case, the fear of not being "with it" is being used to drive home the notion that homosexuality is "normal." The ultimate, unspeakable goal is to weaken instinctive repugnance, especially among teenagers. The prospect of the next steps is not only sickening, but downright frightening. The French poet Paul Valéry once noted that civilizations can die. They can also commit suicide.

The question now is how long people will tolerate being manipulated and treated like morons by madmen claiming to be philanthropists. It is not true that François Hollande won the last presidential election because he promised to legalize same-sex unions. The French merely (and narrowly) rejected the incumbent. Equality does not mean that males and females are interchangeable. Hope and faith that the future can be better cannot consist in depriving the word "marriage" of its significance, but in betting on reason.

French Church leaders have done their duty by pointing out the predictably disastrous effects of the legalization of gay marriage. It is up to the people now to finish the job by making it clear on the political stage that this is definitely not the kind of "advance" that France or the world need.

19. The Life of B.

ROBERT ROYAL

During the recent elections, the Obama campaign developed a series of vignettes involving a cartoon figure name "Julia," showing the ways government would help her at every point in her life.

We thought that Catholics ought to be ready, should the possibility arise at some far distant future date, to be equally clear about what they see as a desirable alternative. So here is a sketch of one such possible life, the life of "Beatrice," hereafter B.

Despite already having an older brother Benedict, B. is actually born because her Catholic parents believe in God's words in Genesis: "be fruitful and multiply." And the One Child Policy legislation is stalled in Congress owing to a split between environmentalists worried about the earth's "carrying capacity" and ruling party strategists worried about a shrinking political base. For years afterwards on her birthday, B. and her multiple siblings giggle when their mother tells how a very earnest nurse in the formerly Catholic maternity hospital gave her a copy of Bill McKibben's *Maybe One* as she was taking B. home.

B. is read to and taught by her parents until age five, after which she and her brother are home-schooled, helped by an informal association of neighborhood women, some with advanced degrees in languages, science, or math. Julia, who lives next door, teases B. and Benedict because *she* attended Head Start with most of the other kids in town, while the "Bs" had to stay home. Still, they're friends. B. and Benedict often read children's chapter books to Julia until she learns to read herself in third grade. After that, they only help her with the hard words.

At seventeen, B. receives the highest SAT score in town and faces a decision where to go to university. Julia's choices are simpler. Like almost everyone else, she's participated in Race to the Top and is prepared to move on seamlessly to State U. The curriculum there respects diversity and, therefore, sticks strictly to government mandated standards and educational outcomes—and qualifies for Federal dollars. After much prayer and thought, B. decides to study at a Catholic liberal arts college with an emphasis on Great Books.

Thanks to generous Pell Grants, Julia graduates owing only $40,000. She immediately finds a job with a large corporation that has an arrangement with State U. and begins paying back the Federal government, like a responsible citizen. B. has no debt at all because her liberal arts college kept costs low by not participating in various Federal aid programs. The money saved in not having "compliance officers" alone is said to have cut about a third off tuition. Her college also found generous private donors who agreed to match what B. herself earned to pay for educational expenses. At graduation, she spends a year teaching for a Catholic religious order at a school in Chichicastenango, Guatemala. About half of her colleagues are considering a religious vocation, and some enter the order. But B. decides, after much prayer and thought, that she wants to do something for America.

Back in the States, people she meets are shocked when she talks about her experiences and inform her that her work in Guatemala would not have met the rigorous standards set by the Lilly Ledbetter Fair Pay Act. They also encourage her to study web design in order to take advantage of small-business startup loans available from the Federal government. "The alternative is the service sector, these days," one of them warns. B. thinks about this until one day she reads a story by Evelyn Waugh, where a headmaster tells a classics teacher:

> "Parents are not interested in producing the 'complete man' any more. They want to qualify their boys for jobs in the modern world. You can hardly blame them, can you?"

> "Oh yes," said Scott-King, "I can and do. . . .I think it would be very wicked indeed to do anything to fit a boy for the modern world."

The headmaster calls this shortsighted. Scott-King retorts, "I think it the most long-sided view it is possible to take." That hits B. like a thunderbolt and she spends the next forty years teaching Latin.

But not before meeting Francis X. in a graduate Latin course. At first they are drawn together because they seemed to enjoy the same poets and philosophers, even the very same passages. Afterwards, they find they have very similar backgrounds and are in complete agreement about the kind of family life they would like to live.

They marry, have multiple children (the ruling party is still divided). Francis X. worked part-time at a plant nursery while he was studying Latin and is offered a chance to buy the business when his childless boss retires. He not only loves the smell of the earth and vegetal matter each morning, but to his own amazement, he finds he enjoys and has a knack for business. His business flourishes and he gains a faithful clientele amused by his casually saying things like, "Here's a perfect *ilex aquifolium* for you."

B. and Francis X. manage to raise a family according to their own lights, support a parish, and donate to local youth activities and poor relief. They are not entirely successful—the culture is powerful—in warding off the false lures of success and security. Some of their children take less than ideal paths. But as they near the end, they look back over the course of their lives with general satisfaction.

They retire. Ill-health forces them into one of the clandestine Catholic nursing homes that went underground because of the Elderly Comprehensive Affordable Care Act known colloquially as ECACA or the "Sayonara System." This was hailed at its passage, in the words of one Federal brochure, as guaranteeing "the responsible social choice of a dignified exit from this life."

B. and Francis X. die, a few years earlier than average. But their children and friends remember them with deep affection and gratitude.

20. Oracular Politics

DAVID WARREN

One of the finest things about ancient Roman public life, Cicero tells us at the outset of *De Domo Sua*, is that Religion and the State are controlled by the same persons. The Roman Senate is a one-stop shop. So when he wants something—in this case, to get his property back, after the government took it, and had it consecrated to a god—he knows where to go.

The same authority can have it de-consecrated, as well as materially restored to its former owner. They can also have the statue of "Liberty" removed from the location where Cicero's house had stood. Yesterday it was holy, but today it might be just an inconvenient pile of stone.

Now, in the political conflict between Cicero and Clodius, I will take no part. Clodius was a rogue, but perhaps Cicero had it coming. The circumstances in which he lost his house have not been an issue for me since I was a schoolboy. Nor, after 2,070-something years, do I think it really matters.

What interests me, today, is the basic structure of pagan Roman politics. In my childhood, it was remote: something to be studied in a "purely academic" way. For that matter, the pagan gods did not impact my life, except as literary allusions. But my disinterest, or non-interest, has become rather dated.

Ancient Rome has become very relevant to our times and to our foreseeable future. For once again we are living in a pagan society; in a society we could not conceive of when I was a child only half a century ago. It is a society in which government has absolute power, as much in the spiritual as in the material realm. And as we know from history, that's "bad news for Jews,"—as well as for Christians.

That the Roman Empire, which succeeded the Republic, collapsed, and Christendom was built over its ruined foundations, we all know too well. Such is the reach of anachronism that we find great difficulty in understanding ancient history—not only because of attitudes that seem unlike ours, but because we're over-informed about where it all led, and how it all ended.

To read Cicero, and other Roman greats, we must suppress this knowledge. We must try to imagine Rome in all her power. At the time of which I'm speaking, she has centuries ahead of her. She has also a teeming population who take all kinds of things for granted, as we have taken (for instance) American power for granted.

The question for the government of this august power is not what can they do, but what do they want to do. The world will accommodate them when they make up their mind; as the world has, until quite recently, been accommodating American power. (Of course, America was a "hyperpower" only briefly; Rome was a hyperpower for a long time.)

Within that Roman State and its metropolis, "the people" may be an occasional problem. But they are a manageable problem. Bread and circuses will buy them off. Pompey's management of the corn supply comes into the background of my present reading, along with the use of free corn, like food stamps, to keep a potentially rebellious population obedient and following orders.

All this actually tells us much about same-sex marriage. The battle against it was lost within a decade of the whole idea being raised, up here in Canada. From Canadian experience, I can often know what is going to happen in the United States. Since 2005 I've known attempts to resist the redefinition of marriage in the USA were hopeless. Polls, including referenda in several dozen states, had nothing to do with it. Once the political class has decided what it wants, the bread and circuses can be provided.

The old definition of marriage—perfectly understood even by the people who did not perfectly practice it—was a product of the Christian civilization that America took in, along with her settlers from old Europe. Its precepts were usually unspoken, because it was seldom necessary to speak them. Until quite recently, the idea of consecrating a "marriage" between two men, or two women, was unthinkable.

But the State, which never established a Church, became one. By slow increments over time, accelerating to quick ones over the last generation, Christianity was marginalized. It is now a "private religion" on a par with Islam, Buddhism, Astrology, and Wicca. It is tolerated, as the Romans tolerated all marginal religious cults—up to the point where the followers refuse to honor the State's gods.

The official religion of the government of the United States—which goes generally under the name "secular humanism"—is replete with idols. They are not rendered in statuary in the Roman style, but mostly in words, for abstract conceptions. Each enunciated "human right" is, for all practical purposes, an Official State God, requiring formal acknowledgement and worship by all, including those with "private religions."

To refuse this worship is to challenge the authority and serenity of the State. To withhold worship of a god, on the grounds that it was not worshipped yesterday, is no defense. As Cicero noted, that State has the ability to create new gods at will, to consecrate and de-consecrate at its pleasure.

And the people are happy with this. Apart from a small, and shrinking body of practicing Christians, and practitioners of other "private religions"—rednecks of various kinds, if you will—the people have always gone along, once clearly instructed. God knows (and I mean that literally) that when Christianity prevailed, many people simply went along. We cannot see into people's hearts, but we can see the outward signs of social conformity.

The State is in the process of decreeing that homosexual alliances may be consecrated. For a god has ruled that this must be so, and the State is the interpreter of the oracles.

21. Steve Jobs and the New Evangelization

FR. C. JOHN MCCLOSKEY

As a priest, part of my job description is to be an agent of the New Evangelization that was proclaimed by Blessed John Paul the Great. Only a few years after leading the Church into the third millennium during the Jubilee year of 2000, his mantle fell to Pope Benedict XVI, who also proclaims very seriously the Church's evangelical mission. I assume that the great majority of my readers are serious Catholics who in these challenging times are as eager as I am to see the vision of Bl. John Paul realized and continued by Pope Benedict XVI: to see the Church recover and flourish in growth and fidelity, in particular in what was once known as the West.

Which brings me to the case of Steve Jobs. Let me be clear, I am not postulating Steve Job's cause for canonization. His biography will convince the reader that he suffered from emotional wounds from his early childhood as an adopted son and, to put it mildly, that sensitivity, generosity, and compassion did not stand out in him as particular virtues. To his credit, he was not particularly avaricious and lived modestly. He entered into a late marriage that produced several offspring. Have mercy on him; after all, he was a product of California in the 1960s, not exactly a breeding ground for saints.

Nonetheless, we evangelizers or modern-day apostles, if you will, can learn from him. The following quotations are from Steve Jobs. The words following each quotation are my comments.

• "The people who are crazy enough to think they can change the world are the ones who did so." Isn't that our goal? To change the world for Christ?

•"Be a yardstick of quality. Some people aren't used to an environment where excellence is expected." Isn't it true that if we are good at what we do professionally or within our family, people will pay more attention when we speak to them about Christ and his Church?

• "We don't get a chance to do that many things, and everyone should be really excellent. Because this is our life. Life is brief, and then you die, you know? And we've all chosen to do this with our lives. So it better be damn good. It better be worth it." Do we work at our spiritual life and try to deepen our knowledge of the Faith and put it in action?

• "Quality is more important than quantity. One home run is much better than two doubles." Are we ambitious to go after the best people to bring them to Christ without any fear of failing?

• "I'm convinced that about half of what separates the successful entrepreneurs from the non-successful ones is pure perseverance." Given that God is on our side, why should we allow ourselves to get discouraged?

• "I didn't see it then, but it turned out that getting fired from Apple was the best thing that could have ever happened to me.

The heaviness of being successful was replaced by the lightness of being a beginner again, less sure about everything. It freed me to enter one of the most creative periods of my life." Whether in our spiritual or apostolic life, we are always, as St. Josemaria put it, "Beginning and beginning again."

• "Do you want to spend the rest of your life selling sugared water or do you want a chance to change the world?" Steve Jobs' famous question to John Sculley, former Apple CEO. Like Steve we should welcome challenges and long for greatness. After all we have the only product—our Faith—that everybody truly needs.

• "Being the richest man in the cemetery doesn't matter to me . . . . going to bed at night saying we've done something wonderful . . . that's what matters to me."

• "Almost everything—all external expectations, all pride, all fear of embarrassment or failure—these things just fall away in the face of death, leaving only what is truly important. Remembering that you are going to die is the best way I know to avoid the trap of thinking you have something to lose. You are already naked. There is no reason not to follow your heart." We should look forward to death and meditate on it frequently, as Christians who look forward to our reward, but still know that we are accountable for the gift of faith that we have received and are now to share with others, in word and deed.

Jobs, who once memorably described death as "very likely the single best invention of life," departed this world with a lingering look at his family and the simple, if mysterious, observation: "Oh wow. Oh wow. Oh wow." Who knows what he saw? After all, he died at 3 p.m. (the hour of hope) on the Feast of St. Faustina.

May God have mercy on his soul, while we use some of his insights and practices in our great commission to carry out the New Evangelization, which will change the world in a way never dreamed of by Steve Jobs when he said, "I want to put a ding in the universe."

22. The Limits of Subsidiarity

PETER BROWN

Whatever the fate of Obamacare, there is no escaping the fact that the great American health care debate is far from over. The debate has been at times so fierce that it has even spilled over into theology, where partisans on either side are armed with cudgels called, respectively, "subsidiarity" and "solidarity." In recent weeks, we've even seen these two Catholic terms, unfamiliar to most Americans, applied to support or to condemn Paul Ryan's budget proposals for the entire country.

In broad outline, "Subsidiarists" are people who are fearful or hostile to the state provision of social welfare—preferring that charity be dispensed at lower levels of society: communities and families. "Solidarists," by contrast, believe that society as a whole is often the best administrator of social welfare, and prefer that things such as health insurance be run by the state.

For the moment, it seems as though the subsidiarists have the upper hand, but the question is by no means settled. For the last several hundred years, not only in the United States but in all advanced societies, the trend has been very much away from "subsidiarity" as welfare states of various forms have sprouted. Let's take a sober look at why this is so.

Subsidiarists speak kindly of social arrangements as they were in the old days, when communities consisted of people who knew and cared for one another and extended families. Why, in this view, should Catholics support a distant, impersonal, bureaucratic welfare state, when for most of Church history Catholics subsisted by taking care of one another? Close to this view—increasingly common in the age of Obama—is that programs such as Medicare, Medicaid, Social Security were adopted by historical accident, or worse, as some sort of progressive plot to subvert communities and families by making them dependent on the state.

In his core conviction, the subsidiarist is not wrong. People *did* use to care for each other more and without state provision.

The original risk-pooling arrangement in the West was the feudal society—with peasants and lords combining resources to take care of the sick and the dying. That system worked adequately, though it was always vulnerable to systemic risks: Crop failures, famines, wars, droughts, and pandemics where many people were affected simultaneously could not be insured against. Despite this, civilization managed to survive.

With the emergence of modern capitalism, the feudal system collapsed. The provision of social welfare was replaced largely by guilds, trade unions, and—increasingly—friendly societies. For a membership fee and active participation, friendly societies would visit sick members while underwriting doctor bills and funeral expenses. Over time, many of them arranged for long-term support for the disabled as well.

These societies also practiced solidarity, with regular member meetings imbued with a specifically religious flavor—prayers, Bible readings, and fellowship. The Knights of Columbus was originally set up along the friendly society model. The arrangement seemed a subsidiarist theologian's dream. People taking care of one another in families and communities in Christian charity. What was not to like?

What happened in a word was modernity. The friendly societies actually began collapsing well before the emergence of the modern welfare state. Understanding why they did so is crucial to seeing why they will probably not return. One problem was the vast improvement in medical care. When the work of a doctor is largely limited to amputating sick limbs, dispensing pain killers, and other (often useless) home remedies, patients are left largely to get better on their own, or not.

A small community could provide for the health care that was available in 1870. It was much harder in 1910. It would be *impossible* today with the cost of care for, say, cancer or heart disease easily running into the hundreds of thousands of dollars. If subsidiarists really want the 1870 community model , then the tradeoff is accepting 1870s health care. Any takers?

Another thing that killed the friendly societies was the other modern capitalist phenomenon: social mobility. With people increasingly moving from farm to city and from city to city, the social solidarity that made the societies work fell apart. *Solidarity is in fact an absolutely necessary (though not sufficient) condition for subsidiarist arrangements to work.* And solidarity simply does not hold up well in a dynamic labor market. Want to move to Texas to accept that great job offer? Then *someone* needs to take care of grandpa and the disabled cousin back home.

The final blow to the societies was a capitalist innovation for dealing with risk: privately underwritten insurance. Insurance companies recognized both the rising cost of medical care and the social mobility; they could offer better rates to younger, healthier, more mobile people. This left the friendly societies with the older, sicker and less mobile. We know how that ends.

But what would replace the friendly societies after the world wars and the Great Depression delivered the *coup de grace*? There was really no one left but the state and some private insurance beset by the same adverse selection problems that killed the societies. As the adverse selection problems inherent in private insurance have grown, the state has assumed an ever greater role. Subsidiarists have not yet come up with a modern model that better manages risk.

Consequently, we have a health care system that is not very subsidiarist—or solidarist. The only solidarity is the ersatz solidarity of both employer provided health insurance and the elderly voting bloc marching under the paradoxical banner: "Keep government off my Medicare."

I do not know what the ideal health care system would look like. But I do know that theological terms such as "subsidiarity" and "solidarity" *of themselves* provide relatively little insight into where we should go. There are great dangers in turning power over to the state, but also in leaving people in modern societies without practical recourse. On this issue as many others, the complexity of the modern age defies simplistic theological sloganeering.

23. The Shell Game in Modern Culture

BEVIL BRAMWELL, OMI

The day before John Paul II died, Cardinal Ratzinger (now Benedict XVI) said: "a new moralism exists today whose key words are justice, peace, and conservation of creation—words that call for essential moral values of which we are in real need. But this moralism remains vague and thus slides, almost inevitably, into the political-party sphere. It is above all a dictum addressed to others, and too little a personal duty of our daily life." This was in his speech on *Europe's Crisis of Culture*. It was really a speech on the continuing effects of the Enlightenment.

If you are a religious in the United States, however, his words also describe some religious life right now. We hear about justice, peace, and creation. But something is missing. We see religious orders and dioceses riven by political affiliations. Ratzinger deliberately spoke of "moralism." For example, religious who focus on interior decorating more than on prayer. It is the spirituality of the restaurant rather than the community table. These are Enlightenment religious. This Enlightenment effect can be discerned in Enlightenment bishops, Enlightenment dioceses, Enlightenment clergy, and Enlightenment laity.

Ratzinger was speaking of a morality that does not include God: "Political moralism, as we have lived it and are still living it, does not open the way to regeneration, and even more, also blocks it. The same is true, consequently, also for a Christianity and a theology that reduces the heart of Jesus' message, the 'kingdom of God, to the '*values* of the kingdom,' identifying these values with the great key words of political moralism, and proclaiming them, at the same time, as a synthesis of the religions." (Emphasis added.) This is the result of losing God as the One, the Good, the True, and the Beautiful, to whom all must be referenced. Failing that words become part of a shell game. They can mean anything that we want them to mean.

This produces a culture of calculation where "it is the calculation of consequences that determines what must or must not be considered moral. And thus the category of the good, as was clearly pointed out by Kant, disappears. Nothing is good or bad in itself, everything depends on the consequences that an action allows one to foresee." We have, what, half of the U. S. Church calculating when to follow the Church and when not? How much calculating went on in creating the scandals? This is not just sinfulness, but knowing Church teaching and deliberately acting against it

Moreover, as Europe and America might discover, we have "the cynicism of a secularized culture that denies its own foundations." Then further, "Enlightenment culture is essentially defined by the rights of freedom," which are good up to the point where they start contradicting each other, such as the rights of the mother and the unborn child within her. The contradiction lies in the lack of a reference to God, as the God of life.

The forgotten outside reference point also produces a weird notion of freedom that "leads to dogmatism, [and] which is showing itself increasingly hostile to freedom." He means real freedom as it is referred to God.

Before Ratzinger lists some of the intricacies of Enlightenment culture, "we must first finish describing it. It is part of its nature, in so far as culture of a reason that, finally, has complete awareness of itself, to boast a universal pretense and conceive itself as complete in itself, not in need of some completion through other cultural factors."

The pretense of this intellectually, morally, and spiritually closed culture is opposed by the Catholic Church, which is intellectually, morally and spiritually open to God because it conceives of intellect and will in ultimately theological terms.

Ratzinger concedes that "the Enlightenment is of Christian origin" in the sense that it seeks a society with a certain egalitarian vision of man. But it was also a reaction against Christianity as the religion of the state. In Christianity, however: "Only creative reason, which in the crucified God is manifested as love, can really show us the way." This is the alternative to the irrational Enlightenment view of the world in which the nature of the world cannot teach us anything so we can only think in terms of values or rights, imagined our way.

In broad strokes, then, is there any move to identify the Enlightenment currents—in that narrower sense—in the American Church? How about looking at such Enlightenment influences on the disciplines taught in seminaries? How about looking at how Enlightenment thinking has influenced decisions to teach Catholics throughout their lives. Or how it influences the way dioceses choose and design their programs? Ratzinger's speech should be the start of something and not a footnote in history—which would be the Enlightenment way to handle it.

24. The Sound of Faith

ROBERT REILLY

There is no intellectual in public life today who understands the essence of music in a more penetrating way than does Benedict XVI. He is a musician himself and his brother Georg is a musician and a composer. But his appreciation goes well beyond mere technical knowledge, and is beautifully expressed in *The Spirit of the Liturgy, A New Song for the Lord*, and various remarks on the occasions of concerts.

For the pope, the purpose of art is to make the transcendent perceptible. In 1985, then Cardinal Ratzinger wrote, "Whether it is Bach or Mozart that we hear in church, we have a sense in either case of what Gloria Dei, the glory of God, means. The mystery of infinite beauty is there and enables us to experience the presence of God more truly and vividly than in many sermons."

How does this happen? He went on to say: Faith becoming music is part of the process of the word becoming flesh. . . .When the word becomes music, there is involved on the one hand perceptible illustration, incarnation or taking on flesh, attraction of pre-rational powers, a drawing upon the hidden resonance of creation, a discovery of the song which lies at the basis of all things. And so this becoming music is itself the very turning point in the movement: it involves not only the word becoming flesh, but simultaneously the flesh becoming spirit.

Where does inspiration come from to create music at this exalted level? Ratzinger's answer: "The Holy Spirit is love, and it is he who produces the singing. . . .The Holy Spirit leads us to the Logos, and he leads us to a music that serves the Logos as a sign of the *sursum corda*, the lifting up of the human heart." That's exactly it, even if not every inspired composer could put it in these profound words. Even an artist as vaguely religious as Sibelius said, "the essence of man's being is his striving after God. . . . [Composition] is brought to life by means of the Logos, the divine in art. That is the only thing that really has significance."

In a similar vein, the pope explains that: "It is not the case that you think something up, then sing it; instead, the song comes to you from the angels, and you have to lift up your heart so that it may be in tune with the music coming to it." Scottish composer James MacMillan, who composed the *Mass of Blessed John Henry Newman* for the 2011 papal visit to Great Britain, concurs: "The great composers were like angels who fell to earth to give the rest of us a glimpse of heaven."

This vision has important implications for liturgy: "But above all this is important, the liturgy is not a thing the monks create. It is already there before them. It is entering into the liturgy of the heavens that has always been taking place. Earthly liturgy is liturgy because and only because it joins what is already in process, the greater reality."

That's why the liturgy and the music that accompanies it must be beautiful. Otherwise, it disfigures the greater reality it is supposed to reflect and participate in. Benedict XVI has said that not every kind of music is appropriate for worship: "it has its standards, and that standard is the Logos."

When music serves its hieratic function, it is the sound of faith. The pope has described his experience at a Bach concert, conducted by Leonard Bernstein, after the death of conductor Karl Richter. He was seated next to evangelical Bishop Hanselmann.

"As the final tones of one of the great cantatas of the Cantor of St Thomas died away triumphally," he recalled, "we looked at each other spontaneously and, just as spontaneously, said to each other: anyone who has heard that knows that faith is true."

This is more than a pious sentiment. It helps explain the numerous conversions to Christianity in Japan when conductor Masaaki Suzuki and his Bach Collegium performed a series of Bach Cantatas.

Some of the pope's views on music may occasionally seem too Platonic, but they are not. They are incarnational, because Logos became flesh: "Thus we come to the paradox that it can be said of Christ that 'you are the most beautiful of all men,' even when his face was disfigured. . . .Just in that disfigured face, the true and final beauty emerges; the beauty of love that goes to the last and shows itself stronger than lies and violence. . . .for together beauty and love form the true consolation in this world, bringing it as near as possible to the world of the resurrection."

We should be "overpowered by the beauty of Christ," which "is a more real and deeper perception than mere rational deduction. . . .[T]o have contempt for, or to reject therefore the shock of the heart's encounter with beauty as the true way to perception impoverishes and makes empty faith as well as theology. We must find our way back to this way of perception—that is an urgent demand of this hour."

Benedict XVI believes that music is the most profound medium for this encounter: "To sing with the universe means, then, to follow the track of the Logos and to come close to Him. All true human art is an assimilation to the artist, to Christ, to the mind of the Creator."

To meet the demand of this hour, we must listen. To what? Not necessarily liturgical music. The important thing can be found in the great secular compositions of Bach, Beethoven, Bruckner, and Mozart. There, as well, you will hear what St. Clement of Alexandria called "the New Song" of the universe, the base of all things. When you hear it, you will know whence you came, where you are going, and to whom you belong.

25. The Real News about Stem Cells

DAMIANO RONDELLI, M.D.

The press recently reported on research at the Sloan Kettering Cancer Center in New York, which showed how human embryonic stem cells can improve Parkinson's disease in mice.

News like this always brings to mind images of John Paul II and the many others who have been devastated by this disease: uncontrolled movements of their hands, increased difficulties walking or, even worse, paralysis of facial muscles—taking away their smiles or normal expressions.

Ultimately, the muscles cannot sustain the body and a slow path to death ensues. Memories of relatives and friends affected by this disease are for many of us an open wound and a reminder of how impotent we find ourselves when someone we love fades away.

So news of a possible cure makes us hope that sometime soon Parkinson's and other neurologic diseases will only exist as a chapter in books about the history of medicine. Similar hopes are periodically raised in the war against cancer.

As a physician, I hope daily for new answers for our patients.

As a researcher, all this is inspiring and exciting, although many details still need to be worked out.

But as a man and a father, I have questions.

I have three children and I wish I could protect their every breath. I am often amazed at how they develop. They are much more than what I could have designed or predicted in advance.

I also had a daughter who survived only forty days. She was born with the whole spectrum of parental hopes, dreams, and plans. But faulty genetic machinery was her speedy return ticket to Heaven. Still, she taught us something very important. Her life, as well as the lives of other healthy children, are, quite simply, not ours in the way we often think.

Our hopes for our children would be meaningless if life and death were not bound together. Our children have a meaning that goes beyond us. We love them as a gift and we are dedicated to spending our life to help them from the very beginning to wherever the possibilities lead us.

So how could I use the early stage of a full human life—an embryo, which as a scientist I don't see as any different from my wonderful children, or from my little angel who left us so young—to cure another person? Is this a fair trade? I don't think so.

It reminds me of the old stories, which appear in the histories of medicine (with little actual evidence), of little children being bled so that the powerful might drink their blood in the hope of acquiring health, joy, and a young spirit. Even if it worked, the treatment would not have been human.

People think they can make such a trade because there is a blind spot about the process by which an embryonic assemblage of a few cells turns, within a few months, into the ugly undeveloped face in a 3D ultrasound image, which makes us cry with joy the first time we see it. But just because my heart and mind don't recognize him/her yet as my child, can I use it/him/her to save or cure another person?

Proponents of the use of embryos for medical progress reject religious considerations and base their efforts on a rational and sincere desire to help patients. But this rationale depends on a certain blind spot. More sophisticated genomic studies may soon demonstrate changes in the DNA of genes strictly related to brain development, in that apparently insignificant assemble of embryonic cells a few days after fertilization. Would that discovery remove the blind spot?

And at the end of the day, does that blind spot really matter? We love our ill child/sibling/parent/spouse so much that we are ready to give our lives to save them. To use an embryo doesn't seem a big deal, if it will work. So the problem may not be the invisible point of demarcation when an embryo is usable versus an early baby.

The trade seems fair even if someone defends the rights of that embryo. If this is the accepted approach, then we have a new therapy called embryo—and then fetus. We should not be hypocritical about this, and baldly proclaim our intention to use it at any time. Why not?

Well, I go back to my little daughter who only spent forty days on this earth. She shows us that we are not in control and that her early passing from this world did not mean unhappiness for us (and certainly not for her either), but a deeper understanding of the value of any life.

I appreciate everything I have, my healthy children most of all. But the only way to reconcile my being a doctor, a researcher, and a man is to regard the dignity of any human being the same as for one of my children. We're all of greater worth than our endowments—physical, mental, or social. Any human embryo claims that dignity, regardless of its stage of development.

That dignity, I admit, is clearer to me because I'm a Christian. A great priest (Luigi Giussani) once said: "Christ is everything in everyone." That reality eliminates all scientific blind spots and offers a universal human dignity before and beyond all later rationalization.

Does it rule out stem cell research? Not at all. Alternatives to embryonic stem cells, such as adult or induced-pluripotent stem cells are promising alternatives—and morally sound. The Vatican itself has just entered into partnership with a small biotech company, NeoStem, Inc. to support the development of new therapeutic strategies using adult stem cells.

The language in our public debates about these issues is somewhat misleading. The distinction lies not between being for or against life, but rather on definition and wise realism—about the dignity of all human life.

26. Obama Proposes a Toast

WILLIAM SAUNDERS

In 1942, C. S. Lewis published *The Screwtape Letters*, advice from a senior "tempter" to a novice about how to confuse us poor mortals, which may be summed up in a single sentence: "Your job is to fuddle them, not to encourage them to think."

In 1959, Screwtape appears again, in an essay titled,

"Screwtape Proposes a Toast," in which the senior tempter reflects on the state of the world and on what can be done to make it even worse. Those who listened to President Obama's Oval Office address on March 9 lifting President Bush's restrictions on stem cell research may be pardoned for thinking the old tempter has returned.

Under Bush, restrictions were placed on federal funding of research using stem cells derived from human embryos after August 10, 2001, the date on which he imposed the ban. But that was all—it was a ban on federal funding of research using those lines. It was not a ban on that research as such, which could still be conducted in any state (e.g., California) which did not ban it, and which could be conducted with state government or private funds. Nor was it a ban on research using pre-August 10 lines (though many of us felt it should have been), or on scientific research using other sources, such as adult stem cells, which pose no ethical concerns.

Far from inhibiting research, as Obama suggested, these restrictions, in the judgment of many observers, spurred scientists to seek ethical alternatives, resulting, a year and a half ago, in spectacular success when different teams of researchers, working independently, found ways to re-engineer adult cells to the embryonic state (these are called "induced pluripotent stem cells"). In other words, scientists can get embryonic stem cells now without destroying embryos. Thus, you would think, there was no need, from any perspective, to force taxpayers to subsidize a practice many find morally repugnant.

Not so, according to Obama. Bush's policy, he said, created "a false choice between sound science and moral values." Huh? Western civilization has always insisted there is a choice to be made, but it is not "false." It is basic. From the Hippocratic Oath to the Nuremburg trials, we have struggled to maintain principles such as that the end does not justify the means, that we may not sacrifice some human beings for the benefit of others, that all human beings are of equal dignity. Science is not a god, but a good, and like every other good, it must be subject to ethical constraints. The Tuskegee experiments, the worldwide embrace of eugenics, and the forced sterilizations conducted in the United States, all of which took place during the twentieth century, should have made this point clear to everyone.

While Obama said he "respected" those of us (more than half of Americans) who feel embryonic stem cell research is morally wrong, whether on theistic, atheistic or non-theistic grounds, what his "respect" amounts to is this: he will force us to fund it.

Obama pledged that his administration would be "open and honest with the American people about the science behind our decisions." If that was his intention, he got off to a bad start.

For instance, if he wanted, as he said, to be honest with the American people about promising treatments for Parkinson's, diabetes, cancer, and heart disease, he should have announced that he was proposing increased funding for already-existing, proven treatments for all of these conditions—that is, research using adult, not embryonic, stem cells. What are we supposed to make of Obama invoking the name and memory of Christopher Reeve to suggest that embryonic stem cell research might help with spinal cord injuries, when it is adult stem cell research that has enabled some with such injuries to walk? (Don't take my word for it; check out the scientific references at stemcellresearch.org).

Obama assured us his administration would never support the funding of "cloning for human reproduction." He neglected to mention the obvious corollary—he will support and fund "cloning for research." In fact, he doesn't even mention cloning for research. Why? Because while cloning "for reproduction" simply results in a twin being born alive, cloning "for research" necessitates the killing of an embryonic human being, and he has already shown that his administration favors that by rescinding the Bush restrictions.

The facts are simple: human embryos are human beings; deriving stem cells from them kills them; doing so is utterly unethical; other sources for stem cells exist and are proven to help human beings; every kind of successful human cloning produces a living human being (whether in a Petri dish or a womb or a bassinet); the aim of human research cloning is not to produce a twin to walk the earth but a source to be exploited for stem cells through embryo destruction. Yet Obama evades all these facts. He demonizes President Bush, while misleading us about the true results of his own policies.

Like a certain tempter, it appears his aim is to fuddle us. He certainly does not encourage us to think clearly about what he is up to.

27. The Divine Child

ANTHONY ESOLEN

Everywhere outside of Christianity, wrote Hans Urs von Balthasar, the child is automatically the first to be sacrificed. Only for Christians is the adult the imperfect child. Everywhere else the child is the imperfect adult, and falls subject to our lust for domination.

It is easy to see why. Men who do not know the true God, or who turn away from Him, do not therefore cease to worship. For God Himself, as Augustine says, gives us the delight in praising Him: He has made us for Himself, and our hearts are restless until they rest in Him.

We turn then to the false gods, and since no man bows down before what he believes is beneath him, we inevitably turn towards what is in our eyes great, powerful, even ruthless. Men summon demons not because they find their company agreeable. They summon them, Chesterton noted, because they believe the demons have no nonsense about them. They get things done.

What use, then, can we have for the helpless child? We have, from Carthage, no delightful amulets portraying the god Moloch in an attitude of joy, for having received from the people his quota of children. Moloch wants the child-flesh, roasted or broiled, but not the children.

Even the Greek gods, those glorious forms of male and female beauty, do not condescend to take note of children, at least until the boys are old enough to compete in the games at Olympia or Delphi. "Children are our greatest resource," goes the ghastly and insincere saying, as if they were minerals to be mined and put to use.

Many among us are ready to deny children their full humanity, on the grounds that they can't *do* anything. And because we worship the demonic getting-things-done, instead of the almighty God who chose to dwell among us as a weakling babe, we are now reverting to the weary old pagan wisdom.

Precisely because the child is weak, we allow it to be vulnerable to our designs. It is not yet one of us, and so we can exert upon it our sovereign power, to mold it as we will.

True, we don't inhale the narcotics and beat the timbrels, while placing in Moloch's arms the poor man's baby we've "adopted," to cut the economic deal with that horrid king. What point would there be in that? We all agree now that Moloch was only a demon of man's fevered imagination. Moloch can't get anything done.

But if getting things done—accruing raw power for ourselves—is the aim, then the child is either constantly in the way, or is the one who suffers the exercise of our power. We murder children in the womb. Why? The child would, in his very helplessness, destroy our aims.

We can't drop out of school now. We can't quit our important work. We can't tie ourselves down with marriage. Or, to consider the decision from beforehand, we will do as we please with our bodies, and if something unfortunate happens despite all our technological precautions, we have a technological solution for that, too.

We haven't yet regressed so far as to murder children outside the womb. We retain a superstitious regard about that. The ancients believed that the lion was too noble a creature to kill a sleeping man. We are in this regard the reverse of the lion. We are those cowardly beasts that will kill a child sleeping in the womb, but will duck and shrug and grouch once it has come awake.

But if we can't murder children yet, we can certainly murder childhood. That murder follows naturally upon our decision to worship the false god of prowess. When Macbeth murdered the good King Duncan in his sleep, it wasn't just the single man's death he was guilty of. No, the doughty Thane of Glamis and Earl of Cawdor hears a voice crying out:

> Glamis hath murdered sleep, and therefore Cawdor
> Shall sleep no more: Macbeth shall sleep no more.

In killing the sleeping man, Macbeth has murdered the very principle that allows us to sleep in peace: our trust that our weakness will be honored, and that we will be protected.

So too, once we agree to subordinate the child to our dreams of power, then childhood itself is scotched as it were in the egg. We wish to design our children, as we draw up blueprints for a banking house or a factory. We institutionalize them as early as possible, because we want to "make something" of them, or because we want them out of the way while we are "making something" of ourselves.

We are the tools of our tools. We subject these simple children to batteries of tests, regardless of the waywardness of the child's developing mind. We murder their innocence every day by exposing them to what is lewd, vicious, and demeaning, justifying it because, we say, that's the world they're going to have to live in. Is the child sensitive to the holiness of his body? Too bad, kid.

How far this is from the family huddled in the stable, and the child wrapped in swaddling bands! In the child Jesus we do not see God hiding his power so much as revealing what it is, really, to be mighty: for power divorced from the magnificent self-lavishing of love is demonic, and is finally futile and empty.

Rummage for human empires in the garbage heap of history. "Unless you become like little children," said Jesus, "you shall not enter the Kingdom of Heaven." It must be so, since He, who was once a child, never ceased to be that child. He wants for us that innocence, that wonder before the glory of God, because then we will be filled with that mighty and Holy Spirit that plays forever in the love between the Father and the Son.

28. How Civilizations Die

MATTHEW HANLEY

I have a pop quiz for all of you, likely the minority, who fully appreciate that virtually the entire developed world is threatened by severe population implosion even as many still prattle on about overpopulation (and costs to the "system" that could be averted by preventing births).

To take just one example, there are only forty-two grandchildren in Greece today for every one hundred grandparents. Apparently it does take a whole village to raise a child, but at these rates such villages won't be thriving—or even around much longer.

Which country is presently experiencing the most rapid rate of fertility decline ever recorded in world history? I'd love to draw out the suspense, but will cut to the chase: Iran. A lot must be going on beneath the surface when the total fertility rate in this Muslim country has fallen to a very European-like 1.5 children per woman.

Back in 1970, Iranian women had seven children on average. That steep a decline—over five children per woman—in just a short couple decades is as if a mighty cold front blasted demographic winter down into the tropics.

This is but one eye opener in David P. Goldman's thought provoking new book: *How Civilizations Die (And Why Islam Is Dying Too)*. Islamic countries, like the West and Japan, are choosing decline, as many other peoples and civilizations have done in times past.

St. Augustine felt that "in order to discover the character of any people, we only have to observe what they love," his explanation for the fall of Rome or, indeed, for any nation. Goldman offers approvingly: "peoples fail because they love the wrong things."

He argues that Iran, aware of its decline, is like a "wounded beast"—dangerous and unstable. Facing the prospect of demise or extinction, it may be more inclined to lash out, sensing it doesn't really have anything to lose.

But Goldman's analysis is more than a deft admixture of statistics and geopolitical considerations. In ways that open new horizons of thought, even for those already sympathetic to his arguments, he gets to the heart of the matter: the spiritual undercurrents of population implosion.

The arrangements of our various secularized cultures, despite their comforts, fail to meet our most fundamental human need: "When men and women lose the sacred, they lose the desire to live." This is because our lives absolutely require meaning that transcends death.

Perhaps that's one reason why he calls population implosion not only "the underreported story of our time," but "the elephant in the room." It's harder to talk about the deepest things even if they are also our deepest needs.

Goldman attributes population decline today to a "Loss of Faith," which he calls the Fifth Horseman of the Apocalypse (the others being War, Plague, Famine, Death): "As traditional societies give way to modernity, faith and fertility vanish together."

Epidemic levels of suicide among Native American peoples from the Inuit in Canada to the Guarani in South America are another sad manifestation of this deep dislocation.

The Iranian collapse is not so different in kind, he argues, than that which occurred recently among ethnic pocket populations once identified as strongholds of the Catholic faith.

Quebec's fertility rates, long notably higher than those in the rest of Canada, plummeted by two-thirds in less than a generation as it transitioned into modernity. By 1982, more than 42 percent of men and women there had sterilized themselves.

The fertility rate in Poland —"the nation whose faith and heroism won the Cold War"—has now hit an astounding low of 1.25. Spain went from having the highest fertility rate in Western Europe, by far, in the 1970s, to having the lowest, in a mere twenty years.

His point is that religion tied too closely to ethnicity—to blood and soil and notions of special elect status with God—has led to great conflicts and tends to be more fragile in the face of modernity, especially compared to religion based on individual conscience. This forms a large part of his discussion not only about Muslim culture—"tribalism elevated to a universal principal"—but also notable differences between Europe and America, despite their common Christian heritage.

America's fertility rate—right around replacement level—is not so much an indicator of great health as it is a grace period. We are still growing and capable of maintenance, whereas Europe and Japan are approaching "a point of no return." By 2050, there will only be half as many prospective mothers in Japan as there are today.

Earlier this year, a report revealed that more than half of all children born to American women under age thirty today are born outside marriage. The precise long-term demographic implications of this deep rift in human equilibrium may be debated. But ultimately all of human life's "dignity and balance depend," John Paul II argued in 1980 remarks that would come to form his *Theology of the Body,* "at every moment of history and at every point of geographical longitude and latitude, on who she (woman) will be for him (man), and he for her."

Perhaps the late Cardinal Dulles, whom Goldman quotes, was right to worry that the Christian residue in America may not be strong enough to resist the forces of secularization that have overtaken Europe.

Lacking connections to the past and confidence in the future, individuals trapped in a dying culture "dull their senses with alcohol and drugs," and out of existential despondency "embrace death through infertility, concupiscence and war."

The wages of sin, St. Paul wrote, are death. The flip side seems to contain a truism of its own: knowledge of death, without faith in the gift of eternal life, drives people and cultures to greater sin.

What we need most today, where sin and stress, despair and decay abound, is faith in the knowledge that grace abounds even more.

V. Conversions and Conversations

1. Third Person Singular

BRAD MINER

When I was a Protestant kid, mention of the Holy Ghost unnerved me; made we want to shriek and look behind me for the spectral form coming to . . . well, I didn't know what it might be up to. My people believed in the Trinity, but you never heard much in church about the Third Person. And I confess that Roman Catholic emphasis on the Holy Spirit (a term that doesn't spook me) was not among the reasons why I "poped."

After my conversion, I spent time among some Charismatic Catholics, who in the course of a meeting one night in a church basement in Columbus, Ohio, exploded into what they swore was genuine glossolalia, the Spirit manifest in their yammering, but which none could actually understand. There were flushed faces and tears and elevated pulse rates and not a few angry looks at me, because I bore an expression of bemused skepticism.

And I suppose it didn't help that every artistic depiction of the godhead in churches and galleries I saw throughout the world depicted the familiar human forms for the Father and the Son but for the Spirit tongues of fire or more likely a dove but never with eyes you might gaze into and always, it seemed, in a supporting role. All in all, I had a rocky start when it comes to understanding and loving the Holy Spirit.

And how fascinating that, although the Spirit has spoken through the prophets and is that power of God who makes us Christians, he does not speak for himself. As the Catechism puts it: "[W]e do not hear the Spirit himself." We speak daily of the Father in prayer, and we celebrate the Son in our holiest of days, Christmas and Easter, but Pentecost, when we acknowledge God's full and final revelation of himself and the real beginning of our Church, seems slighted, because it falls on a Sunday. All Sundays are Holy Days of Obligation, of course, but just compare attendance on Pentecost with any Christmas Day.

And it seems as though this has always been so. Until that moment fifty days after the Resurrection, the followers of Jesus of Nazareth had heard their rabbi speak of the Spirit, but they surely did not know the Spirit. At the last Passover Seder they shared on the night before he died, Christ had told them: "I will ask the Father, and he will give you another Advocate." The "Spirit of truth," he called it, and he promised it would always be with them. *What comfort!* And yet he also told them the world cannot accept the Spirit, "because it neither sees nor knows it. But you know it, because it remains with you, and will be in you." *We know it*, they must have thought. *He has told us so.*

Wait. What do we know again?

Peter, John (whose Gospel relates the story), and all the others could not have known that their Lord was speaking to them of the Trinity. They did not know it until they were together that day seven weeks later and a whirlwind swept among them, like the pillar of fire in Genesis, splitting into fingers and singeing their souls, sending them tumbling onto the streets of Jerusalem speaking whatever tongues the astonished people they met spoke themselves—languages, in other words, that people actually understood, not the gibberish I heard in that church basement in Columbus.

Thirty-five years ago—before I'd returned home to Ohio and was still living in California—I'd been reading about Catholicism and visiting churches, and one morning in bed I prayed to God for guidance. I said the prayer to the Father that Jesus taught. And I lay there—more than half asleep, it must be said—and suddenly felt the sensation of a silent explosion, of something entering almost violently from outside inside, like a vacuum filled, and then, yes, felt-heard a fluttering of wings. Terrified, I tried to wake up and did and then wept with joy, because . . . I *believed*.

I got up, threw water on my face, got into my car and drove to the nearest Catholic church, walked up to the rectory door and rang the bell. An Irish priest stood there with his spectacles in one hand and a book under his arm.

"Yes?"

"I want to be Catholic," I said, and he stood to one side and let me come in.

I would never have done it had the Spirit not given me the knowledge of things not seen. At some point, you can read and read, and listen and listen, and visit and admire the literature, liturgy, music, art, and even the singular odors of a Catholic church, but, if you're a pared-down Protestant, the distance between where you are and where exotic Rome is remains a chasm too wide and deep to cross *alone*. It's the Spirit who gives you faith in these things—who steels your soul for a journey you never imagined taking, not in your wildest dreams. "Because," as the poet/priest Gerard Manley Hopkins wrote, "the Holy Ghost over the bent/ World broods with warm breast and with ah! bright wings."

2. Finalmente: Coming into the Church

HADLEY ARKES

It was last October, the Red Mass, said on that first Sunday in October just before the opening of the Supreme Court on the first Monday. My wife Judy and I were at the service at St. Matthew's in Washington, and we were on the way to the Hilton on Sixteenth Street for the lunch following the Mass.

Suddenly, and happily, we were joined on the walk by Fr. Arne Panula, whom I'd met years ago at the Opus Dei house in New

York. He had moved over to direct the chapel and programs at the Catholic Information Center at Fifteenth and K. In a bantering way, Fr. Arne confronted me: "You, the most notable figure at the threshold, never quite crossing it." (Never actually coming into the Church.) "What's holding you back?" I dipped into the repertoire of Bert Lahr from the *Wizard of Oz*: "C-c-c courage! It's what puts the 'ape' in 'apricot'; it's what I haven't got."

That move deftly got me out of a challenge posed here in an affectionate way. But only for a moment. One month later I dropped in to a noon Mass at the CIC and Fr. Arne, in the homily, remarked that "the one thread that connected these two readings today is c-c-c-c courage." That was the hook that finally worked. We had lunch, we mapped out a series of five or six sessions of instruction, for the decision was finally made. And just yesterday (as I write this), on April 24, I came into the Church in Fr. Arne's chapel, with Michael Novak as my sponsor.

To my astonishment, friends were willing to fly in from Boston and Cleveland and places even more exotic for this occasion. The chapel was filled with dear friends, and it was deeply moving to see them coming up to take communion. Fr. Arne's service was elegant and lovely, his homily deeply thoughtful. And sure enough, he managed to weave in a note about "c-c-c-c courage."

But even Fr. Arne professed to be moved by the friends gathered there. To me they had come to represent the "body of the Church": every one of them marked a moment, or even a chapter in the story, for they each revealed to me, in their own character, what it meant to lead a Catholic life. Each in his own way, taught me something of the teachings of this Church, and each showed me the welcoming face of the Church.

It began with Dan Robinson, when we were on the faculty together at Amherst. I was beginning to think in a probing way about the issue of abortion, and Dan showed me that the Church's position really depended on a combination of empirical evidence (embryology), woven with moral reasoning. It was natural law reasoning. As Aquinas said, the divine law we know through revelation, but the natural law we know through that reason that was natural for human beings. The Church's moral position here did not depend on faith or belief. One didn't have to be Catholic to understand it. And that was precisely the teaching of the Church.

As I began to write myself on abortion and marriage and the issues of the day, I was filling out a natural law perspective, and drawing to myself a constituency certain that I was a Catholic writer. Joe Reilly, in Boston, was the first one to tell me years ago that I was becoming a notable "apologist" for Catholic teaching. Dan Robinson would say, "Yes, but your problem is that you're pre-Vatican II." As a Jewish Catholic, I was too severe a Catholic.

One friend, who converted at Oxford, told me that the resonating line for him came from our friend Dermot Quinn. Dermot said that you can believe everything the Church tells you and not be a good Catholic. The question is, "Do you believe in the Church as a truth-telling institution?" And I thought: I do, I really do. When the Church stands *contra mundum,* against the currents of relativism in the world, my inclination is to think that the Church has it right.

As Fr. Jim Burtchaell used to say, the Church draws on vast experience and lifts a mirror to put in one's face: it shows you what you are going to look like if you proceed along this path. The Church has become the main enclave to preserve the sobriety of moral reasoning, natural law reasoning, when the currents of relativism have inundated and corroded the academy and other institutions.

I've come to this matter then through the Church. But the Church cannot be understood apart from the one who planted the Mustard Seed from which it grew and took its shape and character. Nor can it be detached from the Spirit that managed to preserve the discipline of its moral teachings even through times of trouble and disarray.

We had, clustered around us, the friends who had formed and nourished the journal *First Things,* and the band of brothers, led now by Robert Royal, who held together in bringing forth the *The Catholic Thing.* There is more to the story, of course, than I can relate in this space; it will have to come later. But to take a line from Richard Neuhaus, it may be a story about, "How I became the Catholic I was."

3. Outreach to the Homeless

CHARLOTTE HAYS

Many Catholic converts speak of coming home. Not me. For years, I felt I had left home and cast my lot with strange, argumentative folks. I missed the incomparable language of Tommy Cranmer (most vacillating of martyrs), Anglican plainsong, and that wonderful hush in an Episcopal church right before people go up to the altar rail. And I detested schmaltzy, sentimental music, rabid exchangers of the peace, and choir robes that looked like seconds from a Baptist supply house. I longed to tell the dear crucifer in the Catholic processions that he was holding the cross in an incorrect form. So what was I doing here?

A certain kind of Episcopalian always becomes a Catholic. I guess I was that kind of Episcopalian—starting with being overly interested in the Anglican nuns at Sewanee, which looks like Oxford and serves as a sort of Vatican for southern Episcopalians. My father was alarmed. I became a Catholic many years later, while working for the *National Catholic Register* as the token Prot. In the early 1980s, I was exposed to things that should have proven fatal to conversion—deviant nuns first and foremost. But rather than running away, I became fascinated with an institution that could withstand such assaults and aberrations.

It had a raw intensity. But the aesthetics were awful. I lost a little of myself in becoming what my cousins call "Roman." My family was southern and Episcopalian. I always suspected that Christ would have won a classics prize, played football at Sewanee, and spoken to servants just like Uncle George, a clergyman. My great-great grandparents were married in the church where Patrick Henry uttered his famous either/or. My grandparents were joined in holy matrimony in Natchez, Mississippi by Tennessee Williams' grandfather, the Rev. Walter Dakin. Mr.

Dakin got roaring drunk after and was neither seen nor heard from for decades. During my vaguely atheistic adolescence, I still could not skip one of the most satisfying events of the Christian year. I once entered St. George's Episcopal Church in Germantown, Tennessee, having been driven through a snowy countryside, to an evening Ash Wednesday service. I pushed open the door and it struck me: *This has been going on for 2,000 years.*

I know what you're about to say, without a dollop of our Anglican charm, null and void. Let me assure you: I know, or I would never have crossed the Tiber, a difficult swim in patches. The other bank was dear to me and also so very beautiful. I was fortunate to have been given instruction and received into the Church by a wise and kind Dominican. Father Raymond Smith, O.P. was learned, generous, and a fine teacher. The Dominican friary supplied my aesthetic needs, important to me (then, and, yes, now). Who, I wondered, converts without instruction from a scholar in flowing white robes and a fifteen-decade rosary dangling from his belt?

Why did I stick with it? Well, because it's true. Don't laugh, but one of the books I found quite interesting was the Tan volume about the incorruptibles—saints who don't decay after death. I'm told that they can look awful, but they indicate that sacred history still continues. Episcopalians had history, but not living history. The Catholic Church was history, but more—it still lived, after 2,000 years, in some organic way that was fresh and new and startling.

Nonetheless, the music at St. Matthew's Cathedral was frequently more sentimental than Lawrence Welk (I applauded when they announced an organist was retiring, but things did not improve). And yet slowly, one becomes not just a Catholic, but a cultural Catholic. One knows the Hail Mary and it feels natural to say it. One goes into small boxes with grilles. The Mass and the confessional turn you into the real thing. I've rarely been to confession when I didn't get a drop of wisdom (in addition to grace). Finally, you are standing in the confessional line at Old St. Mary's, the Washington church with a Tridentine Mass, singing the words of Immaculate Mary without a hymnal as the choir processes, and you realize: I've made it. I belong. I'm here.

Although an arguer myself, I was often irritated by the argumentativeness of my fellow conservative Catholics in my early days—I used to think they were arming themselves with "proofs" against unsuspecting Baptists. They'll argue papal infallibility with a tree stump. But the arguments are important.

After the Episcopal General Convention last summer, a clergy-blogger noted, "I know that this church may head in some directions that may be uncomfortable for me." *Uncomfortable?* Fine, in social matters, but you've got to fight for truth. Episcopal friends tell me they can live with what is going on in the larger community—not in their parish or diocese. But how can a Christian congregation remain a part of a body that no longer adheres to the tenets of western Christianity? (An Anglican priest once began a sermon, "St. Paul said—and I partly agree with him . . . .") And it seeps down to the parishes.

I asked a friend why one church never gets male rectors: "They aren't coming out of the seminary." The Episcopal clergy has been significantly feminized. The younger women seem quite sweet, a contrast with the early battleaxes. Katherine Jefferts Schorri, leader of the Episcopal Church in America, has called the concept of personal salvation a "western heresy." Staying in such an ecclesial body is outside my comfort zone.

So, it was worth living through a little bad taste. Even at its tackiest, the Catholic Church has not rejected the Founder. It's good I found a new home, because my old one no longer exists. It brings me great joy that Pope Benedict XVI is welcoming Anglicans into the Church. Think of it as outreach to the homeless.

4. Then I Confessed, I Can Do No Other

FRANCIS BECKWITH

On April 29, 2007, five years ago this Sunday, I was publicly received into the Catholic Church at St. Joseph's Parish in

Bellmead, Texas. My wife, Frankie, stood beside me, as we both faced Fr. Timothy Vaverek, who presided over the brief ceremony between the homily and the recitation of the Creed at Sunday Mass. Frankie was received as a candidate, since, unlike me, she had not been baptized and confirmed as a youngster.

Frankie could not wait to become Catholic, and she thought it a bit unfair that we reverts had a loophole: All I had to do was partake in the Sacrament of Confession. Fortunately for her, Fr. Timothy gave her a private crash-course RCIA, which culminated in her reception the following August.

When I went to confession on April 28 at St. Jerome's in Waco, it was the first time in over thirty years that I had partaken in the sacrament. My younger brother, James, emailed me earlier that week and volunteered to assist me in recollecting my sins.

When I entered the confessional, I sat face-to-face with Fr. Rakshaganathan Selvaraj (or "Fr. Raj"). I closed my eyes, made the sign of the cross, and said, "Father, forgive me, for I have sinned. It has been over thirty years since my last confession. I'm not sure I can remember all of my sins." Fr. Raj, in his thick Indian accent, replied, "That is alright. God knows them all." "I was afraid of that," I quipped.

Fr. Raj then heard my confession and granted me absolution. My penance, if I remember correctly, consisted of one "Our Father" and one "Hail Mary." When I told this to Frankie, she thought the priest had let me off easy. She was right. She knew my sins.

After we had decided to become Catholic, we sought counsel from trusted friends. For I was, at the time, President of the Evangelical Theological Society (ETS), an academic association of Protestant biblical scholars, theologians, philosophers, historians, and ministers that in 2007 had a membership approaching 4500. This is why we initially decided to postpone our entry into the Church until after my presidency had ended in November 2007.

Our Protestant friends thought this wise, and recommended we keep our intentions private until after November. Our Catholic friends looked at it a bit differently. They were concerned that news would leak out and cause scandal. So they suggested that I just make an announcement of what we intended to do post-presidency. Not knowing which counsel was wiser, we prayed about it.

Two weeks after we made that petition my wife and I were having breakfast with my parents in Washington, D.C. We were there for the wedding of my cousin, Jimmy Sclafani. My cell phone rang. It was my sixteen-year-old nephew, Dean, eldest son of my brother James. Dean asked me to be his Confirmation sponsor. Several months earlier his aunts, uncles, and grandparents were asked by his mother Kimberly to compose letters to Dean, explaining why he should receive the Sacrament of Confirmation.

Although when I wrote my letter I was a Protestant (though one clearly moving in the direction of Rome but not quite there yet), I saw Confirmation as a way by which a Catholic publicly announces his allegiance to Jesus Christ. I saw my task as serious business. Several years earlier, when Dean was twelve, he was struggling with issues about God's existence and the overall rationality of Christian belief. I knew I had to write a letter that appealed to both his heart and his mind.

I began by telling him that Jesus Christ was the smartest man who ever lived. I then went on to explain the scope of his influence and that of his disciples—in literature, art, the sciences, law, medicine, philosophy, theology, and politics. I told Dean that by placing his trust in Christ he was entering an intellectually and spiritually rich tradition unparalleled in human history.

When he called me that morning he said that it was my letter that had finally convinced him to receive the sacrament. I took the phone away from my ear, turned to Frankie and said, "I think our prayer has been answered." Dean's confirmation was only four weeks away, and I could not be his sponsor unless I was in full communion with the Church. A week later, on April 28, I entered the confessional. The next day I was publicly received into the Church.

That evening I wrote a letter to the other members of the ETS executive committee, telling them what I had done. Nevertheless, I assured them that I could remain as ETS president since there was nothing in the society's statement of belief with which a Catholic could not agree. It was naïve to believe that this was possible. Within a week I resigned, realizing that I could not remain as ETS president without causing scandal.

When I was elected ETS president in November 2006, I could not have imagined that I would return to the Church fewer than six months later. To be sure, I had moved closer to Catholicism over the prior decade, but there still remained a few issues that were impediments, and I was confident that they would remain so. I was mistaken. Within months, obstacles dissipated at an alarm ing speed. The scales fell from my eyes.

Then I confessed, I could do no other.

5. A Banquet of Truth

TODD HARTCH

Like many converts, I spent years examining Catholic teaching and entered the Church only when I could accept it all. It's been difficult, therefore, to find that many Catholics do not believe all that the Church teaches, but to a certain extent their views make sense. They probably were confirmed as teenagers at a time when catechesis in this country was at a low ebb.

The part of their attitude that doesn't make sense is that we live at a time when Catholic teaching is more accessible than ever. Vatican II, the guiding light for today's Church, produced sixteen documents, all of which are written in an accessible style and are available at the Vatican website. Popes Paul VI, John Paul II, and Benedict XVI have developed the teachings of the council in a rich corpus of writings, also available from the Vatican. Finally, and most importantly, *The Catechism of the Catholic Church* (CCC), presented to the Church in 1992, contains "the essential and fundamental contents of Catholic doctrine" (CCC 11) and can be purchased in Catholic bookstores or consulted online.

The Catechism is a great treasure of the Church. As a Protestant interested in Catholicism, I found it incredibly helpful to have every major Catholic doctrine explained in a clear and compelling manner. I went through all the issues that Protestants find difficult—Mary, justification, the Sacraments, the priesthood, the papacy—and discovered a symphony of truth that finally won me over. Then, when I was convinced that I needed to become a Catholic, I read it cover to cover so that I would know exactly what I was signing up for.

For previous generations there was no one place to find all that Catholics were to believe, but today's Catholics have in the Catechism "a sure and certain reference text for teaching catholic doctrine" (CCC 3). Reading the Catechism is thus a clear next step for many Catholics. By reading two pages a day, they can slowly digest it and still finish the whole book in less than a year.

There are many Catholics, though, who know what the Church teaches but reject those teachings. Such an attitude places them in a grave position because the faithful "have the duty of observing the constitutions and decrees conveyed by the legitimate authority of the Church." (CCC 2037) If they fail to accept what is clearly taught by the Church, they cannot compensate by, for instance, doing well in some other area of the faith. They are saying, in effect, that the Church can err in a matter of doctrine. Logically, then, if the Church can err in one matter, it can err in others as well. In the end, they will be left with de facto Protestantism.

To insist on the necessity of believing all that the Church teaches is not to make light of the real difficulties that many experience in the process of studying doctrine. For many Catholics the hardest teachings are those dealing with sex, marriage, and family. There is simply no support from the broader culture for Catholic doctrines such as "the moral evil of every procured abortion," the intrinsic evil of contraception, divorce as a "grave offense against moral law," and the disordered nature of homosexual acts. (CCC 2271, 2370, 2384, 2357) Because of the cultural consensus in support of the opposite positions, there is a tendency to see these moral issues as somehow too complicated for definitive judgments. But, of course, the Church has spoken definitively on these matters.

What's the solution for those who insist on dismissing the

clear doctrines of the Church? Just as it was for those did not know their faith, one answer is the Catechism. It might seem facile to suggest reading doctrine as a remedy for dissent, but encountering Catholic doctrine is intrinsically different from reading the newspaper. Truth is inherently attractive and the Catechism is a banquet of truth, presented in such a way that what might seem unwarranted when viewed as a singularity becomes more reasonable when seen in context. It is hard to read the Catechism without appreciating that its truths are part of a greater Truth; and it is hard to dismiss one part without understanding that one is dismissing the whole thing, rejecting not just some small point but the councils and the fathers as well.

What about Catholics who insist on beliefs and actions that clearly contradict Church teaching? Let's follow the example of a former chairman of my department. Whenever someone came into his office to ask for special treatment, he pulled out our policy manual and read the applicable section. Who could argue against the manual? It became clear that the chairman was not being unreasonable, but was simply applying established policy.

We can do the same with the Catechism. When Catholics propose ideas that contradict Catholic doctrine, we should refer to the applicable section of the Catechism. Some will change their minds and many more will think twice before publically opposing "the essential and fundamental contents of Catholic doctrine." A few may start arguing against the Catechism. In such cases, it's best not to say too much. Let the dissenters waste their breath in attempts to refute the clear words of the Catechism. In the end, the splendor of the truth who came into our world at Christmas will shine through.

6. Come, Let Us Reason Together

EMINA MELONIC

Can Western democracies have successful dialogue with the Islamic world? As both a Westerner and a Muslim, I might be someone who could answer that, yet almost everything I hear and read leads to bewilderment. I search in vain the libraries and bookstores for new scholarship and sensible social commentary on Islam but find myself being led into a maze of ideology. To most leftists, Muslims have become another protected class under the aegis of multiculturalism; to some on the right, Islam is a monolithic and implacable enemy, as bad as or worse than communism or Nazism.

Then I picked up Robert R. Reilly's new book, *The Closing of the Muslim Mind: How Intellectual Suicide Created the Modern Islamist Crisis.* Finally some clarity!

Mr. Reilly has written a work of precise and exhaustive research about Islamic theology and philosophy. And he superbly explains that foul and unbearable perversion of the faith called *Islamism.*

I often hear that Christianity and Islam will never be able to reason together because Islam is inherently unreasonable, and this is certainly true today in many Muslim countries. Christianity's doctrinal roots in Hellenism allow faith and reason to flourish together, and, for a student of Catholicism as I am, it is one of the most significant aspects about the faith. I now understand why what is happening in much of the Muslim world leads many to assume that Islam (in both its early development and its current manifestations) is irrational. What will surprise readers of *The Closing of the Muslim Mind* is that Islam also has Hellenistic roots. In order to defend their faith in encounters with Christians and Jews, Muslim scholars employed the philosophical methods of the Greeks, and this led to conflict among Muslims over the question of whether and to what extent God may be known rationally.

Those who welcomed the question and answered it affirmatively were rationalist theologians known as Mu'tazilites. According to Mr. Reilly, they "created the first fully developed theological school in Islam." For them, reason had a significant place in faith because Man is endowed with free will. Al-Kindi, an important Mu'tazilite philosopher, said that "nothing should be dearer to the seeker after truth than truth itself." The Mu'tazilite school believed that God gave us the use of reason so that we can "come to know moral order in creation and its Creator." Mu'tazilite teaching agreed with St. Thomas Aquinas that man "can apprehend the created things with his mind because they were first *thought* by God." In other words, the fact that God *is* intelligible gives rise to the intelligibility of creation.

What a difference from what we encounter with Islam these days! How is it that the Muslim world (primarily Arab) seems to be so backward? Mr. Reilly discusses the emergence of another theological school, the eleventh-century Ash'arites. In contrast to the Mu'tazilites, they denied the primacy of reason and free will and placed God's will at the center of Islam: Allah is the "Doer" and "Effecter" of anything He wills. If God wills it, only He can change it. As Mr. Reilly points out, an all powerful God is part of all monotheistic religions, but the Ash'arite interpretation pits God's omnipotence against God's reason. Unity between faith and reason is impossible, and God becomes a kind of "legal positivist."

If God wishes to misguide us, He will. Al-Kindi would certainly disagree with this, but by the thirteenth century, the Mu'tazilites lost standing as an intellectually vigorous authority, and the Ash'arites triumphed.

It is, of course, Ash'arite Islamism that is the source of contemporary terrorism. But a distinction must be made. Islamism's strange theology (or lack thereof, depending how one looks at it) is really an ideology, not a religion. In fact, Mr. Reilly writes that Islamism is structurally quite similar to Marxism.

The most significant modern philosopher behind Marxist Islamism was Sayyid Qutb, one of the founders of the Muslim Brotherhood. He saw the West as a debauchery that must be saved *and* obliterated by Islam. He applied Marxist rhetoric to a religion, calling Islam an "emancipatory movement" with "an active revolutionary creed." Such an unreasoning and ahistorical view yields nothing but the most dire consequences for the world.

In its emphasis on political salvation, Islamism is in many ways similar to liberation theology, which was also comfortable with Marxism. Coercion through "salvific politics" is the way to achieve the "inner perfectibility of history" and with it justice. But we cannot have justice without truth.

The Closing of the Muslim Mind generates many questions: How much of the current situation in Islam is merely a cultural and political trend? Is Islamist ideology limited to Arab nations and their satellites? How can Islam most effectively and quickly enter the democratic public square?

The answer to the last question is to recognize individual liberty and, above all, human dignity. But in order to adopt and *accept* such ideas, many Muslim groups (perhaps Islam as a whole) will have to undergo a kind of reformation.

As Mr. Reilly suggests, someone needs to do for Islam what Aquinas did for Christianity. But *can* anyone do this? Being fully aware of the evil and hatred behind the terrorism that has seared our imaginations and altered our lives, I am inclined to skepticism. But I also believe there is always hope.

7. A Dialogue Between Christ and a Muslim

ROBERT REILLY

Scene: Before the heavenly Throne.

Muslim (upon seeing Christ): "Is this a dream?"

Christ: "No. Something much better."

Muslim: "I didn't expect to see you here far above everyone. I thought you were coming back at the end of time to break the Cross, as we Muslims believe."

Christ: "No, I'm not coming back to break the Cross. Rather, I was broken on the Cross, which is why you're able to appear before me today."

Muslim: "But we believe that the all-powerful God would not allow one of his prophets to be treated that way. That is why we refuse to believe you were crucified. It was some other man, or a shadow."

Christ: "But I am not simply one of the prophets. I am God. I chose to allow myself to be treated this way to fulfill what the prophets foretold of the Suffering Servant."

Muslim: "But God can't do that! He can't suffer and die."

Christ: "Who are you to limit what God can do?"

Muslim: "But we are the true defenders of God's absolute omnipotence. God is *whoever* is all powerful."

Christ: "So, right is the rule of the stronger?"

Muslim: "Yes. God decides because He is the strongest."

Christ: "And He can decide anything?"

Muslim: "Yes, anything, and *whatever* He decides is just."

Christ: "He is not bound even by His own word?"

Muslim: "No, not by anything."

Christ: "But I *am* the Word. I am true to Myself. Pure will and power are arbitrary, tyrannical. I would be a despot."

Muslim: "But we were taught that God cannot be confined by our human ideas of justice."

Christ: "From where did you think you got those ideas of justice in the first place, if not from Me?"

Muslim: "I don't know. Islam tells us to submit without questioning. The great al-Ghazali taught us that, 'the mind . . . once it testifies to the truthfulness of the prophet, must cease to act.'"

Christ: "That is a betrayal of Me. I seek rational consent, not cowering subjection. Tell me: can the all-powerful God enter his creation?"

Muslim: "Yes, but only through his word to his prophets to give us his commands."

Christic "But, as I said, I *am* the Word."

Muslim: "But you are flesh."

Christ: "Yes, the Word made flesh, because God is also Love and wishes to save you. Though I am the strongest, I made myself the weakest out of love for you."

Muslim: "We are taught that God can only *favor* us (if we obey Him) because He is complete in Himself, and loving us would indicate some lack in Him. So, this kind of love cannot be. It is a forbidden thought."

Christ: "You cannot forbid Me. I suffer no lack from this love. I do not need to complete myself, but to complete you. You have a hole in your soul. Only I can fill it. I became man for this purpose."

Muslim: "Yes, we thought you were a man, certainly not the son of God. That would be blasphemy."

Christ: "I know. You have a false idea of Me from the Qur'an, just as it mistakenly tells you that the Trinity is composed of Father, Son, and Mary. Neither did you believe that God is your Father, but some infinitely distant, unknowable Being, who could not possibly be in relation to you, except as a master to a slave."

Muslim: "Yes, that is my name—Abdullah, 'slave of God.'"

Christ: "But I am the Son of God, who made you my brother. I became human, so you could become divine. That's how you became children of God. You have no idea how dear you are to me."

Muslim: "But I can't possibly be a child of God! God is infinitely above me."

Christ: "But We made you in our own image and likeness."

Muslim: "We say in Islam, '*bila kayfa wala tashbih*'—which is: 'without asking how and without comparing.' It is forbidden for us to compare *anything* to God, much less ourselves. So, I find all this inconceivable."

Christ: "I know. In fact, it required Conception—my Incarnation. But I am not telling you anything against your reason."

Muslim: "We abandoned reason and submitted ourselves to the text of the *Qur'an*."

Christ: "In doing that, you abandoned me, for I am *Logos*. I *am* Reason. That is why my pope, Benedict XVI, proclaimed that, 'not acting reasonably is contrary to God's nature.' This is why so many of you have behaved unreasonably, and why you could not find Me."

Muslim: "Since we do not believe any of these things, how did I get here then?"

Christ: "You got here by the merits of the very things you deny, my Sonship and my sacrifice, because you had no chance to accept them. You knew nothing but Islam. And yet you lived a good and decent life by the lights you were given. I love you none the less for that. I died for you, too."

Muslim: "I thought there would be only Muslims here, and that the Christians would be in Hell. But now that I see what the Christians said is true, why am *I* not in Hell?"

Christ: "I only send to Hell those who choose it. In fact, they send themselves."

Muslim: "How can you forgive me for being so blind?"

Christ: "You knew not what you were doing."

Muslim (falling on his knees, forehead to the ground): "My Lord and my God, how can I adore you now?"

Christ: "By loving me back. Now that you see me as *I Am*, you can do this. Welcome. One of my priests martyred in Algeria in 1998, Fr. Christian, prayed before his death that he 'could con-

template with the Father his children of Islam as He sees them.'
He is with my Father doing that now. You may join him and see
for yourself. Then pray for your fellow Muslims that they, too,
may see. I want them all for Myself."

8. In the Beginning . . .

WILLIAM E. CARROLL

The Jewish philosopher and theologian, Moses Maimonides
(1135–1204), observed that Jews, Muslims, and Christians share
a common belief that the world is created by God. Maimonides,
following in the tradition of many Muslim thinkers, was not sure
that Christians were monotheists, given the doctrine of the Trinity,
but he was sure that Christians recognized that all that is depends
upon God's creative act. With most believers, Maimonides identified creation with temporal beginning, as do most people today.
But this has to be carefully examined to avoid unnecessary conflicts between faith and science.

Muslim and Jewish thinkers in the Middle Ages wrestled with
the relationship between Greek science (especially Plato and
Aristotle) and revelation in the Koran and the Hebrew Bible.
What appeared especially troublesome was the common Greek
view that the universe is eternal, a claim that contradicted the generally accepted belief in creation as a beginning of time. The discussion of the relationship between science and faith in medieval
Islam and Judaism anticipated (and partly formed) the later
debate among medieval Christians. The discussion continues
today, especially as contemporary thinkers reflect on the implications of evolutionary biology and cosmology for religious belief.

The identification of creation with a temporal beginning
tempted some in the Middle Ages to think that we can know
that the universe must have a temporal beginning and, therefore,
that the universe is created and has a Creator. Some famous
Muslim theologians (the *kalam*) made this argument, and similar
arguments exist today among those who think that Big Bang

cosmology, in its usual acceptance of an initial "singularity," offers scientific warrant, if not strict proof, for the absolute beginning of everything. If there is such a "singularity," a point where our notions of space and time collapse, and natural sciences can offer no further explanations, then, so some claim, we have evidence for an act of creation.

But recent developments in cosmology seek to explain the Big Bang in terms of "quantum tunneling from nothing," or offer various scenarios for a pre-Big Bang universe, or speak of a series of big bangs, or even entertain the possibility of an infinite number of universes—a "multiverse." All seem to challenge traditional belief in creation. Maimonides admitted that if science could demonstrate that the universe was eternal (without a beginning), then Biblical accounts that seem to affirm a beginning would have to be read metaphorically. For him, God's revelation and the truths reachable by reason cannot be in contradiction. God, after all, is the author of all truth. Maimonides, however, did not think that it was possible for science to know whether the universe had a beginning. He believed it an error to think that one could reason from the current state of affairs to such a beginning.

Among medieval Muslim thinkers, the discussion about creation and science was especially sophisticated. Avicenna (980–1037), for example, argued that creation needs to be understood essentially as the dependence of all that is on God as cause, apart from any question of temporal beginning. In fact, Avicenna thought that he could demonstrate that the world is eternal and, therefore, Islam ought to affirm creation as complete dependence on God, not the beginning of time.

Thomas Aquinas (1224–1274) learned a great deal from Maimonides, Avicenna, and other Muslim scholars, as well as from Christian predecessors. Thomas believed that the world has a temporal beginning, but that reason alone cannot prove it. The Bible reveals such a beginning, as the Fourth Lateran Council (1215) reaffirmed. Thomas did not agree with Avicenna that the world is eternal, but he accepted that the fundamental sense of creation is that all existing things depend upon God as cause. Furthermore, he recognized this dependence as ongoing. Creation is not some distant event. If God were not causing all that is to exist, as it exists, there would be absolutely nothing. The expression "creation out-of-nothing" does not mean, first of all, "after nothing." Rather, it means that in creating God does not use anything; creation is sheer exercise of divine omnipotence.

Thomas clearly saw the difference between the origin and the beginning of the universe. The universe has its origin in God. A temporal beginning concerns the kind of universe God creates. Thomas thought that an eternal universe would still be created. Although Thomas believed the universe had a temporal beginning, he advised against using scientific arguments to prove such a beginning. He always warned against using bad arguments in defence of beliefs.

If he knew contemporary cosmological theories that reject the need for a Creator by seeking to explain the world scientifically or to deny a Big Bang, Thomas would say such an analysis fails on two counts: 1) to deny a beginning is not to deny creation—whatever kind of universe (or multiverse) there is it would still require a cause; 2) speculations about a universe without a beginning (or with a beginning, for that matter) cannot be more than speculations, since, in principle, science cannot know whether there is a beginning. Cosmological theories can neither confirm nor deny creation. To the extent that creation can be grasped by reason, it is through metaphysics, not the natural sciences.

The "singularity" in traditional Big Bang cosmology may represent the beginning of the universe, but we cannot conclude that it is the absolute beginning, creation as believers understand it. Some contemporary cosmologists recognize there could very well be something before the Big Bang.

Discussions of creation and beginnings can provide opportunities for dialogue among Jews, Muslims, and Christians, and such discussions can help to clarify the relationship among the natural sciences, philosophy, and theology—important distinctions among these disciplines, as well as their complementary truths. Whatever "beginning" cosmology addresses, it is not the absolute beginning that faith affirms. Believers can admit, with St. Thomas and without fear of scientific contradiction, that even were the universe to have no beginning it still would be created.

9. Where Pride Masquerades as Compassion

Tom Bethell

The *New Yorker* has published a fascinating article about the problem of evil by James Wood, an excellent writer who formerly reviewed books for The *New Republic*. Titled "Holiday in Hellmouth," it continues with deliberate illogic in the subhead: "God may be dead, but the question of why he permits suffering lives on."

Wood says that the problem of evil has undermined the faith of many thinkers, himself included. If God "has the power to alleviate this suffering but does not, he is cruel; if he cannot, he is weak." Such reflections eventually separated him "from the somewhat austere Christian environment" of his youth.

He reflects on a new book by Bart D. Ehrman, a professor of religious studies at the University of North Carolina: *God's Problem: How the Bible Fails to Answer Our Most Important Question—Why We Suffer*. That sounds as if it should be "furiously triple underlined on the dust jacket," Wood says, and those who accept the problem of evil as a serious argument against God's power or goodness often do begin to get very angry—with Him.

In fact, the argument itself is more an expression of rebellion than of disbelief. It is also rebellion at a profound level because it pits itself against the very structure of creation. The argument really goes like this: An all-powerful God could have made the world differently, could have left out the pain and suffering. But he didn't. Why not? Maybe because, in the end, he is not so great, or not so good.

All this amounts to "permanent rebellion," according to Wood. "It is not quite atheism but wounded theism." It is "condemned to argue ceaselessly against a God it is supposed not to believe in."

Obviously, I am not going to resolve the problem of pain here. But it is not a problem to be "solved," as though it were a test of our logical skills. The error of those who allow their thoughts to be restricted to these paths is to imagine that human understanding can exist on the same plane as God's. From that vantage point, some then actually look down on God. In C. S. Lewis' phrase, they put God in the Dock.

Such people re-imagine a kinder, gentler world, devoid of suffering, then give themselves moral credit for their sensitivity. It's not hard to see why such an attitude is favored in our time. Pride masquerades as compassion.

Many in the contemporary world cannot accept that human understanding, on its own, has real limits and is often little more than a meager candle in the dark. Medieval theologians described whole hierarchies: angels and archangels, principalities and powers, cherubim and seraphim. And they distinguished what could be achieved by reason and what comes to us only by faith. That has all been leveled by the modernist wrecking ball.

And just as there's nothing higher, so there's nothing lower. The same people who want to show God how the world could be better organized also aspire to teach chimps sign language. We are even-handedly disdainful of the Higher and the Lower. Animals are not on our level? That is species-ism.

Egalitarian sentiment peeks through, now dressed up as theology. Sometimes what we object to is not so much the existence of evil as its maldistribution. We can hardly deny that we all suffer and sooner or later we all die. But suffering appears unevenly rationed. "For the lucky few," writes Wood, who acknowledges that the problem of evil really only gained traction in the post-Enlightenment era, "there is reason to hope that life will be a business of evenly rationed suffering."

It's worth noting that this view of Creation—we could have done a better job—is frequently used in an almost identical way to support evolution and denigrate intelligent design. Often anti-design arguments have nothing to do with science but are veiled theological claims. They go like this: "If God had designed the organ, he would have done a much better job than that!"

The influential Darwinian theorist George Williams, for example, says that the eye was "stupidly designed," because a smart designer would not have placed the wiring of the retina on the side facing incoming light. Among other things it created a blind spot. But how well have they done? Even with the help of GPS, their dim driverless robots blunder about the Mojave Desert at 15 mph and tumble into ditches. The fact is, the best engineers and computer scientists haven't been able to produce anything remotely comparable. But they can imagine something better, so they feel entitled to call existing structures poorly designed.

"Creating 'successive species of crocodiles?' God wouldn't have wasted his time in that way!" (That paraphrases an actual argument used by Thomas Henry Huxley.)

The anti-design frenzy mocks heaven, while the problem of evil rails against it. Both are forms of the same argument. Both are condescending, prideful, and thinly veiled displays of rebellion against the Creator.

10. The Problem of Good

Howard Kainz

The number of man-hours spent by philosophers in analyzing and writing about the "problem of evil" would certainly come to an astronomical figure. I have spent a considerable amount of time on it myself, including the second chapter in my book, *The Existence of God and the Faith-Instinct*. But the problem of *good* is well-nigh ignored by philosophers. And most people are probably unaware that there is such a problem, and that it is formidable.

In my book, I separate the problem of evil into three subdivisions—natural evils, such as tsunamis and earthquakes; moral evils, such as brutal massacres of innocent persons; and physical/psychic suffering, especially hereditary diseases and handicaps, such as Huntington's Disease and Sickle-Cell anemia.

The problem of good can be similarly subdivided:

I. Natural Goods

Certainly to be included in the list are the perennial goods in nature that keep poetry from becoming a dying profession: The beauty of the natural world: awe-inspiring beauties of land and sea, and the infinitely variable loveliness of fauna and flora.

Those of us who are living in the modern age have also benefitted from the awesome scientific discoveries of the last two centuries: opening up for us the intriguing complex harmony of the microscopic world, from quarks to DNA to stem cells; the physical laws which make possible the investigation into the secrets of the cosmos, and even probes of other planets and solar systems; and the marvelous "fine-tuning" of all possible variables after the "big bang," situating us in a universe that seems to be made for the production and protection of human life, even down to the details of our place in the Milky Way and the solar system.

And in the realm of "everyday" poetry, who can even begin to explain the beauty and innocence of babies and young children, preserved—we hope—by the adults entrusted with their nurturance and upkeep; or the literally stunning beauty of the opposite sex, which can cause occasional "distractions" as well as moments of aesthetic contemplation and, for the lucky ones, the wonders of romantic love, by which unexpectedly a person, ignoring our obvious faults and imperfections, can find us somehow attractive enough to want to spend a life with us.

II. Moral Goods

Charles Darwin viewed the existence of monstrosities and parasites in organisms as evidence for the random nature of evolutionary developments. But the opposite also needs explanation. Evolutionary psychologists strain themselves to figure out how "selfish genes" and "memes" and all the chance developments leading to "survival of the fittest" can explain the almost unfathomable love of mothers and fathers—as well as the concern of other persons in our lives who seem to be impelled as if by an ineradicable instinct to spend themselves for our benefit; and the helping hands willing to extricate us from situations in times of trouble or dire distress (sometimes situations we have ourselves created).

Over and over we hear in the news, and sometimes witness, evolutionarily inexplicable cases of heroic individuals willing to give up their lives to save others—often perfect strangers.

And evolutionary theories about reciprocal and group solidarity help very little in explaining the patience and good humor of the sick, handicapped, and elderly, often suffering quietly from painful diseases or serious disabilities.

III. Physical/Psychic Goods

The extraordinary healings, "remissions," and cures that doctors, the media, and people at large refer to as "miracles"—natural miracles—offer us evidence of the extraordinary ability life and immune systems have at times to overcome seemingly insuperable challenges.

And let us not forget even the bodily signals of pain or distress without which we would not be able to find a diagnosis and remedy for disturbances in our physique or psyche.

On the psychic level, our lives are essentially sustained by the joys of love and friendship, and the constructive sharing of ideas and ideals that can take place at the right time and place—leading to immeasurable intellectual enhancements.

We might add "transcendent" moments to this list—those rare but welcome surges of joy that arrive unexpectedly, which sometimes can even be religious experiences; but most of all, there's the overpowering religious realization that, for some strange reason, God himself wanted to share his divine life with us, and was willing even to send his Son to become man, and live and die among us, so that we could, in turn, be divinized.

In sum, while evil gets the lion's share of free publicity, we children of Adam and Eve have entered into a world with a consciousness of both good *and* evil.

On the one side, we encounter Nature with its unpredictable upheavals, and "red in tooth and claw." In the other, we see the magnificent ordering of physical laws, which led to the existence of humans on a planet with marvelous beauties.

We are shocked by incredible atrocities in the news, confirming the belief, *homo homini lupus* ("humans are wolves to one another"); but we are also consoled by the unending strange stories of human love and sacrifice by persons who seem to belong, as it were, to a different species.

We puzzle over tragic cases of hereditary diseases and pandemics, which medical science has not been able to combat; but we find equally baffling stories confirming the remarkable human powers of homeostasis.

It is indeed shocking and sad that there is so much evil in the world. But if you think about it, it is strange and exhilarating that there is so much good. In fact, the amount of good is mysterious and has been made even more mysterious by the considerable advances of modern science.

The proper response, even for the melancholic among us, might be to sit down once in a while, forget about our troubles for a moment, and wonder how on earth there is so much goodness.

11. An Ancient Letter

JOSEPH WOOD

Archaeologist's Note: Around three years ago, we announced in this space the discovery of a document from a Near Eastern kingdom dating back to approximately 2000 years ago. Written, it appears, just before the winter solstice, that memorandum from the bureaus and agencies responsible for foreign affairs to a royal priest of the kingdom—a magus, as they seem to have been sometimes called—urged him not to join with counterparts from neighboring kingdoms in a proposed journey to Judea, whereto the magi apparently believed a mysterious star beckoned them. Today, we report the uncovering of a second document from the same kingdom, written a few years after the first and also in the winter period. This later letter from one of the foreign policy advisors who had opposed the Judean expedition to the same magus provides further insight into the events of that era.

To: Royal Prisoner #1027, formerly known as The Magus
In Care of the Royal Correctional Facility, Block A

Your former highness,

At this time of year, as we celebrate the return of lengthening days thanks to the generosity of the gods and goddesses, let me extend my warmest hopes for your welfare. I trust that the conditions of your confinement are satisfactory.

While I understand that you have expressed no remorse for your ill-fated trip to Judea, I and many others retain our profound desire that you might admit the error of your decision, renounce those conclusions that you drew while traveling (and which have been rightly suppressed for reasons of security and royal prestige), and open the way for your reinstatement to your station and your original position of authority.

I offer this wish for the sake of your family's reputation as well as your own.

But I write you now with a specific question. As you may have heard, my next service to our kingdom will be to write my personal memoirs of my years in government. With the advantage of various consultancy arrangements and speaking fees that assure my family and myself the financial security appropriate to former senior officials, I now have the time to focus on this challenging effort.

I have given my new book the tentative working title, *How Right I Was*. Naturally, I want to give you and all the others who served our government the full benefit of fair consideration of their views, however wrong and misguided their disagreements with me may have been.

I will not review in detail the events of your journey to Judea and its tragic aftermath. As you know, I and every other member of the National Foreign Policy Committee recommended unanimously and strongly that you not undertake such a trip.

Subsequent events vindicated our advice to the fullest. Your clumsy mishandling of the relationship with King Herod resulted in his condemning to death all the male children under the age of two in Bethlehem and the vicinity.

Of larger import, your actions provoked a crisis between our kingdom and both the Roman authorities and the local Judean tribal officials, which cost enormous time and energy to contain, all for no positive outcome.

Fortunately, the coming to power of King Archelaus in place of his father has given us the opportunity to reset our relations in the area and pivot towards the region in a way that has preserved and advanced the interests of our kingdom.

But the entire crisis was foreseen by myself and other experts. That your trip resulted in far fewer deaths than it might have without my own diplomatic skill and exertions only deepens your personal responsibility. It saddens me that one of the greatest demonstrations of my strategic prowess had to come in the wake of your poor judgment.

But that is all behind us now, though our intelligence sources in the region continue to pick up occasional data points regarding a family, like the one you described meeting in Judea, that escaped Herod's wrath by fleeing to Egypt and has now returned to the area. We will monitor these rumors closely but do not expect any significant events to emerge from them.

As I say, my point in writing you is to clarify one matter for my book, to make sure the public record of my period in government is complete for future historians and policy makers to study.

As you know, your former highness, I am a person of the world, comfortable in the corridors of power and confident with the affairs of state. I am neither sentimental nor superstitious, always sticking to the demonstrable facts and taking a pragmatic point of view.

So do not misunderstand—my question is purely an intellectual one, with no strange supernatural motive such as the one you claimed for your benighted expedition. But there have been some rumors and rather unprecedented sequels to those otherwise unremarkable events.

So please, former magus, just for the sake of the full historical record, tell me:

What did you see in Judea?

12. Bold, Benedetto, and Bello!

ROBERT ROYAL

As the Second Vatican Council developed, traditional Catholics in England were distressed because they saw Rome giving up the Old Latin Mass for a vernacular both shallow and shabby. Further, as Evelyn Waugh put it, "This was the Mass for whose restoration the Elizabethan martyrs had gone to the scaffold. St. Augustine, St. Thomas à Becket, St. Thomas More, Challoner, and Newman would have been perfectly at their ease among us [at that Mass]." It was a proud tradition, a heroic tradition. And Catholics living in a country where Anglicanism was the official faith and its English liturgy was magnificent in its way, were understandably sensitive to anything that appeared to ignore a Church that had survived much bloodshed and discrimination.

This week, the old Latin High Mass was celebrated in St. Peter's Basilica for the first time since 1969, and by an English-speaking American, Archbishop Burke, under a new ruling of Benedict XVI. This week the Vatican also announced new procedures for Anglicans—whole groups of them, it seems from preliminary reports, who are disaffected with gay bishops and other departures from tradition—to become Catholics while retaining some elements of their own tradition. British papers predict thousands of priests will convert.

If you have been following this news only in secular sources, you will get the impression that it's all a political strategy. The ecclesiologists at National Public Radio, for instance, called it a bold papal move to take the Church in a sharply conservative direction, including the netting of hapless Anglicans. But no Catholic should be so myopic. The proper perspective on this is the whole pilgrimage of God's people through history. The immediate details are significant, but what is truly important in such matters, as Waugh noted, is whether the Church is giving indications of remaining in living communion with its heroic past and is launching a way forward into the future.

The people who are worried whether the Church is veering right also usually wish that the Church would just go away.. But Catholicism has survived plenty of trouble, both internal and external, and has shown itself able to outlast whole civilizations and its own worst moments. As Ezra Pound once said, "an institution that survived the picturesqueness of the Borgias has a certain native resilience." Vatican II was the first time in history that in several ways the Church *secularized itself*. That left us with many unprecedented problems. But a half century later, the Church still stands for something as Protestants—excepting evangelicals, Pentecostals, and very few others—do not. And we may be in for some surprises.

But it takes boldness. The much ballyhooed "ecumenical dialogue" did not produce much beyond greater friendship among Christian and Jewish denominations. It may still have opened up unsuspected possibilities. About twenty years ago, I was invited to speak at an ecumenical event. Back then, I was much impressed with George Lindbeck of Yale, a Protestant who argued that all the churches (even Catholics) were midway through a large historical arc. Pre-modern churches were authoritarian, modern ones had to deal with people who thought themselves autonomous—until they saw the effects on themselves, their children, and their communities. The church's challenge, Lindbeck argued, was to rediscover how, in modern circumstances, to be *authoritative*. A little too schematic, perhaps, but even back then the basic direction of things was clear enough. When I presented my own version of this scenario to surprisingly warm agreement, no one responded more enthusiastically than a female Methodist pastor who acutely felt her church's footlessness.

Benedict will take criticism for his gutsy moves, but he's playing a masterful hand of new and old cards while preserving the fundamental authority of the Church. Some secular stories said he's trying to undo what Henry VIII did. Such is the poor education of our young investigative reporters. Henry had his sexual peccadilloes, of course, but gay bishops? gay marriages? the Bible largely ignored, except to sprinkle holy water on the idea of inclusiveness *in the church itself*? His church would have been the first to "undo" modern Anglicanism. Ironically, it seems only the pope of Rome can do that now, and it confuses journalists who tend only to think in binary oppositions of left and right that maybe a whole other game is being played.

Our late friend Fr. Richard John Neuhaus often said that history has many ironies in the fire. You could see how maybe God worked, even in the Enlightenment, he would say, to bring Christian truths about human dignity and freedom back into a Christian world that had mislaid them. It's more difficult to see what God was doing in letting the "king's great argument" take England out of the Catholic fold for half a millennium, a defection that guaranteed the survival of the Reformation and continues to trouble the unity of the West.

But when several dozen Anglican bishops send inquiries to the Vatican, thousands of priests stand ready, and whole dioceses and parishes may enter into full communion with Rome, it does shows a conservative thread in Western Christianity that many reporting on it don't like. But it shows perhaps even more importantly what may be a historical pendulum swing, which is never supposed to happen according to progressive history, and a renewed vigor in the Vatican and among the British Anglicans—that we American Catholics often miss in our brothers and sisters abroad who seem too aware of living *in partibus infidelium*. The pope is having an astounding effect on all that, *Viva Benedetto!*

VI. Personal Portraits

1. JFK: Charm or Character?

GEORGE MARLIN

Forty-five years after the assassination of John F. Kennedy, speechwriter Ted Sorensen has written *Counselor: A Life on the Edge of History*, his fourth book sanctifying the thirty-fifth president and only Catholic to occupy the White House. Mr. Sorensen's devotion to the memory of his sainted hero is embarrassing. Like a court troubadour, he continues to sing of "Camelot," ignoring the mountain of documents exposing the earthier side of President Kennedy and his administration. That side is so well known by now that it is difficult to know how Sorensen or his publisher, in good conscience or even in mere good sense, let these pages see the light of day.

He truly believes that President Kennedy was a philosopher-king who embodied nearly every virtue. In addition to being "honest, idealistic and devoted to the best values of the country," J.F.K. "never lost his temper . . . was most always calm . . . was superb at handling criticism . . . [and] unfailingly deferential and respectful of all women."

Despite this implausible hagiography, occasional lapses into candor in Mr. Sorensen's memoir undermine the myth of shining armor he has been polishing since November of 1963.

As for honesty: Sorensen admits that Kennedy suffered from the adrenal insufficiency known as Addison's disease and concedes that J.F.K. and his inner circle were "generally misleading on the matter"; that, in fact, there was a "conspiracy to conceal" the president's condition.

Mr. Sorensen also reveals that J.F.K. was not the sole author of *Profiles in Courage*, the Pulitzer Prize-winning book published solely under then Senator Kennedy's name. "I did the first draft of most chapters," says Sorensen, and "privately boasted or indirectly hinted that I had written much of the book." Such a confession is startling and confirmed by the further admission that he had an agreement with Kennedy to split the royalties fifty-fifty.

As for idealism: Mr. Sorensen concedes that the censure of Senator Joe McCarthy was "an issue [J.F.K.] wanted to duck" and he admits, in this regard anyway, that he "cannot in good conscience" defend his hero.

As for devotion to best values: Sorensen writes that J.F.K.'s references to God in speeches were "more a matter of political convention than religiosity." And he admits that with regard to sexual ethics the President "was not exercising due caution in his private life," as, for instance, when he had an affair with mafia chief Sam Giancana's mistress, Judith Exner.

As for J.F.K. never losing his temper and superbly handling criticism, Sorensen appears to have forgotten that President Kennedy constantly complained to editors about news stories critical of him. In 1962, the thin-skinned president cancelled the twenty-two White House subscriptions to *The New York Herald Tribune* and in 1963 unsuccessfully pressured *The New York Times* to remove correspondent David Halberstam from his Vietnam post for writing unflattering stories.

Midway through his book, perhaps realizing he's on thin ice, Sorensen confronts the character issue directly and asks "Was J.F.K. a moral leader?" His answer: "[He] was in my book a moral leader regardless of his private misconduct. Public officials should be judged primarily not by their Puritanism in private, but by their public deeds and public service, by their principles and policies."

This is the Bill Clinton school of ethics, and it goes against the historic norm.

For centuries, character—"the actualization of the human potential for excellence"—was seen as the prerequisite for anyone interested in public service. Plato, Aristotle, Thomas Aquinas, the Renaissance humanists, and the American Founders all agreed that character matters; that it is essential for public officials to cultivate the moral virtues of justice, courage, honesty, patience, and temperance. For them, a leader with character is one who can keep irrational appetites under control in both public and private life.

Presidential historian James David Barber concurs. In his classic work, *The Presidential Character: Predicting Performance in the White House*, Barber describes character as ". . . the way the President orients himself towards life—not for the moment but enduringly. Character is the person's stance as he confronts experience. And at the core of character a man confronts himself."

Barber argues that a president's personal history—his lifelong character traits—is key to predicting presidential performance.

How does John F. Kennedy measure up to these standards?

Another J.F.K. biographer, Thomas Reeves, has reached this conclusion about Mr. Kennedy:

> Jack was pragmatic to the point of amorality; his sole standard seemed to be political expediency. Gifted with good looks, youth, and wealth, he was often, in his personal life, reckless, vain, selfish, petty, and lecherous. Jack's character, so much a reflection of his father's single-minded pursuit of political power and personal indulgence, lacked a moral center, a reference point that went beyond self-aggrandizement.

These character traits not only explain Mr. Kennedy's reckless sexual behavior in the White House, but also his approval of assassination plots and clandestine activities, and his manipulation of reporters to whom he gave classified documents in return for good news stories.

The record shows John F. Kennedy was not the philosopher-king the "Camelot School" would have us idolize.

Sad to say, it appears an infatuated Ted Sorensen has mistaken Kennedy's superficial charm for true character.

2. Remembering Fulton J. Sheen

GEORGE MARLIN

Today is the thirtieth anniversary of the death of Archbishop Fulton Sheen, who was revered by millions of Americans because of his great gifts in preaching and writing about the truths of the Catholic faith—and about the great heresies of the twentieth century.

Fulton John Sheen was born over his father's hardware store in El Paso, Illinois, on May 8, 1895. An outstanding student, Sheen attended St. Victor's College in Bourbonnais, Illinois, and later, realizing he had a religious vocation, entered Saint Paul Seminary in Minnesota.

Ordained a priest on September 25, 1919, he was not assigned a parish, but was sent to The Catholic University of America for graduate studies. Upon earning his Master of Arts degree, he traveled to Europe for additional education. After earning a doctorate of philosophy from the University of Louvain and a doctorate in sacred theology from the Angelicum in Rome, Sheen was offered teaching positions at Oxford and at Columbia University. Sheen sent a letter to his bishop asking, "Which offer should I accept?" The answer was, "Come home."

In the summer of 1926, Father Sheen was summoned to the bishop's office, who informed him, "Three years ago I promised you to Bishop Shahan of The Catholic University as a member of the faculty." Sheen asked, "Why did you not let me go there when I returned from Europe?" "Because of the success you had on the other side, I just wanted to see if you would be obedient. So run along now, you have my blessing."

Sheen was to teach for twenty-five years. During this period, his reputation as a preacher and Catholic apologist grew, and invitations to speak and preach throughout the nation poured in. In

1930 the American bishops invited him to represent the Church on NBC's nationally broadcast show "The Catholic Hour," and he appeared on that show until 1951, when he switched from radio to television.

Many believed Sheen had the ability to become the greatest Catholic philosopher of the twentieth century. His duties at The Catholic University, however, became minimal; he eventually taught only one graduate course a year. The chairman of the philosophy department, Father Ignatius Smith, explained, "I was often criticized for not giving him more work, but I felt he was doing more good on the outside."

Sheen accomplished much on the outside. He produced at least one book a year, wrote two weekly newspaper columns, became national director of the Society for the Propagation of the Faith, and edited two magazines. Also, he was instrumental in numerous conversions, including Clare Booth Luce, Henry Ford II, Communists Louis Budenz and Elizabeth Bentley, and violinist Fritz Kreisler.

Sheen had the rare ability to take complex philosophical and theological concepts and translate them into language the person on the street could understand. Witness this from 1933:

> Never before in the history of the world was there so much knowledge; and never before so little coming to the knowledge of the Truth. Never before so much straining for life; never before so many unhappy lives. Never before so much science; never before was it used so for the destruction of human life.

Or this from 1944:

> In religious matters, the modern world believes in indifference. Very simply, this means it has no great loves and no great hates; no causes worth living for and no causes worth dying for. It counts its virtues by the vices from which it abstains, asks that religion be easy and pleasant, sneers the term "mystic" at those who are

spiritually inclined, dislikes enthusiasm and loves benevolence, makes elegance the test of virtue and hygiene the test of morality, believes that one may be too religious but never too refined. It holds that no one ever loses his soul, except for some great and foul crime such as murder. Briefly, the indifference of the world includes no true fear of God, no fervent zeal for His honor, no deep hatred of sin, and no great concern for eternal salvation.

His insights went beyond strictly religious questions. The books—e.g., *Liberty, Equality and Fraternity* (1928), *Freedom Under God* (1940), *Whence Come Wars* (1940), *For God and Country* (1941), *A Declaration of Dependence* (1941), *God and War* (1942), and *Communism and the Conscience of the West* (1948)—educated Americans on the evils of Nazism, fascism, and communism.

In 1951, now Bishop Sheen appeared at Manhattan's Adelphi Theatre and said to America, "Thank you for allowing me into your home." It was the beginning of his award-winning television show, "Life Is Worth Living." He was the first (and possibly only) religious leader with a show sponsored by a major corporation.

"Life Is Worth Living" was up against "The Milton Berle Show." Every week America asked, "Shall we watch Uncle Miltie or Uncle Fultie?" Sheen's ratings skyrocketed, and Mr. Television was knocked off the top of the ratings chart.

The show continued until 1957 and had an estimated audience of 30 million. The bishop, who covered various subjects from psychology to Irish humor to Stalin, received 8–10,000 letters a day. In 1964 Sheen appeared on a weekly show entitled "Quo Vadis America," and in 1966, "The Bishop Sheen Show."

On October 2, 1979, seven days after celebrating the sixtieth anniversary of his priesthood, in St. Patrick's Cathedral in New York, Pope John Paul II embraced Archbishop Sheen and told him, "You have written and spoken well of the Lord Jesus. You are a loyal son of the Church."

On December 9, 1979, Archbishop Fulton Sheen died in the Lord. He was buried beneath the main altar at St. Patrick's Cathedral, where he had preached for many years. In a nation that still harbored anti-Catholic sentiments, Sheen gave Catholicism a public face that made the Church and its teachings acceptable to millions of Americans.

Archbishop Fulton Sheen, God love you—and pray for us.

3. Our Brother, Paul

PETER BROWN

In the information age, bad interpretations of Scripture flourish faster than good ones can replace them. The Bible can then become a warrant for all manner of dubious moral and theological claims. In this Year of St. Paul—and especially in this Holy Week—we can be grateful for many things about Paul's example, but especially that his modern interpreters have not done an even worse job with him than we might fear.

There is plenty of material to work with. Paul called the Galatians "stupid," (Gal 3:1) and then wished their Judaizing opponents would circumcise themselves and have the knife slip. This was after he bragged of having opposed the first pope to his face, not caring whether he really was a "pillar" of the Church. (I suspect Paul lost that verbal confrontation because otherwise he would have bragged about his victory.) He mocked the pretenses of the Corinthians (1 Cor 4:8), belittling them by calling them babes, while refusing to accept their support for fear of being tainted. He insulted the Cretans by repeating the hoariest stereotypes of their lying beastly gluttony. (Tit 1:12)

The Thessalonians probably never took literally Paul's instruction to starve those who would not work, but was this the best way of encouraging his flock to work quietly for a living? When the servant of the high priest Ananias slapped him, Paul did not turn the other cheek but instead threatened him with divine vengeance, calling him a whitewashed wall and a lawbreaker.

(Acts 23:3) Paul did not mince words either, referring to his past pre-Christian glories as so much "dung," (Phil 3:8) and I would not be surprised at all if one his secretaries inserted this euphemism for a more scatological term.

And all this was *after* Paul became a Christian.

The interpretive tradition has always been reserved in obeying Paul's command to "imitate me" (1 Cor 11:1) and in identifying the times Paul is really "imitating Christ." Perhaps it is too much to say that had others done these things they would have been committing sin. But we cannot ignore the fact that Catholic mothers and schoolmarms would not tolerate some of Paul's antics.

Things are quite different with Our Lord. Jesus exercises what media types today would describe as perfect control over His public persona. Even the potentially embarrassing stories about Him in Mark—friends and family calling Him mad or His inability to work miracles in Nazareth or His having to try twice to heal a blind man—seem strategic "leaks," which in our skeptical age give the Gospel stronger claims to authenticity.

Not so with Paul. His writings reveal a man with no idea that readers would be wrangling over his words two millennia later; that he reveals so much of his own character is quite incidental to why he wrote at all.

His raw letters posed a major problem for readers from the start. He was "hard to understand" (2 Pet 3:16) and he himself has proven difficult for the Church to domesticate.

One large theological consequence is the split in western Christianity, basically over the meaning of Paul. The practical consequences are significant as well. We know more about Paul's life than any other first-generation follower of Jesus. And yet his life has had little influence in popular piety, especially compared with saints such as Therese of Lisieux or Padre Pio.

This is unfortunate. Luke and Paul's own letters portray a man whose mission was to suffer so that Christ might be exalted. Even Paul's greatest glories go unmentioned. He suffered martyrdom though Luke opted not to tell us and drops Paul's story in Rome years before he died under the Neronian persecution. Paul is credited with a few signs and wonders, but mostly these seem to have been used to keep the natives from getting too restless.

As it happened, the natives got plenty restless, and Paul spent the lion's share of his career one step ahead of Jewish and Roman enemies, suffering lashings, beatings, and imprisonments. Jesus' ministry seems mostly to have drawn admiring throngs. Paul's seems mostly to have drawn angry mobs. Our Lord was so impressive in death that he is recorded to have made converts by the way he died. Few were much impressed with Paul's sufferings; indeed Paul's afflictions actually seem to have harmed his reputation *even among the churches he founded.* Paul's poor eyesight and bodily afflictions did not prevent the Galatians from troubling him and embracing another gospel. (Gal 4:15; 1:6)

The Corinthians had the gall to ask Paul for letters of reference (2 Cor 3:1), so put off were they by his inarticulate speech, his meager appearance, and his embarrassing refusal to accept their financial support. And Paul's protestations that his sufferings actually made him more Christ-like seem to have only made things worse.

Yet there is much of value in Paul for us. We may easily identify with someone who is an ardent Christian, but does not seem very effective in the main passion of his life. We who work at child-rearing or housework or jobs where we are underpaid or underappreciated can identify with a man who spent most of his adult life in that condition. We who are unlikely to become martyrs and must pursue our Christian vocation incrementally can admire a man who follows God mostly in fits and starts and with nearly constant setbacks.

Paul's life reminds us of an old truth that, provided we make Christ crucified our center, God will show forbearance for the rough edges and personal flaws at our perimeter. That should give us greater comfort as we approach Easter: holiness is not the same as success, and lies within closer reach than we think.

4. Rediscovering St. Mugg

DANIEL MAHONEY

The journalist, writer, and latter-day Christian apologist Malcolm Muggeridge (1903–1990) was once well known by the cultivated public on both sides of the Atlantic. His television programs and BBC documentaries drew huge audiences (his 1971 documentary and accompanying book on Mother Teresa of Calcutta—*Something Beautiful for God*—first brought her to the attention of the larger world). Muggeridge wrote sparkling prose in works such as his autobiography *Chronicles of Wasted Time* and in his beautiful meditation on the enduring human and theological significance of Christ in an age of skepticism and ideology, *Jesus the Man Lives*. The latter conveys far more spiritual insight than all of contemporary scripture scholarship, but is, alas, out of print.

Muggeridge's life was dramatic without being self-dramatizing. Muggeridge was a faithful friend of people who mattered from Evelyn Waugh and George Orwell to William F. Buckley, Jr. (he was a particularly delightful guest on Buckley's "Firing Line"). Muggeridge had been a reporter in Moscow for the left-leaning *Guardian* in the early 1930s and was among the first to tell the truth about Soviet Communism and all its works. He also served as a spy for MI-6 during the Second World War. Obviously, Muggeridge was no ordinary journalist. He was a man at the center of the intellectual and political life of the century who nonetheless knew that happiness could not be found solely through human efforts. An astute student of politics, he coolly assessed power and sharply chronicled dislocations and decadence (his work *The Thirties* is still very much worth reading).

A mordant wit and somewhat tortured seeker, his spiritual search carried him in the 1960s into a non-denominational Christianity of a decidedly Augustinian cast (see *Jesus Rediscovered*) and then in 1982 into the Roman Catholic Church. There he found his long-sought spiritual home. The luminous spiritual witness of Mother Teresa—whom Muggeridge never confused with a mere humanitarian—and the Catholic opposition to abortion led him to accept "the great boon and blessing" that is the Catholic Church.

Some secular critics derided him as "St. Mugg," an aging man of the world who turned against worldly pleasures just as he was no longer able to enjoy them. For many years, Muggeridge did lead a tempestuous personal life. Even his supremely happy sixty-year marriage to Kitty Dobbs Muggeridge was marred in earlier years by infidelities on both sides and no small dose of tragedy. But as the essays edited by Nicholas Flynn in the recently published *Time and Eternity: Uncollected Writings, 1933–1983* make clear, Muggeridge's late embrace of Christianity was not a dramatic departure. His early turn away from socialism and secular radicalism stemmed from his first-hand observations of the Soviet Union and his growing awareness that "The Kingdom of Heaven on Earth is all pretence, a denial of the very nature of life." In 1938, he wrote that "if an epigraph were required for this sad and terrible time"— Communism and National Socialism were then in full bloom—"it might well be found in 'The Kingdom of Heaven on Earth.'"

As the nephew-in-law of the famous Fabian socialist Beatrice Webb and the son of a prominent Labour-Socialist activist H. T. Muggeridge, Malcolm went to Moscow expecting to find "the green stick," the fabled this-worldly source of human happiness. Instead he discovered unprecedented tyranny based upon a "General Idea" that had no place for human fallibility or the liberty and dignity of ordinary human beings.

Muggeridge describes in painful detail what was at stake in "class warfare" that showed no mercy for peasants trying to scratch out a meager existence as the regime "collectivized" them and confiscated their grain. Millions perished in a "terror-famine" in Ukraine and southern Russia, which was denied by George Bernard Shaw and Walter Duranty, the *New York Times* reporter who won a Pulitzer Prize for his mendacious reporting from Moscow. The "dictatorship of the proletariat," Muggeridge tells us, hated traditional Russia—the peasantry, the church, the independent intelligentsia—and was bent on destroying it even if it meant ultimately destroying itself. Muggeridge lost his job at the *Guardian* but would later gain the respect of other honest men such as George Orwell and Aleksandr Solzhenitsyn for his courage and dedication to truth. Muggeridge wrote with particular lucidity and insight about Solzhenitsyn's Christian-inspired opposition to the totalitarian degradation of man (satisfying a longtime wish, Muggeridge interviewed the Russian Nobel Laureate when Solzhenitsyn visited London to receive the Templeton Prize).

The experience of utopia-in-power in the Soviet Union cured Muggeridge of ideological illusions and taught him that western civilization was eminently worthy of defense. No longer believing in the prospects for the self-deification of man, Muggeridge's soul opened to belief in the one, true God. But even after becoming a Christian he refused the fashionable conflation of Christianity with secular humanitarianism, with what he mockingly called in a 1972 piece reproduced in *Time and Eternity*, "The Gospel of Jesus *Égalité*." He did not become a Catholic near the end of his life, he wrote, because the Church offered a "panacea for contemporary ills, or the promise of future happiness." That is to confuse Christian wisdom with utopian ideology, and to forget the true lesson to be drawn from the death and resurrection of Christ—the *logos*, the word made flesh—that "provides the bridge between mortality and immortality, between man and his creator and between time and eternity."

There is a great deal to be learned from the life and witness of Malcolm Muggeridge, not least the fundamental and enduring distinction between Christianity and ideology. Let us hope that an American publisher has the good sense to make *Time and Eternity*, Nicholas Flynn's remarkable collection of Muggeridge's writings, available to the American public. Muggeridge should not become just another once-important but now forgotten figure. His voice and example still have much to say to us, who face many of the same threats under different guises.

5. A Singular Ordinary Man

ROBERT ROYAL

One of the most unusual men I ever knew died last week. He wasn't a national figure or much noticed outside the circle of his family, friends, and community. He didn't graduate from a prestigious university and, since he was a teenager during the Great Depression, barely made it out of high school before he had to go to work. But he lived an honorable life, and even a life that may have touched—in the way of the vast majority of ordinary people—on holiness and heroic charity.

His name was Nello (an odd moniker that he was so proud of it that he offered his children a large sum to name one of the grandchildren after him—without success); he was one of my mother's brothers and therefore my uncle. I bring him to your attention not for that, but because he's the kind of person who used to be commoner in our culture, but has become all but invisible today. If a man or woman like this is brought to our attention now, it's as a slightly offbeat "human interest" story in the media.

In my view, most of the leaders in Washington and elsewhere are more or less interchangeable, with educations and attitudes that, like all human things, have their value, but reflect a very narrow slice of humanity. As a nation, we could swap out our entire political and intellectual class with less loss than we could afford to lose sight of people like Nello.

He took an eccentric path into adulthood. He got married, had kids, bought a house—but not like everyone else. His brothers got jobs and had considerable success in big companies: General Electric, the railroads, manufacturing. My first memories of him were when he showed up at the house, as he did at thousands in the area, as what I think ought to be frankly called a peddler. He'd started a business selling laundry bleach, Starwater, which he delivered directly to people's homes on a regular basis, the way milkmen used to home-deliver milk. He also had trays of sundries: clothespins, shoelaces, ribbons, thimbles, needles, and more substantial items, which every household needs and he made easy to buy.

Out of this unashamed, humble entrepreneurship, he must have done pretty well because by the time I came back from college, he'd bought a number of rental properties and even a small dance hall that he rented out for weddings and other celebrations. As I was struggling to find my way, he'd always ask kindly in the old fashion, "you making a buck?" Later, he would tell me and my kids that you couldn't make money "just working," you had to figure out something people needed and offer new services.

I don't know exactly when he got into local politics, but what first moved him was prayer being taken out of schools. Once he decided to enter the fray, he was relentless in the local culture wars—and his adversaries have the scars, physical and psychological, to prove it. A first-generation American, he acted in public forums with the confidence of someone whose family came over on the Mayflower. Abortion naturally vexed him, but since there was little he could do about that locally, he set up a shrine to Our Lady and prayed. Meanwhile, he was re-elected to the town council repeatedly for almost half a century.

His most famous fight involved a Christmas crèche on town property. After the lawyers and judges were through wrangling, a decision came down that a crèche could go up on the town green at Christmas—but only if someone was with it at all times. Why someone present made the display legal may be a puzzle to those of us untrained in the law. Presumably, opponents thought this requirement would be impossible to meet, given that almost everyone wants to be indoors with family and friends during the cold Christmas season. But Nello didn't bother about that. He put up the crèche with his own money and sat by it in his van for days in the cold well into his eighties and nineties.

Though by the end he was quite well off, he lived all his life in the same modest house, which was fitted out with oddities in the garage and yard that were like some strange backcountry to a young boy. One I particularly remember—something I have not seen anywhere else in the world—was a product of the old *paisan's* arts. Since he didn't have a big backyard and wanted two fruit trees, early on he grafted a plum tree into a peach tree and it continued to produce both fruits for decades, one on one side, one on the other.

Something that only came out at his funeral is that in addition to his public defense of religion, charities, pro-life labors, and other works of mercy, he had fitted a cot and heater into a shed in his yard, and even in his last years was bringing homeless people there for the night. I have no doubt this violated multiple zoning laws, housing regulations, and basic federal requirements for professional caregivers. But that says more about how we've changed as a society in the way we help the poor than it does about anything else.

He was not without flaws, and an outsider watching him and his brothers playing a hand of pinochle or a game of *bocce* might be forgiven for calling the police—since we've lost the living experience of common people who enjoy arguing and even force themselves to argue face-to-face as an expression of pleasure in competing against each other.

Towards the end, he had the habit of saying to people, "May the Lord take a liking to you." Amen, and *requiescat in pace.*

6. Nino: A Memoir

HADLEY ARKES

The voice came over the phone, a voice with energy and welcoming comradery, from one I had not yet met: "Hadley, this is Nino Scalia." It was the spring of 1977; I was a Fellow at the Smithsonian, about to present a paper for my final seminar. Antonin Scalia had just left his post as head of the Office of Legal Counsel at the Department of Justice with the end of the Ford Administration—or as he would put it, "when the people threw us out."

He was at the American Enterprise Institute now, just before he would begin a distinguished career as a teacher of law at the University of Virginia and my own University of Chicago. Of all things, he was being recruited as a discussant for my paper. It was a wonder that he would be willing to carve out time to do that, but he engaged himself in this seminar with characteristic wit and gusto. The whole thing could be understood solely as an expression of his large, good nature, which would never fade. His friends have glided happily over the years in the currents generated by that nature and by his spirited family, in the lives they have drawn in with them.

In the banter and laughing—and arguments—over the years, he has tilted with some of his friends over the matter of "natural law." The Justice has been famously dubious, at times scathing. My own argument has been that he has shown us handsomely, in his work, how a jurisprudence of natural law may be done, even while professing up and down that it cannot be done. As Aristotle noted, the distinct nature of human beings is marked by the capacity to give and understand reasons over matters of right and wrong. As Aristotle saw, there is something approaching the divine in the capacity to grasp propositions not bounded by space and time, truths that would hold in all times and places and not decompose, as all material things decompose.

The natural law may be shown in the disciplined engagement of the "laws of reason" in the cases that come before us. My friend has boasted that he had never taken a course in logic, and yet he has been the most relentless logician on the Supreme Court. And he has done the most important work of natural law as he has challenged, in the most demanding way, the premises that the Court has put in place as it removed protections of the law from unborn children, created novel licenses in sexuality, and undermined support for marriage as an institution.

In cases prosaic and grand, he has managed to use the key of propositional logic to expose the vacuities that may beguile lawyers and judges. In one case, he posed this Talmudic question to Justice Kennedy: "[W]hat possible linguistic usage would accept that whatever . . . *affects* waters of the United States *is* waters of the United States?" It was a simple flexing of propositional logic, but one that could limit the reach of a federal statute.

Scalia's supreme achievements, in this vein, have come at those moments in which he has shown certain claims to rights as so exquisite that they virtually extinguish themselves. One of my favorites was *Lee v. Weisman* (1992). The Court struck down, as an establishment of religion, a non-denominational prayer, offered by a rabbi, at the graduation of a public high school in Providence. Justice Kennedy thought it was an unwarranted psychological coercion that a girl, a professed atheist, should be compelled to sit in silent acquiescence and respect while others invoked God.

Scalia pointed out, in dissent, the famous flag-salute case. Parents who were Jehovah's Witnesses were faced with jail for parental neglect if their child refused to salute the flag and speak the pledge. But that case did not involve a claim of religious belief; the Court had protected the student and his family from the imposition of a *political* orthodoxy.

As Scalia pointed out, the combination of the two decisions was now explosive. The student in Providence had not been compelled to do or say anything. And so we would gather now that a student objecting, say, to Jesse Jackson as a speaker could not merely absent himself from his commencement; he could invoke his right not to suffer the presence of Jackson on the platform. The only thing more bizarre than this implication is the example of judges, entranced by high sentiment, and heedless of the logic they are putting into place.

In the case of assisted suicide in Oregon, Scalia invoked the Hippocratic oath—that the purpose of medicine and drugs is to preserve life, not to speed the death of the patient. Justice Kennedy allowed that this venerable principle was "reasonable." Yet it was but "one reasonable understanding of medical practice."

Scalia was incredulous. *One* view among many? Three times in his dissent he insisted that the opinion of the attorney general, in rejecting use of drugs for assisted suicide, formed the "most natural interpretation." "Natural"? As in reflexes? No, because Janet Reno, as attorney general, had different reflexes. She had approved the use of drugs for assisted suicide. Scalia must have meant "natural" as *in accord with the laws of reason.*

With those laws of reason ever in him, he has never been detached from the natural law.

7. Karol Wojtyła, Bishop

BEVIL BRAMWELL, OMI

One book that I read each year is George Weigel's biography of Karol Wojtyła, *Witness to Hope*. A remarkable person—and the holy man who would become Blessed John Paul II—shines through the clear narrative, but also a remarkable bishop. Wojtyła became auxiliary bishop of Krakow in Poland (1958), archbishop of Krakow (1963), and then pope and bishop of Rome on October 16, 1978.

He was first a bishop under the cloud of the Communist oppression of his country. Yet in the midst of that vicious situation, he took the truth with him into everything. As Weigel puts it: "For him, the episcopate is preeminently an office of preaching and teaching." His episcopate is striking because he took the Incarnation so terribly seriously. The Word had to become flesh in every circumstance.

By long practice and with much effort Wojtyła integrated in himself and understood for himself his role in the intellectual and cultural life of the city of Krakow: "He was a Polish patriot in a city where the nation's history was enshrined in the cathedral church." He was a writer and he "was a priest and bishop in a city of great witnesses to the faith." He lived out the integration of Church and country and he understood it intellectually. He needed to embody that living integration for his people because, if he did not do it, then who would?

The Incarnation integrated God and human history. In Wojtyła, a human being lived out that integration in an exemplary way. He knew that he was successor to "great witnesses to the faith, [Saint] Stanisław; the model for his successors . . . . Piotr Skarga sixteenth century preacher of national renewal through spiritual renewal. . . . Adam Stephan Sapieha," his saintly predecessor. They all lived an integration of devotion to the saints and to the intellectual life. In Wojtyła the integration arose because of his spiritual discipline: "Wojtyła was a bishop who governed his diocese (and did his philosophy and theology) 'on his knees'—or at a desk in the sacramental presence of his Lord." And he managed to achieve all this in a diocese with 1.5 million Catholics.

Wojtyła kept in constant contact with the intellectual community with whom he could speak as an equal. He connected with the parishes, the university students, and the workers in the city. When the authorities would not allow a church to be built in the new town of Nova Huta, he began to celebrate Christmas Midnight Mass there each year. The authorities were ultimately worn down and the church was dedicated in 1977. He said at the opening Mass: "This is not a city of people who belong to no one, of people to whom one may do what one wants. This is a city of the children of God."

A stunning, perhaps even surprising perspective, but it shows his profound sense of the actual solidarity amongst the children of God even while they were embroiled in the hostile and brutally secular—I won't call it a culture—way of life contrived by the communists. Communist rule was one of divide and conquer. Instead, Wojtyła brought unity to diocesan life, the practical implementation of the Body of Christ. He lived it out himself and expressed it at every opportunity. His stance was rooted in the Church's dogma of the assumption of human nature by the Divine Son. And it was manifested at hundreds of Eucharists, Eucharistic processions, Opłatek celebrations at Christmas, and on and on.

Ironically, it helped that Wojtyła had lived through the horrendous Nazi occupation. He started early learning how to do his job no matter what. It's a lesson we need to learn here in America. Government interference in Church life and an aggressive secularism have rapidly increased in recent decades. But a courageous and complete response has yet to happen.

Wojtyła took part in every session of the Second Vatican

Council and not only made formidable contributions, but then made sure that his diocese studied and understood precisely what the Council had to say. During the Council he made several addresses by radio to Krakow. He also worked with Polish journalists, encouraging them to dig more deeply into truly understanding the Council, unlike their Western counterparts. Many of the study groups that he started still continue to this day. In Krakow, there was never the rupture and disorder after the Council which occurred in many parts of the world.

For the future Blessed John Paul, the Council was a "great gift to the Church, to all those who took part in it, to the entire human family." In Wojtyła there was no concession to the bland materialism and growing secularism that is drowning us in the West. The incarnate Word is the incarnate Word. A real bishop stands by that Word with no apologies. Wojtyła showed both that it can be done, even in unfavorable circumstances, and how to do it.

8. When Life Is Intolerable

DAMIANO RONDELLI, M.D.

As a teenager, I was fascinated by political campaigns. The most fun to watch on TV were the figures of the extreme right or left, who were always fighting. One of these was a member of the Italian Chamber of Deputies Lucio Magri. Magri founded the most popular Italian communist newspaper, *Il Manifesto*, and never gave up the communist label even when in 1991 the historic Partito Comunista Italiano (Italian communist party) dropped its name for more social-democratic harbors.

Lucio Magri's name dropped off my radar until a couple of months ago when national and international newspapers reported that, at seventy-nine, this gentleman went to Switzerland to commit—or assisted to commit—suicide.

Over decades, his ideals never seemed to flag, though Italian society had lived strongly rejected Communism. But idealism was not enough when he faced the most human cause of suffering.

Three years ago his beloved wife died of cancer. He could not tolerate this loss, and while still active and surrounded by friends and family, his life entered a dead end.

He asked for and obtained a doctor's permission to stop his pain by putting him asleep—forever. The reaction of friends and former opponents was regretful and sympathetic, and respectful of his record and bright intelligence, for which he was especially known.

But Magri's story is far from being an isolated case and the clinic near Zurich where he went is doing a brisk business. Moreover, on January 5, a U. K. Commission reported to Parliament that assisted suicide should be legal for terminal patients with less than a year to live.

In my medical practice, I'm sometimes the one to whom cancer patients, who have exhausted the therapeutic options, or their families, ask for a last possible last cure that does not yet exist. I feel great frustration, but offer my time and compassion, and volunteer to be with them and help them in living through their remaining time.

They care about having someone with them. This time is, for patient and family or close friends, a supreme experience of love.

Lucio Magri wrote in his last letter that life was no longer tolerable. Suffering becomes the mirror from which our naked humanity cannot hide. In that mirror, the mystery of a whole life is seen and suddenly reveals the urgency of some greater meaning, of an answer that has to be reasonable and at the same time cannot leave anything or anyone out.

When this meaning is not found, someone who refuses the superficiality of our society may indeed come to think life intolerable. From experience, I know that it is not for me or anyone else to judge patients who succumb to disease or families left with painful scars due to the loss of a beloved member. God will know all, including second thoughts and requests hidden from us, to weigh what is returned to Him, even in the desperate act of one who voluntarily enters a hospital with a one-way ticket.

I find it deeply wrong, however, for a physician who has committed his life to help improve or prolong the lives of patients to turn to an extreme pain-killer such as assisted suicide. It might seem an act of help, or even love, for a doctor unable to treat breath-taking pain with any medical procedure. But it is not.

To me, the problem is the same, both for Lucio Magri, who ran out of reasons to go on, and for his doctor, who ran out of reasons to oppose to his patient's will—and even helped him to die. I imagine Magri living his last period of life going to the Parliament, writing his last book on the history of communism (*The Tailor of Ulm*), entertaining his friends and young granddaughter in his apartment in the heart of Rome, but always with a living memory of his wife and what she meant for him.

That memory definitely prevailed over his long-time ideals and hopes for social justice. His wife had really become a significant other: so significant as to make him decide to forfeit his life, so other that he was lost in remembrance.

Is the hardest physical or psychological pain, when it is resistant to medical intervention, ultimately a good reason for a physician to help someone commit suicide? Isn't that life already "finished"? Don't I know that nothing else can be done?

This is where assisted suicide and euthanasia (from Greek: *euthanos*, good death) are seen as merciful human acts. But would terminating someone's miserable life make me feel better? Absolutely not. In my experience, the mystery of suffering ("Doctor, why me?") relates to something beyond my medical authority.

It is a living memory that calls forth our acts, regardless of intellectual theories or politically correct public statements. It was a living memory of a real person that led Lucio Magri to his decision. It is a living memory that guides me when I face unfixable or intolerable medical circumstances.

Christ is a living memory, based on stories, challenges, and people that directly changed and keep changing our lives. Euthanasia or assisted suicide cut the thread of living memory when happiness seems to have disappeared due to illnesses, intolerable events, multiple hopeless failures, or any other disastrous scenario that you may imagine.

But that thread was known to Christ. And He took it, lived it fully, and transformed it. He then returned it to us, not with less pain, but with an extension of meaning and hope, here and now.

Lucio Magri planned everything for his last trip. He was buried close to his wife in a small cemetery in Central Italy. He chose Mozart's Requiem for a very private ceremony. I am not sure why but like to think that he was still listening to a few lines of the *Recordare*: "Seeking me thou didst sit down weary, thou didst redeem me, suffering death on the cross. Let not such toil be in vain."

9. William F. Buckley against the World

JEREMY LOTT

After the walloping Republicans took in the 2012 elections, my first printable thought was, "Man, where is William F. Buckley when you need him?" The likely answer to that question is "in Heaven" or at least well on his way through Purgatory.

If he were still with us, he would turn eighty-seven today.

In life, Buckley's political adversaries regularly slandered the man about as readily as they use his name now to bash conservatives. (Sample title, from just this week in the Politico newspaper: "Conservatives at a Crossroads: Harold Hill vs. William F. Buckley.") Yet to those people who knew him, Buckley's work on behalf of countless others added up to a kind of rough and tumble, vulgar saintliness.

We could use his wit and his perspective now. With the founding of several organizations and campaigns and the magazine *National Review*, Bill Buckley did more to create the conservative movement than any other man. Without Buckley, it's hard to conceive of a Goldwater campaign, a Reagan presidency, a Giuliani mayoralty, or many other historical benchmarks that proved there was a real alternative to liberalism.

There were conservative currents in America before Buckley. Starting with the publication of his breakout book *God and Man at Yale*, Buckley's vision turned about half the country into Conservative America. Conservatives shared a suspicion of elite opinion and a faith in America's founding that could rival the twentieth century's default progressive politics.

Even for those of us who are not movementarians (as I am not, for Marxian reasons—Groucho, that is), his was an achievement worth toasting. American conservatives, radically different fish from their continental European counterparts, insisted that certain hard truths need be proclaimed loudly.

These conservative truths were: 1) that the Soviet Union was monstrous and aggressive; 2) that the United States was heroic to oppose the spread of world Communism; 3) that government is necessary but dangerous; 4) that peaceful exchanges of goods—markets—make us better off and this result ought to be celebrated, not deplored; 5) that Original Sin is the only empirically verifiable dogma; and, latterly, 6) that we ought to follow "the heresy of your own eyes," as Tom Wolfe has rightly called it, and ban the organized barbarity that is abortion-on-demand.

If most of those truths sound consistent with Catholic teaching, this is no accident. An interviewer for *Playboy* once asked him how he could be so sure that his deepest convictions would stand the test of time. Buckley replied by simply quoting the book of Job: "I know that my Redeemer liveth."

He was both small c and large C Catholic. He did not think it absolutely necessary for one to believe in God to be a conservative, but it sure helped. Outright mockers of religion were effectively excommunicating themselves from his movement. Occasionally, he added a good shove.

Great political conflicts, Buckley argued in his bestselling first book, are really spiritual conflicts. "I believe the duel between Christianity and atheism"—opposites manifest in the free West and the Soviet bloc—"is the most important in the world. I further believe that the struggle between individualism and collectivism is the same struggle reproduced on another level."

Liberal Catholic anti-Communist critics got after Buckley for his likening of the struggle against an obvious menace to the less obvious one of liberal improvements. He later confessed it was not his idea at the first. Buckley wrote that his Yale mentor, Willmoore Kendall, "was responsible for the provocative arrangement of a pair of sentences that got me into more trouble than any others in the book." Yet it was his call to run and take abuse for those words, because he saw in them a truth worth defending.

In hindsight, Buckley looks simply way ahead of the curve. As we have seen most recently with Obamacare's HHS mandate and European courts' assault on Jewish ritual through banning circumcision, progressive polities prove ultimately quite intolerant of religious difference. They might not pound their shoes on the table and threaten to bury those of us who are religious dissidents, but sometimes it sure feels that way.

It would be good to have Buckley back with us now because of his accumulated wisdom that political change is a long struggle with brutal, heartbreaking setbacks. The Goldwater campaign lost in a Camelot-fueled landslide, but Reagan eventually took the White House. Buckley's mayoral candidacy for New York City didn't even manage to keep Rockefeller Republican John Lindsay from being elected, yet notice that Rockefeller Republicans are pretty scarce on the ground these days.

The chief lesson of Buckley's life—if we are to reduce it to that—is that one ought to stand up and tell the truth with as much intelligence, wit and passion as he can muster. Eventually, somebody will have to listen.

10. Marie Dolan, Guerrilla Catholic

KRISTINA JOHANNES

When someone we love dies, we find comfort in talking about events in their lives with other friends and relatives who knew and cherished them. I've discovered lately that when a loved one's memory dies, you can find comfort in relating those events to the very person who enjoys hearing about exploits she can no longer remember.

The stroke that robbed my mother of her memory has not totally altered the personality that made her the great lioness of the Faith that I remember. In another column, I shared her role in founding CREDO, but her involvement in that apostolate was not the sum total of her courageous efforts to defend the faith.

She had a personal apostolate as well which, to my mind at least, made her deserving of the title "Scourge of Heretics." She attended daily Mass from the age of twelve on, so she was well fortified in this undertaking.

The campaign she waged was relentless. It involved attending "Catholic" lectures around town, where known dissenters were to appear, and then challenging them with the truth of the Faith in the question-and-answer period. She was strong yet civil, always making her point in the form of a question in order to present the Church's teaching on whatever topic the speaker had just tried to undermine.

But she was not shy. If the speaker avoided recognizing her raised hand she would ask her question anyway, whenever the opportunity arose.

Although she hoped to enlighten the speaker, she soon realized that her target audience was more likely members of the audience who might be uneasy about what they had heard—but weren't sure why. She hoped her intervention would reaffirm such persons in the faith.

To her, even one person thus informed was enough to warrant these frequent jaunts, and quite often at least one such person would approach her at the end of the lecture, thanking her for what she had said. This added fuel to the fiery passion of her faith.

At first she and my father were collaborators in the effort. But he soon departed the campaign, quoting St. John according to Polycarp: "Let us flee lest the room should fall in, for Cerinthus, the enemy of the truth, is within." Having heard the stories, though, I'm sure it was rather a fear of coming to blows, such was the anger these "Catholic" speakers aroused in him.

My mother, however, soldiered on, simply finding willing friends to accompany her. Brave friends, I might add, because as time wore on, she became a known entity and efforts were made to head her off at the pass. She was resilient and resourceful and more than once scribbled her name on the sign-in sheet so that it was illegible.

At one particular talk, she was recognized and the "bouncer" tried to keep her from entering the hall by telling her that she was not a parishioner and therefore not allowed to attend. The brave friend who accompanied her that evening was a parishioner and informed the woman that my mother was her invited guest. The two of them passed unhindered.

Returning home from these events, she would tell my father about everything objectionable that the speaker had said. In response, my father would yell at the speaker through my mother, often starting the argument with, "Doesn't that jackass know. . .", and then quoting the applicable doctrine, pope, church father, or saint. She would excitedly reply, telling him the points she had previously presented in her dogged but ladylike duel with the dissenter. It was fascinating to listen in—and impossible not to—owing to the decibel level these "debriefing" sessions reached.

As a young adult, I knew more about my faith than many of my friends, who wondered how I had accumulated the knowledge. "Applied apologetics" was my response. I heard so many of these conversations between my parents that I am certain every major Church doctrine was covered in depth at one time or another.

I've always thought fondly of my mother as a "guerrilla Catholic." And I'm grateful that in addition to her efforts to defend the Church, she also passed the flame of faith to her daughters. But the staid catechetical lessons she and my father dutifully arranged could not hold a candle to those late night, wild and woolly apologetic sessions they unwittingly held for us.

These have been perilous times for the faith and at an important time in their children's lives her generation was suddenly deprived of the trustworthy assistance they had been heretofore receiving from the local church in educating them in the faith.

I find myself praying these days that the sacrifices of my parents and many more of their generation may serve as an offering for the salvation of the many children and grandchildren whose faith patrimony was squandered by the revolt of the scholars.

11. Fathers and Sons

Brad Miner

I'm a member of St. Joseph's Parish in a suburban community in New York. We have a lovely church with several thousand parishioners, which is why we have six resident priests, a deacon, and seven Sunday Masses, at least four of which are often SRO.

There is a statue of St. Joseph behind the altar. He holds the infant Jesus—in this depiction, the Savior is about six-to-ten-months-old. And the apse is filled with angels, because as our pastor told me: "I love angels."

Angels played an important role in the life of Joseph. They were the link between his previously quotidian existence and the miracles to come. When he discovered that his teenage soon-to-be wife was pregnant, "he had in mind to divorce her quietly." (This, of course, goes to the heart of the Church's teaching on divorce, since the situation Joseph thought he was in is the only one Jesus would later allow as grounds for a divorce: adultery committed during a betrothal.) But an angel gave Joseph understanding, as Matthew explains: "Son of David, do not be afraid to take Mary home as your wife, because what is conceived in her is from the Holy Spirit. . . ."

And twice more an angel would speak to Joseph.

The second and third times had to do with Herod: flee to Egypt; return to Israel. Knowing by then not to doubt these messengers, Joseph first saves the savior from Herod's swords, and then, upon the tyrant's death, returns Jesus to the nation through which salvation will come to the world.

During the great eras of Christian painting, which for 1500 years meant Roman Catholic or Orthodox art, depictions of Saint Joseph—often with the infant or boy Jesus and in portraits of the Holy Family—were among the most common motifs in sacred art. (A few of my favorites illustrate this column: by Guido Reni, John Everett Millais, and Georges de la Tour.)

Joseph is often portrayed as white-haired and elderly, especially when we see him at work as a carpenter (the Millais is an exception: Joseph is bald with dark, dangling payos). In pictures of the Nativity his hair may be black, but the age difference between him and Mary is usually evident and pronounced.

One thing that until recently never registered with me about Joseph is his silence. He plays such a significant role in God's drama, yet he has no lines—not in Scripture anyway. We hear from Christ's mother, his aunt, uncle, and cousin, but never from his earthly father. As Pope Francis put it in his homily upon receiving the pallium and the Fisherman's Ring, Joseph is (as all fathers must be) a protector:

> How does Joseph exercise his role as protector? Discreetly, humbly and silently, but with an unfailing presence and utter fidelity, even when he finds it hard to understand. . . . As the spouse of Mary, he is at her side in good times and bad, on the journey to Bethlehem for the census and in the anxious and joyful hours when she gave birth; amid the drama of the flight into Egypt and during the frantic search for their child in the Temple; and later in the day-to-day life of the home of Nazareth, in the workshop where he taught his trade to Jesus.

Every father—especially so the father of sons—learns that there are times when simply being there—cheering, explaining, scolding, but often silent—is at least half the job.

In the New York City playground where my sons cavorted as tots, they would often stop in the middle of frolicking and run to me. They would touch my hand or lean against me breathless before running back to whatever game engrossed them. It was if I were a battery charging station—but not a boost to their energy, which was boundless, but to top-off their souls. *Daddy's here; we're safe.*

Compared to Joseph, Mary, and Jesus, my wife and I and our sons (now grown men) have lived like aristocrats. When His parents presented Jesus to the temple, their offering was not a lamb but a couple of birds—a poor folks' sacrifice. When we presented our younger son to the temple of higher education, we laid out six figures. But I think the boys know their principal education—courtesy of the parents—was gratis, as love always is.

My sons touch base less often now, but that's the way of the world, isn't it? They have grown strong.

At the end of his inaugural homily (celebrated simply as the Feast of St. Joseph), Pope Francis said:

> Here I would add one more thing: caring, protecting, demands goodness, it calls for a certain tenderness. In the Gospels, Saint Joseph appears as a strong and courageous man, a working man, yet in his heart we see great tenderness, which is not the virtue of the weak but rather a sign of strength of spirit and a capacity for concern, for compassion, for genuine openness to others, for love. We must not be afraid of goodness, of tenderness!

I've never been able to grasp why some fathers are abusive towards or competitive with their sons.

And we recall that, despite his humble estate, Joseph was of royal lineage, descended as he was from King David, himself a humble shepherd. There is in this something of what C. S. Lewis was getting at in *The Chronicles of Narnia*, namely that each of us, no matter how humble (and we are dust after all), is offered a crown if we follow Christ, which we do when we are strong in love.

12. The Importance of Vocation

ANDREAS WIDMER

When I entered the Swiss Guards, I was twenty years old and, like my fellow guards, in peak physical condition. But as fit and energetic as we were, John Paul II could still run rings around us.

That running began before 6:00 every morning when he would rise, pray, dress for the day, then head to his private chapel for more time in prayer. At 7:00 a.m., small groups of visiting dignitaries, Catholic pilgrims, or Vatican staff would join him for Mass. After Mass, guests joined him for breakfast. An hour or two of office work followed. Before greeting official visitors at 11:00, he would meet briefly with linguists to review the finer points of whatever language he would be using to speak to the visiting crowds or dignitaries. Then the audiences began.

Sometimes he spoke to thousands, sometimes only a select few; yet these audiences lasted until one or two in the afternoon. Then it was on to lunch, where various Vatican staff joined him, followed by more time for prayer, with John Paul II often heading to the rooftop gardens of the Papal Palace to walk and talk with God.

After that there was more office work and more audiences, lasting right up until dinner at 8:00 p.m. when guests often dined with him. After the meal ended he would return to reading and writing and working well into the night. Sleep came around midnight or even later. Somewhere in all that, he also found time to ask a Swiss Guard about his day, chat with the sisters who cooked for him, and keep up with old friends.

That was just his Rome schedule. Compared to his schedule while traveling, it was comparatively light. I have often tried to remember times I saw that schedule taking a toll on the pope. I couldn't. I recalled plenty of occasions when I was worn out with exhaustion. Not once do I recall him being bleary-eyed. In fact, it was just the opposite. The reason he could do that, joyfully and unfailingly, was because he knew what God had made him to do. He knew his vocation.

The term "vocation" means much more than the standard dictionary definition of "a career path or line of work." It is more of a "calling" than a "job." According to John Paul II, your vocation answers the question, "Why am I alive?" Moreover, he believed, only when you're living out your vocation can you find fulfillment in this life. Your vocation, understood, embraced, and lived, is what makes you feel truly and fully alive.

There are three different levels of vocations.

The first of these three is the universal vocation. It doesn't matter who you are or where or when you live, you have the same universal vocation as every other human being on the planet: To know, love, and serve God in this life so that you can know, love, and serve him eternally in the next life. Your objective is to receive grace now so that you can receive glory later, or even more simply put, to cooperate with God in his work to save your soul.

After the universal vocation, it starts to get more specific. How we live it, the way of life in which we love and serve God and others, is our primary vocation. According to the Catholic Church, there are three primary vocations: married life, the priesthood, and consecrated life (brothers or sisters living in community and consecrated singles living in society at large).

Each of these vocations is a permanent and freely chosen way of life. Each also entails a gift of self. In choosing a primary vocation, you make your inalienable and non-transferable "I" someone else's property. In other words, you give priority in your life either to God and the consecrated life or to your spouse and family.

Our modern notions of freedom can confuse us about the value of this kind of vocation. So often, we see the type of limitations to our freedom that a permanent commitment brings as impediments to "being who we are." But real freedom isn't freedom from outside restrictions. Real freedom is the freedom to love and give ourselves fully. Freedom in fact exists for the sake of love. It is the means to the end we all desire - loving communion with God and others. It is when we give ourselves most fully that we're truly free.

The third level of vocation, your secondary vocation, is what you do on that path. It's how you use your gifts and talents in service of God and others while living out your universal and primary vocations. For most of us, this means our work or profession. It also, however, can apply to your civic and community involvement, apostolate work, or simply bearing the various crosses and trials that come your way in life. It's your plan of action for living.

John Paul II realized that through our work we don't simply make more: We become more. Work shapes us, refines us, and pushes us to discover and hone our natural gifts. It enables us to love, becoming a means by which we're able to serve our family, customers, clients, neighbors, and communities. Through that, work becomes a means of giving our life to God.

When you understand all three levels of vocation and the place each one holds in the hierarchy of importance, it becomes much easier to order your life and your priorities, pursuing the virtues you most need, and balancing competing roles without compromise.

John Paul II was living proof of that. All work, not only that of priests and religious, can be holy when done as an act of love, service, and sacrifice according to the mind God. That's what the Incarnation made possible. That's why St. Thomas Aquinas could say with such confidence, "There can be no joy in living without joy in work."

APPENDIX: IN MEMORIAM

Richard John Neuhaus

On January 8, 2009, Father Richard John Neuhaus, a great American and Catholic, passed into the eternal hands of the Father he served so long and so well. He was not only a singular man and thinker, but a personal friend of almost all the writers for **The Catholic Thing**, *most of whom also often write for* **First Things**, *the splendid journal he founded and edited for many years. The good padre was also a friend to our efforts on this site, which he immediately welcomed with generosity when we set out in mid–2008. We thought it only fitting for several of us to set down some brief personal reminiscences, and to give you one long reflection by Hadley Arkes at the end of the queue, on a man who was even greater than his work.*

A More Excellent Way, Robert Royal

Someone once said to me of a forceful person we both knew that he came on strong and stayed strong. That about sums up the Fr. Neuhaus I first got to know in the early 1980s when he was still a Lutheran pastor and serving on the board of a think tank where I worked for almost twenty years. That perfectly pitched and paced baritone, and the even authoritative manner, might put you off—at first—because you'd never heard or seen anything like it. But once he worked the magic on you, you never got tired hearing him exhort an audience to fulfill our secular duty "to deliberate how we should order our lives together" or his various ways of building an argument towards St. Paul's, "But I shall show you a still more excellent way." Many people have been called born preachers. Richard John Neuhaus redefined the category.

His books on death and Good Friday show a side of him that those who only knew him as a courageous public voice might not have suspected. When he decided to become a Catholic, I sent him a letter commending his public calm and dignity in difficult circumstances, and his touching respect towards his longstanding Lutheran friends, some of whom were—to say the least—upset. He wrote back to say thanks, but also that, although he knew it was the right thing, he had never felt more that he was taking a step into the unknown. Still, at his ordination as a Catholic priest, I remember Cardinal O'Connor humorously reminded him several times that he (Fr. Neuhaus) was becoming a priest, but he (Cardinal O'Connor) would remain in charge as Cardinal Archbishop of New York. When he was settled as a Catholic, I once or twice kidded Fr. Neuhaus that people were saying he was the most important convert since John Henry Newman. Of course, Chesterton and many others who have appeared since the great English Cardinal make any such claim a tough call, but we'd both chuckle about it, and I was never quite sure I was entirely joking.

He did have a few limitations. As a Canadian, he had only a weak hold on the fact that there is a National and an American League in baseball, and that grave moral questions hang on the distinction. His political judgments were so clear as to be almost clairvoyant, with one notable exception. We were staying in the same hotel in Havana during the pope's visit in 1998 when the Monica Lewinsky scandal broke and he confidently instructed several of us to note the date of Clinton's demise in our journals— but who in those days truly knew the dark arts of the Comeback Kid? Other than that, he pretty much saw where things were going, but all evidence to the contrary, he could never give up on his firm belief that in publishing magazines, organizing seminars, and entering into debates we were actually doing for our time what the medieval universities did in theirs.

I was saying Morning Prayer after the news of Richard John Neuhaus' death and came upon this Latin line from Jeremiah in the canticle, which describes what will happen when the Israelites finally return from captivity: *Et inebriabo animam sacerdotum piguedine,* "And I will feast the souls of the priests with abundance." We may have a reasoned hope, as he used to say, that Fr. Richard John Neuhaus is indeed now enjoying that feast.

Random Memories of Richard, Ralph McInerny

When Father Neuhaus was preparing for ordination he was tutored by Avery Dulles. Surely these were two of the most formidable Catholic converts of recent times. I first met them in Hartford at a conference meant to show that political differences did not affect the common faith of Christians. A statement was issued. Richard liked statements. At the meeting there was a hybrid liturgy on a Saturday. I asked a theologian if he thought it fulfilled one's Sunday obligation. A waffling response. I asked Avery Dulles. He thought a bit, then said, "I'd go to Mass if I were you."

At the Second Extraordinary Synod of 1985, Richard and I were there as journalists. The *Sala di prensa* provided lush inspiration for future fiction. Once, standing in the Via della Conciliazione, Richard said, apropos of I don't remember what, "Of course the pope is the head of the Church." He was still a Lutheran then—Richard, not the pope—and I thought his conversion was inevitable.

It took me a while to appreciate the capaciousness of his mind. Once in Claremont, he gave a talk on Richard Rorty that was one of the best analyses I ever heard. And who can forget his chairing of those seminars at the Union League Club with the portrait of U. S. Grant on the wall behind? He made one believe that "dialogue" could signify a worthwhile activity. I was privileged to be at his ordination and his first Mass. I gave him as a gift St.

Thomas's commentaries on all the epistles of Paul. Only afterward did I wonder if he read Latin. No matter. Now he has gone to the source. *Requiescat in pace.*

Lunches with Richard, Brad Miner

I first met Fr. Neuhaus in 1989 shortly after I became literary editor at *National Review*, where he was religion editor. Over lunch we talked about a lot of things, and he was especially interested in the story of my conversion to Catholicism. He was still Pastor Neuhaus then, a Lutheran, although it wasn't long after that when he made his transit to Rome. We also talked about his break with the Rockford Institute and about the difficulty of charting a Christian course through choppy political seas.

Jump ahead to 2006 when we broke bread another time, in this case so I could interview him for a book I was writing—specifically, about the torpedoes fired at him by those who claimed his position about the political context of the abortion question made him a revolutionary theocrat. What struck me about him then—as it had nearly twenty years earlier (and was the refutation of the hot-headed charges against him and *First Things*)—was his temperance. This man about whom intemperate words were written was still steering true.

Now he has sailed into port.

A Brother Dies, Michael Novak

It has been a very long time (if ever) since any American Catholic priest had as much influence in the Vatican, in the highest reaches of American life, on the intellectual culture of Christianity here and abroad, on Christian-Jewish conversations of the deepest and warmest sort, on the relations of Evangelicals and Catholics in this land, and on the intellectual life of his beloved New York City, as Father Richard John Neuhaus.

Friends teased him that Martin Luther nailed a mere ninety-five theses in one manifesto on a church door in Wittenburg, whereas Father Richard helped draft not quite as many whole manifestos for different social necessities—on the non-negotiables of Christian Faith, on what was morally wrong with the conduct of the war in Vietnam, on ecumenical study and conversation, on Evangelical-Catholic cooperation, on abortion and other pro-life issues, and so forth.

Brought up as the son of a Lutheran pastor, the younger Neuhaus was nourished from his seminary days by the community of those Lutherans who hold that the aim of Luther was to bring the Catholic Church back to fidelity to its origins, and to contribute themselves to a much-desired reunion of the two separated communities. Painfully, the younger Pastor Neuhaus came to judge that nowadays the Catholic Church was ever more serious about such self-reform, just as a wide body of Lutherans was drifting toward not concretely wanting such unity, in any case not soon. He felt obliged to follow his vocation to join the Catholic Church, not as a conversion, but as a public declaration of what he had always believed. He did so despite a certain cultural resistance from others, even in his new communion.

Father Neuhaus was the most consequential American Christian since Reinhold Niebuhr. He was the most consequential American Catholic since John Courtney Murray, S.J., and Archbishop Fulton J. Sheen. He was a worthy successor in a long chain of great witnesses.

"Everything is Ready Now," Austin Ruse

Some years ago I got into the habit of sometimes taking one of Father Neuhaus's books with me when I would travel to Europe. I have countless times sat in some Roman, Parisian, or Viennese cafe reading or re-reading Neuhaus and simply marveling at his mind and his ability to express himself. I have been moved many times to drop by a nearby church to light a candle for him, and to pray God to grant him a long life. Every time I did, I would send him a postcard to let him know. Though he obviously wrote fast, I would ask him to write faster because I wanted more.

I loved this man. He changed my life, though I only met him a handful of times and spoke to him over the phone a few times more. He knew my work. He mentioned it a few times in *First*

Things and from time to time he would send a check to support my work. I must admit I liked it the most when he was giving it to the Catholic Left, always with good humor, always winsomely (did he teach us that word?). During the Long Lent, which he named so well, he served the Church profoundly, in his unique way, by distilling the issue beautifully. He growled in that warm fire of a voice, "Fidelity, fidelity, fidelity" and let everyone know that the homosexual abuse problem sprang from the culture of disobedience that had grown up in recent decades and there was only one way out of it, which was faithfulness to the teachings of the Church.

Perhaps his most important work, though, was bringing Catholics and Evangelicals together, a long-time project he shared with his friend Charles Colson. The fight for the unborn and the family has brought Catholics and Evangelicals together, and while God wants abortion to end and He wants marriage restored, more than anything He wants His children as one and with Him in Heaven. At no time since the Reformation have Catholics and Protestants been closer than we are now, and this is due in no small measure to Father Neuhaus.

I sat in a Roman park last summer reading his book about dying. I had never read it. I was struck by the scene in his hospital room where he was visited by two "presences" who said to him only this: "Everything is ready now." Neuhaus said he understood this as an invitation to come with them and by saying yes he would have died. He chose to stay. It so happened that I had just read the passage in St. Luke's Gospel about a certain man who hosted a great supper and told his servant to invite everyone and tell them "everything is ready now." One assumes that those who turned down the invitation were in trouble. So, I was stunned when I read these two passages together. Had Neuhaus turned down the invitation? I emailed Neuhaus and asked if this worried him. He said he had not thought about it. But I suspect that he had and I wish I knew what he thought. Neuhaus thought about everything and beautifully.

Yesterday morning the Heavenly "presences" returned and

this time Father Neuhaus said "yes, take me to the supper" and he will be sorely missed by all of us who have loved him.

Faithful and Extraordinary, Mary Eberstadt

Unlike fellow writers for *The Catholic Thing*, I never knew Fr. Neuhaus personally. We shook hands once, quickly, at a noisy cocktail party a few years back. Nothing more than a smile and nod and an e-mail or two ever passed between us. It didn't matter. We were friends nonetheless, and whether he knew it or not, just as he was to so many thousands of others: by virtue of his faithful and extraordinary literary company.

About the Maker he served with such gifts, Fr. Neuhaus presumably knows more now than any of us do. About his personal mark in the world, the eulogies to come will tell us more. But about his public legacy—all those writings that have comforted, cheered, and emboldened the rest of us—this single unknown friend knows one thing. His Catholic mark will outlast all the personal memories. It will outlast all of us reading these notes. A hundred years from now, Fr. Neuhaus will still be making and teaching friends among people who never knew him, or needed to. His true and brilliant prose will be all they need, just as it's been more than enough for the rest of us, too.

A Tug on a Line, William Saunders

In the first issue of *First Things*, in the very first of Father Neuhaus's "Public Square" columns was a reference to the Eucharist that, like Father Brown's hook on the invisible line, caught in my religious imagination and stayed there until, several years later, I came into full communion with the Roman Catholic Church. My ultimate decision was due in no small part to Neuhaus's own conversion and the reasons for it he sent in a brief note to all who asked. One of the great privileges of my life was to get to know Father Neuhaus and to collaborate with him on several projects. One of his greatest projects was "Evangelicals and Catholics Together," which he started with Chuck Colson. This is, in my judgment, the most important development in

American politics in the past fifty years, and as a Catholic working at the evangelical Family Research Council, I have been proud to participate in it. American political life, American religious life, and American intellectual life are immeasurably diminished by his passing.

Eloquentia Perfecta, James Schall, S.J.

Jesuits in the old days were said to educate for a goal known as *eloquentia perfecta*. Fr. Neuhaus, untouched by anything Jesuit, possessed this perfect eloquence. He knew, moreover, that eloquence was useless if not based on truth. What always struck me about Fr. Neuhaus was his voice, his words. He could move souls. He could explain things even to intellectuals. Not only could he explain in his speech, he did so in almost every conceivable forum, print, radio, television. His voice was always the one that said what needed to be said, what was true to say, yet with a wit that made it seem—what? Well, obvious.

In the Shadow of Great Men, Michael Uhlmann

One would be hard-pressed to name anyone during the past thirty years who had a deeper or more lasting influence on our nation's cultural life than Richard John Neuhaus. His only real competitor in that sense was Bill Buckley, who worked somewhat different, if allied, precincts of a more overtly political sort. They are both gone now, and the void they left behind reminds us that we are but Lilliputians laboring in the shadows cast by great men.

Richard's mind was learned, deep, and subtle, an organ of multiple registers that could alternately inform and entertain an audience, rally the faithful to a cause, or, as occasion might require, gain the attention of the heavenly host. He was a superb preacher (even when he wasn't formally preaching) and a writer of surpassing power and eloquence. How many millions of words he poured out, I do not know; but essays he wrote twenty-five or thirty years ago seem as fresh today as when first beheld. He not only left his mark; he will continue to do so, on our hearts no less powerfully than on our minds.

The suddenness of his passing compounds our sense of loss. It was only yesterday, was it not, that he sat right there, at the end of the table, orchestrating the talk, brandies, and the cigars, as only he could over the course of a long evening. To think that we shall not be graced by that warm and vigorous presence again reminds us of how weary and stale the world would have been without him—and of how lonely we shall be.

It is altogether fitting that his death should have come so soon after that of his great, good friend Avery Cardinal Dulles. One suspects that more wisdom was shared in their random private conversations than most of us would likely encounter, working full time, over the course of three or four lifetimes. In the midst of our present sadness, we can take great joy in the knowledge that the two are together again, taking up where they left off and—let us pray—shining a light so that we who are left behind can find our way.

Memories through the Sadness, Hadley Arkes

Only one week into the New Year, Fr. Richard Neuhaus has succumbed to the cancer that struck him hard as we neared Christmas. For his friends this is the kind of loss that tilts the world on its axis; for so many things marking the world around just cannot be the same. How could it be that we'll never have those evenings again in the townhouse in New York with the wine and cigars, and Richard presiding with gravitas and brotherly affection? It has become a cliché, but in this case it hits with a sad, jolting force: His loss just creates a void in the world; how could anyone fill it?

Somewhere in the 1990s, after one of our legendary Ramsay Colloquia, when we were having drinks before dinner, David Novak waxed nostalgic about the years we had all been together. He remarked to Richard that he could take a satisfaction in this "family" he had woven together. The center of it all was the Institute for Religion and Public Life, the institution that sprang from the genius and love of Richard Neuhaus. The remarkable thing was indeed that "family" woven together, drawn from the various religious strands: Catholics, Protestants, Mormons, Jews, with so many variants, and yet all standing against the currents of relativism; all persuaded that there were truths of revelation and reason to declare, and in that sense, standing together against the currents of our own age.

We've heard of that formula before, cast as an aspiration. But Richard actually made it work: He brought together, in some cases, people who would not ordinarily agree to be in the same room with one another. He would bring together the late Christopher Lasch or Stanley Hauerwas with Jean Elshtain, George Weigel, Michael Novak, Robert Wilken, Robert Jenson, Robert George. He would bring in the lawyers on opposite sides of the argument over religious "establishment" and the question of driving religion from the public square. He would bring in Henry Kissinger. For he moved in heady circles in New York; he was respected in circles literary and religious, and people would come when he invited them. And what they found, when they came, was a conversation that was penetrating, serious, theologically informed, philosophically demanding—but civil through and through. No venom, no unbridled attacks. There was a tendering of respect that counseled restraint and kindness even as it enjoined us not to hold back from asking the question that pierced to the core of someone's argument—or his claim to standing in the world of letters.

In my own case, the invitation to join the discussion came in the fall of 1987. Thomas Derr, at Smith College, gave Richard a copy of the book that became my own signature tune, *First Things*. That title would become the source of ribbing that would go on, even as late as a few weeks ago, because Richard borrowed the title and the font for a new journal that we would all make our own. But of course, in taking the name for the journal, he gave that title "First Things" an enduring resonance in our public life that my own book would not have produced.

At the twentieth anniversary of Richard's own signature work, I imagined us, thirty years hence, settled in homes for the aged, and celebrating that important journal, *The Naked Public*

Square. We thanked Richard for his large nature in letting us make use of that title for a new journal. I came into a group that included Ralph McInerny, Marvin Fox, David Novak, Fr. Ernest Fortin. (I recall us going around the table, with people introducing themselves: Ralph introduced himself as "a peeping Thomist from Notre Dame," and Ernie remarked, "I was a Thomist—when I was a teenager.") In any case the chemistry was magnificently right, and I was invited back again, and again, until it became clear, as David Novak recognized one day, we really had been woven together as something close to a family.

If we had to condense the account of the experience, it would run roughly in this way: No one would get away with arguments that were just not good enough, just not up to the standard. But the corrections would come in a jesting, loving way from friends who knew you shared the sense that you could do better. At the same time, nothing was ever lost or forgotten. I recall Bob Jenson ("Jens"), in the midst of a discussion, suddenly pointing out that people were backing into an argument I had sought to press on the group three years earlier. That was a measure of how closely people listened, and how arguments, seriously framed, could linger as we kept weighing them. I had never seen anything like this seminar, even in my days at the University of Chicago, and I've seen nothing like it since.

With the demise of the journal *This World*, Richard launched *First Things*, and we all signed on. We worried initially as to whether we could actually generate enough material to sustain a serious—and I mean serious—journal touching theology, law, and political philosophy. The results speak for themselves. Richard's own writing and editing attracted other writing trying to meet that standard. We discovered that there were even more talents, more possibilities out there than we had imagined. In other words, Richard built it, and they came.

I think the word came to us from Ralph McInerny, the first word, discreetly conveyed, that Richard was on the path of leaving the Lutheran Church and moving to Rome. That could not be a complete surprise. Not at least for anyone who had kept up with his writing and his involvement in the project of bringing Protestants and Catholics together. So much of this was figured in his book, *The Catholic Moment*—the dynamism had clearly shifted to the Church under the leadership of John Paul II. The main axes, the main questions were defined still, defined ever, by Rome. Richard was off to Rome on different embassies, and so the step, when it finally came, was a short step.

But before there had been any announcement, and while the benign gossip had been making its way within "the family," I phoned: "Richard, I just wanted to tell you that I've heard the news, or I've heard versions of it, and I want to be among the first to congratulate you. For the word is that you are about to join the Lubovachers." He said, "Hadley, I'll never forget this conversation." About a year or so later, we were gathered at the seminary at Dunwoodie for his ordination, and Cardinal O'Connor, with his characteristic humor, said, "Richard, you don't deserve this . . . any more than I deserve the honor of being here, ministering to you." Richard was just lit up that afternoon, with a freshness and sparkle rare even for him, as we all gathered in the garden after the ceremony. I noted again "the family" gathered around— George Weigel, Bob Royal, David Novak, Midge Decter, Norman Podhoretz.

And I couldn't help wondering what Cardinal O'Connor would make of it all: Who was this man, with so wide a reach, bringing in with him this contingent so varied that it included Jews? He would offer his prayers to the God of Abraham, Isaac, and Jacob; it was the Catholicism of John Paul II, which incorporated the Jewish tradition. Were the Jews on the way to Rome? Or was it that Rome had brought the Jewish ethic to the rest of the world? As one friend put it, when you're Catholic, you are at least Jewish. And that sense of things, nurtured by Richard, has marked the cast in which I too would find myself moving.

With the journal *First Things*, the testimony came in from every quarter: people read the back of the magazine first. They began with Richard's "Public Square," and "While We're At It." Just a few years ago he was doing an extended essay on his readings over the summer, including a biography of Benjamin Franklin and books on the American Founding. The breadth of his interests rivaled the reach of people who made the study of the Founding their main specialty. But with this difference: his touch was subtle and deft, his judgments quite sound; and his grasp of the issues, in their philosophic root, ran beyond the understanding of most people in the academy who had made this subject their professional work.

Here he was approaching seventy, and it seemed to me that he was getting stronger and stronger. He was not slowing down; he seemed to be on some remarkable roll. The rest of us could look on with a certain wonderment and joy. Even Justice Scalia, himself an engine of productivity, never wanting in wit, asked me, of Richard, "How does he do it?" How did he do so much so well every month, marking that journal ever more as his? So much so, that we'll be faced with a serious question of what *First Things* could be like in his absence. My own thought is that we could still set aside a section of the journal, reprinting some of his many writings from the past, just to keep his voice and his stance present in the pages. But whatever is done, it would be done with the surety that, in sustaining Richard's genius, the journal—and the project—must continue.

When Tom Derr made him a gift of my book, Richard twitted me in print for an argument I had made about the logic of "supererogatory acts," acts beyond the call of duty. We could not define an act as "good" solely because people acted out of a heedless disregard of their own safety. The willingness of commanders in the *Wehrmacht* to die for Hitler was an expenditure of their lives for a wrongful end. I imagined then Pope John XXIII falling on a hand grenade to save people gathered around him, and the people happened to be Vito Genovese, Sam Giancana, and assorted Mafiosi. It would have been, I argued, an unjustified and wrongful sacrifice. Richard pronounced me theologically wrong. But he was so taken with the book that he wanted to see me making my arguments within this ongoing project he had been shaping.

And so I came, without realizing how deeply I would be woven in with the family he had formed. I still think I was right on that matter of John XXIII falling on the grenade. One edge of consolation is that I may see him again, as he expected, and to steal a line from him, he may have discovered in the meantime, that I had been right after all. But none of that would matter so much as the prospect of being with him again.

2. Ralph McInerny (1929–2010)

Everything Is Different, Robert Royal

Our dear friend and regular TCT contributor Ralph McInerny died Friday at age eighty of complications, weeks after surgery for esophageal cancer. To say that he will be sorely missed and that he leaves a gaping hole in Catholic intellectual life are the kinds of things that might be said about several people. But Ralph was like no one else. In fact, given his great achievements in philosophy, fiction writing, poetry, journalism, teaching, translation, and other fields (not least humor), his passing is like the disappearance of several highly talented people.

You can imagine him writing a clever detective story in which friends who knew a person in one capacity are shocked to find out after he dies that they knew only a small slice of a multifaceted character. There may indeed be people who have precisely that experience at his funeral this morning in the Basilica of the Sacred Heart on the campus of the University of Notre Dame, where he was a phenomenon for over half a century.

There are remembrances of those who knew him at Notre Dame and elsewhere below. If Ralph were still alive, he might find this a bit embarrassing because he was the least self-centered of men. To be sure, he knew what he had done and he liked to talk about it, especially the books that had fallen into relative obscurity. But you often had the sense that he, too, was surprised that he'd been lucky enough to create such wonderful things, was happy he had, yet felt as a matter of course that such things are not, in the end, reason to boast, but gifts from God.

We were together once at EWTN to tape some shows. After breakfast, we went to our rooms to work until we had to appear. Ralph emerged about two hours later, a kind of standard writing session for him, with a dazed smile on his face, "I didn't expect it to go that well." All writers have days when they suffer the torments of hell just to produce a few ordinary paragraphs. Ralph seemed to have fewer such days than anyone else.

His autobiography *I Alone Have Escaped to Tell You: My Life and Pastimes* manages to give you in a very few lively pages the history of Ralph and his family—his time in a seminary, his decision to study philosophy, travels around the world, his often nocturnal work habits—as if even he thought of all of it as just interesting material for which he was not bragging or trying to make himself any more than he already was in readers' minds. But almost anyone who picks it up will be "unable to put it down." I gave it to my wife and some of my children, who have quite different tastes and interests, as a kind of experiment to see how Ralph's magic would work outside the usual readership. It worked like a charm.

It was typical of his generous spirit that he told me (after helping, with Michael Novak, to get *The Catholic Thing* off the ground by sending us a small sum still sitting in the account of the Orestes Brownson Institute at Notre Dame) that he didn't need or want any payment for columns. We pay so little that it's maybe not as great a sacrifice as it might seem. But a regular contributor who is not getting paid might be tempted to skip a deadline here and there. Ralph, never. Once he made a commitment, he delivered.

Before he went to the Mayo Clinic for his operation, he sent several columns (you may not have noticed at the time, but re-read "We Lepers" in light of Ralph's own intimations of mortality, with its conclusion "Notionally, mortality is a pretty dull fact. But it is a feature of life that certain limit situations bring home to us its reality. It is no longer notional. What then? Like Damien, we go on doing what we were doing. Yet everything is different.")

He had calculated out how long his convalescence would take and sent enough columns to appear normally in the regular rotation until he could start writing again. When convalescence took longer than he'd hoped, he let me know that he still expected to be back in 2010. I said I'd hold him to that. Sadly, it didn't work out. But his spirit will always be a part of the writers and readers of *The Catholic Thing*, as he's part of the lives of hundreds of thousands of people around the world—now, perhaps, even more than in life.

Rest in peace, dear Ralph, and flights of angels—O lucky angels!—take thee to thy rest.

Professor, Artist, Editor, Publisher, Translator, Holy Man, Gentleman, Friend to a Multitude, and a Helluva Companion for Laughter and Story, Michael Novak

Our friend Ralph has slipped behind the clouds, out where the Sun is brightest. He will still be with us.

I can't think of any man in our time who accomplished more in one lifetime, in more different spheres, with a wider array of talents. He seemed to be laughing all the time. No one was so steady a gusher of puns, not least in the titles of his novels: *On This Rockne, Frigor Mortis, The Emerald Aisle* . . . even in his introduction to the philosophy of St. Thomas Aquinas, his guide for "Peeping Thomists."

A dinner with Ralph was a feast of stories. Also, probes by him to follow up on his curiosities. Also, seeking your opinions. Tales of the latest "progressive" outrages, followed by kind words for the particular persons being singled out. New projects he was thinking of, and what do you think of this? Puns, of course, and an endless appetite for new funny stories and the telling of the latest of his own.

One always left Ralph warmed by his love for the Church. That love may have been his most distinguishing characteristic. It surely fed his zest for the comedic sense of the Divine. It won his gratitude for the great intellectual patrimony it brought him.

He had great patience for me when I was swinging left, both

politically and theologically. Nor did he gloat when experience brought me back toward love for orthodoxy (not passive, but inquisitive and pioneering) and political realism. He wryly smiled at the proposed title for my intellectual journey: *Writing from Left to Right.*

Ralph's course was always steadier. He let people pass him by on left and right, and observed the wreckage as he later passed them by. He changed a lot himself, of course. But often he was just remaining constant as the world veered left and right, to extremes. He watched his hereditary Democratic Party adopt old Republican tendencies such as isolationism, while Republicans (*mirabile dictu*) became pro-life and rather more Catholic all the time. Ralph did not think social justice, the common good, and subsidiarity pointed to ever-larger government. He had a midwestern habit of common sense and a steady observation of results, rather than self-admiring motives.

There is a largeness about the American Middle West, and the sky there is very tall above the silos, water tanks, and trees. What counts there is feet on the ground, and not getting too big for thine own britches. There is a contemplative spirit there, and the steadiness of the rich soil all around. There is a distinctive Catholic spirituality of the middle part of the United States. Ralph lived it.

He suffered a lot from his wife Connie's death. She was always so matter-of-fact, down-to-earth, and a wifely puncturer of dreams too rosy to be true. He missed her terribly, although (so far as I could see) without complaint.

I loved and envied the boldness of Ralph's writing travels: two months here or there to write another novel, eat well, and laugh a lot—in Sicily, on Capri, even in Sarasota, Florida.

Ralph lit my life, kept my compass true, ate well with me (mostly I with him), and made me laugh a lot. Not a few times I kept him from working at his desk, with long telephone calls.

I will never forget founding *Crisis* with him (at first it was *Catholicism in Crisis*). We each put in $2000 to get the first issue out, and trusted in Providence to bring us enough in the mail to let us put out another one, and another. It always came.

Ralph, dear friend, I cannot say that I will miss you, or grieve for you. I know you are with us, even closer than before. I know that you are laughing at our blunders. And pulling for us.

Thanks, good friend.

O Rare Ralph McInerny, Bruce Fingerhut

Ralph McInerny's professional accomplishments are legendary: perhaps 125 books in philosophy, poetry, general fiction, and mysteries—plus thousands of articles and translations of dozens of books from several languages. He edited three national magazines; started an online university before they became passé; founded a book/audio publishing company producing user-friendly versions of Cliffs Notes; directed hundreds and hundreds of dissertations; headed two major centers in philosophy and medieval studies; won awards in mystery writing and, finally, philosophy's greatest award, the Gifford Lectures; all while being recognized worldwide as one of the foremost Thomist philosophers of our time.

I'll let my betters speak to such matters.

The most attractive aspect of this most attractive man was . . . the man. Ralph achieved with easy grace what every academic yearns for: to be the smartest guy in the room. But in his case, he never showed it. He always had time for students, friends, and fans. His goal was to lift people up, not put them down (remember, now, he taught at the university for fifty-five years; to be positive in such a venue is to approach sainthood). He was an outstanding teacher and writer and witness for Christ. But it was as a friend that so many will remember him. I consider him one of the closest, if not the closest, friend I have had, and I'm sure I am one of scores of people who think that. His capacity for friendship was overwhelming, lavish, effortless. His gifts of time and treasure, advice and encouragement, affability and care were all just part of being in the enormous circle of friends whom he helped and laughed with and counseled and prayed for.

He was at ease with Tolstoy and Dante, with football and movies, with Church history and Chinese food. My own mentor,

Gerhart Niemeyer, once said that an educated person should be able to be say something intelligent in any conversation. He must have been thinking of Ralph, a man able to uplift the disheartened, edify the skeptic, and encourage the searcher. To be with him was to be happy.

And humor! Why, heaven itself must be shaking with laughter, now that Ralph is in their midst, bringing wit to the most mundane, and proving once and for all time that puns are the greatest form of humor.

In his final days, when I wanted to see him and wanted not to bother him, when I was self-conscious because I feared making him discomfited in his frailty, he greeted me with his usual kindness, smiling through the pain, talking enthusiastically about books and ideas and family, even though his voice was weak, putting *me* at ease, when I was there, I thought, to put *him* at ease. How fortunate are we who knew him, who know him. God is good to have put such a man in our midst.

A Notre Dame Legend, John O'Callaghan

"Well done, good and faithful servant." No one's life can be counted in earthly words. Even Ralph who wrote so many words could not do so. His life is now recorded in the Book of Life. I once called Ralph "magnanimous." Perhaps the best word that I can think of now is "gracious." Grace-filled, he shared grace with us. Because of his deep and abiding love of God, we can be confident that Ralph lived and died in grace. We who were privileged to know him received the grace of his smile, his wit, his writing, his kindness.

Ralph served Our Lady's University as a faculty member for fifty-five years. His scholarly life began with *Studies in Analogy* and the *The Logic of Analogy*, in which he criticized Cardinal Cajetan's interpretation of Aquinas on analogy. It nearly concluded with his *Praeambula Fidei*, in which he defends the autonomy of philosophy within the context of religious faith, and returns in charity to Cajetan, now to defend him on questions of grace and nature. Ralph never held a grudge.

Ralph's writings on analogy in Aquinas still form the point of departure for all serious contemporary scholarship on the topic. His *Ethica Thomistica* is the best and most accessible introduction to Aquinas' Ethics. And then there's his marvelous translation and commentary on *Aquinas against the Averroists: On There Being Only One Intellect.* His *The Very Rich Hours of Jacques Maritain* won *Christianity and Culture*'s Best Book in Religion for 2003. It was written from the heart.

It would be folly to rehearse his scholarly CV, and even more so the novels, short stories, and detective series, his little book of Shakespearean Variations on the Sonnets, or his other poetry. He once found in his copy of Plato's *Dialogues* from 1948 the outline he had written at seventeen of the dialogue he would write to outdo Plato. Apparently that is one of the few things Ralph ever planned to write, and didn't. He was a writer through and through.

At Notre Dame, he built an international reputation as a scholar of medieval philosophy, serving for several decades on the Pontifical Academy of St. Thomas Aquinas. He was president of the American Catholic Philosophical Association, the American Maritain Association, and the American Metaphysical Society. He was awarded several honorary doctorates and Notre Dame's own Faculty Award. He served in Washington on the President's Council for the Arts. And of course, there are the awards for his fiction.

Most importantly he was a teacher—of thousands of students in almost all areas of philosophy. He focused upon the luminaries in the Catholic intellectual tradition such as Augustine, Boethius, Aquinas, Dante, Newman, Maritain, but also on others outside that tradition such as Kierkegaard. In addition to the normal load of courses, Ralph was always willing to lead reading courses on Aquinas, sometimes two or three a semester. After he ceased to offer official classes a few years ago, he continued to offer them in his home for anyone who asked. Ralph is listed among the top ten philosophy professors in the United States for directing doctoral dissertations. That list, however, only includes dissertations written by students in the Philosophy Department. He would place even higher if that list were to include the dissertations of students in the Medieval Institute. He served the department as its director of graduate studies, and directed the Medieval Institute. And for twenty-seven years as director of the Maritain Center, he provided a locale for intellectual discussion. Despite his very busy schedule of writing, teaching, and speaking, he was always willing to spend hours talking philosophy, if one had a question or two or three.

For the past few decades, Ralph responded almost every year to the requests of undergraduates and graduate students to read informally with him classics of the Catholic intellectual tradition. Quite often these groups went on, at his suggestion, to read the documents of Vatican II. Among the results were crops of adult converts. He sought no recognition for this service. For him, it was simply an act of the theological virtue of charity.

Those of us fortunate enough to have been his students know of his tireless efforts to raise additional money to support graduate students, many with families, as they completed degrees. No one who came to Ralph for help ever went away empty. Many of us would not be in the profession but for his generosity. Ralph can count on the prayers of thanksgiving of all us who spent time in the Maritain Center studying in genuine leisure, not worrying about whether we could feed and clothe our growing families or afford health insurance. He has seven successful children, and countless grandchildren. But our children, his students' children, are his spiritual grandchildren.

Finally, he weighed in on the cultural and political issues of our time, founding *Crisis* magazine, and writing many articles in other places. He was candid about his opinions. Perhaps Father Hesburgh captured Ralph's character best when he said of him, "Ralph McInerny will always tell you what he thinks is true. I knew when I asked him for his advice that he would tell me what he thought I needed to hear, not what he thought I wanted to hear. I have not always agreed with him, but I always knew he would tell it to me straight, a virtue not often in abundant supply in the political or academic worlds. Ralph McInerny is an honest man."

During a recent visit, we talked about his latest project: an edition of the collected works of his teacher Charles De Koninck. Ralph said that working through the papers, "I realized that I did not know what an opportunity I had back then, I wasted so much time, and did not learn enough." I was fortunate enough to be able to echo the sentiment to a treasured mentor.

It is perhaps best to finish with Ralph's own words. After Connie died, he decided to move to Holy Cross Village, "My final address will be Holy Cross Village. (Penultimate, that is, my plot in Cedar Grove awaits me.) I can walk to class and my campus office. My life will be centered physically as well as spiritually in Notre Dame." He now rests with Connie and Michael awaiting the resurrection under the loving gaze of his Mother, Our Mother, Notre Dame, in the serene knowledge that he lived a life of *veritas in caritate*, full of grace. *Requiescat in pace.*

3. Joe Sobran

A Noble Heart: Robert Royal

Michael J. Sobran, Jr., Joe to those of us who knew him, died last Thursday. He was by far the most eloquent, passionate, and witty pro-life writer in America over the last quarter century. And in spite of an intellectual's eccentricities that could drive you crazy and his, at times, stubborn wrongheadedness, he was a rare soul who livened up any room he entered and remained, despite the trials of years, a friend.

His was one of the most naturally brilliant minds of anyone I've ever known. Though he went to Eastern Michigan University, under different family circumstances, he would have ended up in the Ivy League or someplace like the University of Chicago. Fortunately, he came to the attention of William F. Buckley, Jr., when the famous founder of *National Review* spoke at the university amidst protests and was ably defended by a young campus journalist named Sobran. Not long after, Buckley invited him to join the magazine staff in New York.

Joe began his ascent to prominence with a long article demolishing Garry Wills, another *Wunderkind* given a start by Buckley, who early in his public career presented himself as a Chestertonian, but turned rather sharply into a standard—if brilliant—pro-abortion Catholic. In compensation, Sobran himself became a kind of contemporary Chesterton on all the pressing social issues. His book of collected articles, *Single Issues*, which was published in 1983 by *The Human Life Review*, is still illuminating and entertaining on everything it touches: abortion and euthanasia, marriage, family, religion, homosexuality, and many other matters.

When I first came to know him, we were both living in Princeton. I was running a magazine and he was commuting to New York. He'd give me tips on public arguments: "When you see a double standard, look for the single standard behind it." And on the way that government was evolving into a soft tyranny by clever evasions of constitutional limits: "Just think what Stalin could have done if he'd only had the Commerce Clause."

He meant that Congress now claims unconstitutional powers under the Constitutional principle that the Federal government can regulate interstate commerce. (Case in point: Obamacare wades into health insurance, which is not sold across state lines.) Some think he singlehandedly restored popular appreciation of the Tenth Amendment argument that anything beyond the enumerated powers remains in the hands of the states or the people. Joe came to regard Lincoln as one of the instigators of power grabs because he ran roughshod over the states in the Civil War— unfair to Lincoln, but indicative of Joe's passion for liberty, and limited government.

Shakespeare was a lifelong passion; he knew the Bard so well that you could give him an obscure line and he could almost always go on a bit from there. Around 1990, he became obsessed with the authorship question. It made no sense to him, once he started to look into it, that a nobody from a small town could have written such convincing scenes about monarchs and nobles. He concluded, for this and other reasons, that Edward de Vere, the seventeenth earl of Oxford, wrote "Shakespeare," the latter being a minor actor from Stratford-on-Avon used as a screen by various figures (playwriting and acting were disreputable activities in Elizabethan England). He also concluded from the Sonnets that de Vere was a homosexual, a hard truth about a beloved writer, which he put into an epigram: "He's here, he's queer, he's de Vere."

Joe wrote a fall-over-dead-laughing novella in the form of a detective story about the clueless Shakespeare trying to figure out who was using him and why. Inexplicably, no publisher has picked it up.

Or perhaps not so inexplicably. Around 1990, he started to think that our alliance with Israel, which he had supported vigorously till then, and powerful Jewish lobbies in America were drawing us into decidedly non-conservative military adventures, as in the first Iraq War. When he started to get pushback from other conservatives, he resented it and dug in his heels. There's plenty to debate about Israel and the Middle East, of course. But Joe started to throw hard punches in rebuttal and even began to flirt with some unsavory publications and organizations that were anti-Semitic in ways that he was not.

I say this as a person who had to stop talking with him for about a year because of his obsessions about the attacks he suffered and the unfair charges of anti-Semitism, a death sentence in respectable circles for any writer. William F. Buckley famously excoriated Joe and Pat Buchanan in an article, "In Search of Anti-Semitism." Buckley concluded that neither man was a classic anti-Semite but that they were providing fuel for the old canard about Catholics and conservatives harboring anti-Semitic attitudes. Joe retaliated and they broke with each other, but reconciled a year before Buckley died. Still, the accusations damaged Joe's reputation and some publishers were gun-shy about him.

This was unfortunate in several ways, not least because it hurt him financially. And as a man who was not married—two marriages had failed—and was a textbook-case impractical intellectual, his health declined. Fortunately for him, his business affairs were run by the saintly Fran Griffin and her Griffin Communications the last few years. Fran literally prolonged his life.

I saw him in a nursing home last Sunday. He perked up when my wife told him she was leaving this week for Egypt to study icons and he asked about the book I'm working on. But with diabetes and double renal failure, we all knew it was a matter of time. He died the day after the Feast of the Archangels. The lines from *Hamlet* come unbidden:

> Now cracks a noble heart. Good-night, sweet prince.
> And flights of angels sing thee to thy rest.

4. Avery Dulles, S.J. (1918–2008)

A Faithful American: Robert Royal

Today's column was supposed to be about the birth of Christ, but I feel obliged instead to commemorate the death of a cardinal: Avery Dulles passed to his reward last Friday, and was beyond all dispute one of the great Catholic churchmen and theologians ever produced by America.

"Beyond all dispute," however, needs to be understood literally in this case, because many disputes arose around Dulles in the 1970s and again when Pope John Paul II made him a cardinal in 2001. His 1974 *Models of the Church* (institution, mystical communion, sacrament, herald, and servant), was often cited by liberals and dissidents for its allegedly Americanized understanding of the Church as the People of God. When Dulles got the red hat almost thirty years later, though it was clear that his work had developed along lines very similar to Karol Wojtyla's and Joseph Ratzinger's, many people still groused. But he was one of our great men.

I first met him in the early 1980s when he was teaching at the

Catholic University of America. By then, he had settled into a familiar pattern. He was robustly orthodox and his catholicity on any question he addressed was close to exhaustive. If he was writing on the death penalty, he would read everything in the tradition and the contemporary debate, and would produce impeccably balanced conclusions. In this he reminded you of the Aquinas of the *Summa Theologiae*, a figure who helped draw him into the Church.

Dulles was also notoriously dry, though a good teacher and enthusiastic about youth renewal movements. And he was humble. His family, of course, were *the* Dulleses. John Foster (father), was secretary of state under Eisenhower, and Allen (uncle) headed the CIA. Longtime Presbyterians, with clergy and missionaries in the mix, they were surprised when he converted at Harvard, a story he tells with a simple charm in *A Testimonial to Grace*, which he wrote while serving in the Navy during World War II. The fiftieth anniversary edition (1996) contains an addition that begins, "In a sense I could say, as did John Henry Newman in his *Apologia pro vita sua*, that there is no further history of my religious opinions, since in becoming a Catholic, I arrived at my real home."

Of course, this is true, but not the whole truth. Part of the controversy over *Models of the Church* had to do with the fact that, like Ratzinger, Wojtyla, and others prior to Vatican II, Dulles became impressed with the more personal view of the Church in the *nouvelle théologie* of De Lubac, Daniélou, Congar. Unfortunately, other admirers of these quite orthodox thinkers moved towards the radical sides of Karl Rahner, Hans Küng, and lesser known figures. John Paul II was the pope who finally separated the sheep from the goats.

Dulles himself became skilled at this task. In a seminar at the Catholic Theological Society of America in 1995, he laid out fifteen criteria (I told you he was thorough) by which we can tell whether a theology is truly Catholic. He was a past president of CTSA and knew where the bodies were—and are—buried.

I went to Rome when Dulles was made a cardinal along with

the archbishops of New York and Washington, D.C. It is a rarity for a priest to be so elevated, though De Lubac and Hans Urs von Balthasar had received similar recognition. We scheduled a telephone conversation a bit later so that I could write a long piece on his work. I wish there were space to transcribe parts of the tapes, but there were two points I particularly wanted him to clarify.

First, St. Augustine wrote his *Retractationes* in his old age. Did he, Cardinal Dulles, have anything that he would put in that category? Without hesitation, he said no. And for an interesting reason: in the 1970s, a lot was in flux, and he didn't want to close off any possibilities that the magisterium might decide to pursue. Some might regard this as rationalization. But Dulles convinced me that his aim, then as always, was "to think with the Church." To anyone who knew Dulles, this sort of humility was entirely in character. I once even saw him embarrassed when he had to mention Dulles Airport (named after his father).

The second thing I wanted was to get the old Presbyterian to do something out of character: tell me, when you got that call from the Vatican, how did it *feel*. No trick known to man could pry that out of him. He was with a student, the secretary buzzed, he excused himself briefly, and took the call. The only thing he asked: could he be dispensed from being a bishop (he was), and had the Jesuit superior general agreed? Yes. They didn't ask him if he would accept—I'd say because they knew he would do what he was asked.

The great story of his conversion and growth into one of America's premier theologians cannot be told in a column. You have to read through several of the books and a lot of the masterly essays. One of my favorites among the later books is *The New World of Faith*, where he writes: "The world disclosed to faith is immense. It opens up vistas that extend beyond the world of sense and into a realm not reached by telescopes and astronomical instruments, however powerful. . . . Its population includes the living and the dead, saints and angels, and even, at the summit, divine persons. . . .We cannot even sketch it, still less enter it, unless we receive and accept God's loving revelation."

Avery Dulles received and accepted and, we can hope, in God's good graciousness has now entered into that world.

5. R. Sargent Shriver (1915–2011)

George J. Marlin

Fifty years ago this month, American Catholics watched proudly as John Kennedy was sworn in as president of the United States.

J. F. K. was flanked by the first Catholic Senate majority leader, Mike Mansfield, and the first Catholic House majority leader, John McCormack. Catholics knew they had finally arrived. And when the young Cold Warrior told the tyrants in Moscow, Warsaw, East Berlin, Bucharest, and Budapest that "we shall pay any price, bear any burden, meet any hardship, support any friend, oppose any foe to assure the survival and success of liberty," the souls of ethnic Catholics were stirred.

Last week one of the last and most honorable members of the Camelot era, Robert Sargent Shriver, Jr., husband of the late Eunice Kennedy, died at the age of ninety-five.

Shriver was born on November 9, 1915 in Westminster, Maryland. His ancestors, David and Rebecca Shriver, settled in Frederick County, Maryland probably in 1761, and had 8 children, 64 grandchildren and 265 great-grandchildren. The first U.S. Census conducted in 1790 listed 50 families headed by Shrivers.

David Shriver was a signatory in 1776 on the Maryland Constitution, and he helped write Maryland's Declaration of Rights. (Thomas Jefferson borrowed heavily from the document when he composed the Declaration of Independence.)

In the nineteenth and twentieth centuries, the Shrivers became prominent members of Maryland's Catholic establishment, which was centered on Baltimore, the nation's first Catholic Diocese. The family founded numerous organizations and societies including the Catholic Evidence League—dedicated to teaching Church fundamentals to the faithful—and the National Convert League (later the Society of St. Vincent de Paul), which provided financial support to married Protestant ministers who converted to Catholicism.

America's primate, James Cardinal Gibbons (1834–1921) stayed at the Shriver home in Union Mills, Maryland, during his summer and winter vacations. Sargent was not only baptized by Gibbons, but often served as his altar boy at Masses held in the Shriver family chapel. Shortly before his death, Gibbons said his final Mass on December 9, 1920 at the Shriver home.

After earning bachelor and law degrees from Yale, Sargent served in the Navy. In 1945, after a brief stint in the New York law firm of Winthrop, Stimson, Putnam, and Roberts, Shriver, who had chaired the *Yale Daily News*, took a job as a *Newsweek* editor.

In 1946, he was introduced to the woman he would marry seven years later, Eunice Mary Kennedy. Her father, always on the lookout for young talent, hired Shriver to work for Joseph P. Kennedy Enterprises and sent him to Chicago where he eventually became manager of the gem of the Kennedy financial empire, the Chicago Merchandise Mart—then the nation's largest commercial building.

Shriver was active in Chicago's Catholic and political circles and went on to serve as president of the city's Board of Education and the Catholic Interracial Council. He fearlessly tackled the issues of housing, hospital, and education discrimination.

His political ambitions, however, were crushed by the Kennedy steamroller. As early as 1948, old Joe nixed Shriver's move to become an Adlai Stevenson speechwriter. And when he was offered the 1960 Illinois nomination for governor, the Kennedy clan leaned on him to decline. He was also persuaded in 1964 and 1968 to turn down offers to run for vice president on the Democratic ticket.

Shriver, from 1961 to 1966, served as director of the last surviving program of the Kennedy presidency, the Peace Corps.

Thanks to his efforts, tens of thousands of young Americans served as voluntary teachers and workers in the world's poorest nations.

Although the Kennedys viewed it as an act of disloyalty, he accepted President Johnson's offer to become overseer of the "War on Poverty" as head of the Office of Economic Opportunity, which created a host of anti-poverty programs, including dubious ones such as Legal Services for the Poor and the Community Action Program.

Unlike his famous brothers-in-law, Shriver upheld and defended Church teaching in the public square. Although he was a liberal who bought into *Commonweal* magazine's interpretations of Vatican II, nevertheless, when it came to abortion he was solidly pro-life. As the Democratic Party's 1972 vice presidential candidate and in his unsuccessful 1976 run for his party's presidential nomination, he refused to bend.

In a 1976 position paper, he stated, "I am strongly opposed to abortion . . . . I intend to work in and out of government, as I have for the past decade, for the day when abortion will no longer be looked upon by anyone as a desirable or necessary procedure." During the New Hampshire primary campaign, after a four-hour discussion on abortion one participant said, "What impressed me about [Shriver] more than anything else was he just never allowed himself to talk about anything but the substance of what was the right thing to say. He never let go of his principles."

Sargent and Eunice Shriver funded the first international abortion conference and the Georgetown University Kennedy Institute of Ethics to study life issues. They also founded Life Support Centers which Shriver biographer Scott Stossel reported, "provided prenatal care and child-rearing instruction; helped mothers find jobs; and generally tried to augment the incentive for teenage mothers not to abort."

On hearing of Shriver's death, Sean Cardinal O'Malley, Archbishop of Boston, spoke justly: "He changed the world for the better. His commitment to preserving and protecting human life at every stage of existence, especially for the unborn, and working to lift people out of poverty were exceptional gifts of love and humanity. . . ."

R. Sargent Shriver, *requiescat in pace.*

6. The God-Haunted Christopher Hitchens

Francis Beckwith

Contemporary unbelief has lost one of its most gifted apologists, Christopher Hitchens. He, along with Richard Dawkins, Sam Harris, and Daniel Dennett, are often referred to as the four horsemen of the New Atheism. It is called the "New" Atheism because of its evangelistic zeal, an enthusiasm largely absent from the more urbane and engaging infidelities of "the Old Atheists" like Bertrand Russell, John Dewey, or Antony Flew.

But like all undisciplined enthusiasts who confuse wisecracking proselytes with wisdom-seeking pilgrims, the New Atheists seem incapable of completely ridding themselves and their disciples of the metaphysical infrastructure of the creeds from which they claim to have decisively fled. Hitchens, for example, in his book *God Is Not Great*, argues that "religion poisons everything," blaming religious believers and their beliefs for many of the atrocities of history.

Setting aside the question of Hitchens' historical accuracy and philosophical acumen, his thesis correctly affirms that human beings have had their rights violated by other human beings who committed their wicked deeds in the name of God and for bad reasons.

Some of the cases that Hitchens cites involve legitimate governments perpetuating and protecting wicked acts that these states had the legal power to perpetuate and protect. And yet, this fact would have not moved Hitchens to say that the acts he thinks are wrong are now right. Why? Because human beings are beings of a certain sort and thus by nature possess certain rights that their governments are morally obligated to recognize and protect.

In fact, Hitchens writes that he and other atheists "believe with certainty that an ethical life can be lived without religion," thus implying that he and others have direct and incorrigible acquaintance with a natural moral law that informs their judgments about what counts as an ethical life.

But to speak of a natural moral law—a set of abstract, immaterial, unchanging principles of human conduct that apply to all persons in all times and in all places—seems oddly out of place in the universe that Hitchens claimed we occupy, a universe that is at bottom a purposeless vortex of matter, energy, and scientific laws that eventually spit out human beings.

And to speak of an ethical *life* is to say that morality is more than rule keeping, that it involves the shape and formation of one's character consistent with a human being's proper end. But proper ends require intrinsic purposes, just the sorts of things that a theistic philosophy of nature affirms and Hitchens' philosophical naturalism denies.

In the same book, Hitchens writes that "what we [atheists] respect is free inquiry, open-mindedness." Unsurprisingly, Hitchens procures pages and pages of evidence to show how the suppression of open-mindedness has led to the vice of ignorance and thus untold mischief and misery in the history of the human race.

His point is clear: human beings have the power to act consistently or inconsistently with their own good and the good of others, and open-mindedness makes advancing that good more likely.

Open-mindedness, of course, is a good thing. No right-thinking person denies that. But to say that anything is a "good thing" cannot be understood apart from what makes it a good thing for the being who ought to actualize it.

So, for example, it would make no sense for me to say that my dog, Phydeaux, ought to be open-minded, since a canine is not the sort of being for which open-mindedness can ever be a virtue (or closed-mindedness a vice), just as the number three can never be the reddest letter in the alphabet.

Natures matter. Consequently, we learn from Hitchens' commitment to open-mindedness what he thought about the nature of the human being's intellect and the role of its proper functioning in advancing the good of the individual and the community in which he resides.

For Hitchens there is a normative natural end, an intrinsic purpose, to a human being's active power for self-movement to engage in free acts initiated and/or accompanied by thought and reflection. Thus, like Hitchens' allusion to a natural moral law and his commitment to the ethical life, his call for open-mindedness requires a philosophy of nature that his philosophical naturalism cannot sustain.

It presupposes a nature teeming with intrinsic purposes, the sort of nature that the New Atheists tell us smacks at an ancient understanding with which we are no longer saddled—thanks to the ascendancy of philosophical naturalism. So, in order to show us that God is not great, Hitchens relies on the philosophical infrastructure that only this diminished deity can adequately provide.

Hitchens' atheism was a God-haunted atheism. May he rest in the peace in which he did not believe.

7. Robert Bork's Lingering Presence

Hadley Arkes

As the old year is passing—and as if it were not depressing enough, for some of us, to find ourselves in the new year at the threshold of Obama II—some of us are still feeling the loss of our dear friend Robert Bork, who died just before Christmas.

I remarked in a piece I wrote on the morning of his death "Robert Bork, with his bear-like frame, was one of the most sensitive and dearest of men, and for his friends, unrelentingly loyal. . . . [The dark days before us would become] harder to bear without his courage and laughter."

Last October I wrote in these columns a piece marking the twenty-fifth anniversary of those scandalous hearings sparked by his nomination to the Supreme Court. And yet the irony was that Robert Bork emerged an even larger figure, drawing the respect and affection of a public even larger than the audience he had commanded as a professor and judge.

That summer of the hearings on confirmation, I was driving back and forth between Amherst, Massachusetts and our cottage in Bethesda, Maryland, to settle in for a year of academic leave. Back and forth I listened to those hearings and in later years I would remember parts of the hearings that Bork had forgotten.

At only one moment in those hearings did I wish something could transport me to take Bob's place in that seat facing his questioners. That was when Joe Biden asked (and I paraphrase): Judge, can you imagine a case in which a legislature would actually pass a statute barring access to contraception?

And I would have been tempted to say, Yes, Senator: A regulatory body, pursuant to a statute you had voted for, takes the Dalkon Shield off the market, judging it a hazard. A group of women then come forth to say that they found the device economical and safe, and that they should be the sole judges of the risks they are willing to take with their own bodies. And this was well before we would hear serious talk of legislatures making the wearing of contraceptives compulsory for the participants in pornographic films.

Bob Bork and I would tilt over the years on the matter of natural law. He was, to the end, a confirmed "positivist." He professed to find his decisions controlled by the laws "posited," set down in a statute or in the Constitution. He was enduringly dubious about any attempts to engage in moral reasoning outside the text of the Constitution.

To the dubiety of some of his friends he insisted that this reigning "positivism" was not moral "relativism." But then his friends would recall lines of this kind: "Truth," he once said, "is what the majority thinks it is at any given moment precisely because the majority is permitted to govern and to redefine its values constantly." If that wasn't a signature tune of relativism, it would be hard to invent one.

And yet, anyone who knew Bob Bork knew that, in his reactions to everything of moral consequence in the life whirling around him, there was no trace of moral relativism. To adapt a line from Samuel Johnson, Bob was a lawyer by vocation, but a moralist by necessity. And so it could truly be said that, as a judge, his practice was far, far better than his theory.

As I remarked then in these columns, Bob Bork as a jurist offered a steady example of the "laws of reason," or the canons of logic, brought to bear on cases in law in a disciplined way. In that respect, he gave us the most elegant examples of how a jurisprudence of natural law could be done while professing up and down that it could not be done. And with the same wisdom that ran beyond his theory, those powers of reasoning would later bring him into the Church even while his scoffing at natural law remained undiminished.

In that respect, as I used to tell him, he had thoroughly absorbed the style of the University of Chicago as he and I had come to know it. He would make the strongest case he could for an argument he was pondering, and then, viewing that argument at its best, decide that it wasn't that compelling after all. Readers or listeners looking on would be baffled as to what he was doing; but to those of us from Chicago it made eminent sense.

He went from that university into the Marines during the war in Korea. In the barracks, he would be reading Shakespeare while those around him read comic books, and that was enough for his sergeant to call him "Hey, Shakes." A sergeant also asked him what religion to put down on his dog tag. Bob insisted at the time that he had no religion. The sergeant said, "All right . . . 'Protestant.'"

When he came into the Church, in his seventies, he remarked that this was a terrific deal: He could be absolved of all the earlier sins, while being too old to engage in any sins that were especially interesting. But I remarked to another friend that Bob's death can itself impart new confidence in a life after death: For it is just implausible to think that a soul so vivid, so vibrant still among his friends, could really be extinguished.

And that may be Bob's last gift, even at the beginning of this New Year, the gift of consolation—and hope.

8. Mike Schwartz

Son of Thunder: Austin Ruse

In his final days, Michael Schwartz could hardly hold himself up. He had to be propped up with pillows. Though his voice was little more than a whisper, his words bristled with passion.

He sat with radio personality Sandy Rios and between greedy gulps of air whispered out his life story.

You will probably not know his name or heard of him. It is hard to say that he was merely a behind-the-scenes person. He was that, but he was more. Hardly a pro-life leader in America was not at one time welcomed by him, mentored and taught by him, prayed for by him. He was in fact a leader of leaders.

Mike grew up in Philadelphia, poor and in family chaos: "My father was a drunken, adulterous wife beater. I remember my father beat the crap out of my mother frequently. He wanted me to meet his girlfriends. I started driving when I was seven. I took him to their homes. He became for me the permanent image of what I did not want to be. "

This was the seedbed for what became a man of deep and abiding faith: "I think I got all the breaks. I've had a very blessed life."

His life's trajectory was likely set when one of his young friends gave him a copy of *National Review*. Until then, he didn't know he was a conservative. This led to Mike's becoming a charter subscriber to *Triumph* magazine, the smart and combative journal that represented one of the last gasps of Counter-Reformation Catholicism in America.

Triumph led to summer pilgrimages at El Escorial in Spain, the home of the Spanish Monarchs and not very far from the Valley of the Fallen, the monument built by Francisco Franco. The *Triumph* team wanted to imbue their students with what a true Catholic culture was like. Mike drank deeply.

Mike says *Triumph* "became the seedbed for the pro-life movement of the 1960s." He and his *Triumph*-enthused fellow students at the University of Dallas formed the Sons of Thunder, one of the first pro-life groups in America. They promptly occupied a Planned Parenthood facility in Dallas and promptly got arrested.

For his whole professional life, Mike was at the center of all the most important pro-life activities. With Nellie Gray and others, he founded what became the March for Life.

Mike went on to a whole host of important jobs. He worked for Paul Weyrich at the Free Congress Foundation. He became Legislative Director for Concerned Women for America. (He loved saying he worked for a women's group.) He worked for Congressman Tom Coburn in the House of Representatives and later became Coburn's Chief of Staff when he went to the Senate.

Mike was not a namby-pamby Christian. He was salty. Talking about the Supreme Court or the "gutless Republicans in the U.S. Senate," his eyes would narrow, and his lips would tighten across his teeth and he would hold forth like an Old Testament prophet. Sometimes this got him into trouble.

He once said publically that the Justices of the Supreme Court shouldn't be impeached "they should be impaled." He called it the "*Roe v. Wade* Hate Crimes Against the Human Race Decision."

It wasn't just abortion he cared about. Mike said that the scourge of pornography caused young men to become homosexual. He was one of the first in this country to sound the alarm bell about the sex scandal of Catholic priests. He called abortion murder. Mike was salty and fearless.

His last pro-life testament was a strategy memo that he began to float a few years ago and that he presented formally to a large group of pro-life leaders who met in Washington, D.C., around the March for Life—which turned out to be his last public appearance, a few weeks before his death.

The memo is masterwork, a summa of a life spent living and thinking about the cause of the unborn. Mike believed that America is uneasy with the idea of abortion, but has grown comfortable with the reality. Besides the true blue partisans on both sides, no more than 20 percent on either side, was a mushy middle weary of the debate.

He believed that even if *Roe* were overturned we would still be faced with massive numbers of abortions and "instead of eliminating abortion by outlawing it, we first need to outlaw it by eliminating it."

He wrote, "When the total number of commercial abortions committed is no greater than 100,000 and the total number of abortion shops is less than 100, then we can say that the cancer has been shrunk sufficiently to cut it out."

To end abortion Mike called for prayer—specific prayers for women and for abortionists by name—service to the pregnant woman, and legislation aimed almost exclusively at putting abortionists out of business in the states.

He called for "facilities regulations," requiring all abortion workers be bonded so as to expose the criminal past of many of them, establishing an Abortion Injury Compensation Fund to be funded by a tax on all abortions, and several other very clever ideas, many of which are already being carried out.

You may never have met Michael Schwartz, but much of what you know about the pro-life cause first came to life in his head and at his hands.

He was diagnosed with Lou Gehrig's Disease only a year-and-a-half ago. This man who always carried some book about theology in his pocket, knew this was a blessing and was always joyful about it even to the end. It was a final test, a final penance that he carried out with the sporting spirit of a true Christian and a Son of Thunder.

Mike breathed his last on Sunday in the company of his beloved wife of 42 years, his many children and his grandchildren. *Requiescat in pace*, Mike. At only 63, you left us way too soon.

Contributors

Hadley Arkes is the Ney Professor of Jurisprudence at Amherst College. His most recent book is Constitutional Illusions & Anchoring Truths: The Touchstone *of the Natural Law.*

Michael Baruzzini is a freelance science writer and editor. He is also the creator of CatholicScience.com, which offers online science curriculum resources for Catholic students.

Francis J. Beckwith is Professor of Philosophy and Church-State Studies at Baylor University, where he is also a Resident Scholar in Baylor's Institute for Studies of Religion.

Tom Bethell is a senior editor of The American Spectator *and a contributing editor to* The New Oxford Review. *He is the author most recently of* The Politically Incorrect Guide to Science.

David Bonagura is an adjunct professor of theology at the Seminary of the Immaculate Conception, Huntington, New York.

Fr. Bevil Bramwell is a member of Oblates of Mary Immaculate and is Undergraduate Dean at Catholic Distance University. He has published Laity: Beautiful, Good and True *and* The World of the Sacraments.

Peter Brown is completing a doctorate in Biblical Studies at the Catholic University of America.

John W. (Jack) Carlson, who passed away suddenly in 2012, was professor of philosophy at Creighton University. During his career, all at Jesuit-sponsored institutions, he served as a department chair, arts and sciences dean, and academic vice president.

William E. Carroll is Thomas Aquinas Fellow in Theology and Science, Blackfriars, University of Oxford.

Michael Coren is a TV and radio host based in Toronto, Canada. His syndicated column runs each week in many newspapers. He is the author of thirteen books, including Why Catholics Are Right.

Roberto de Mattei is professor of the History of Christianity at the European University of Rome and vice-president of the National Research Council of Italy. He is also president of the Lepanto Foundation.

Fr. Phillip W. de Vous is the pastor of St. Joseph Parish in Crescent Springs, KY, and adjunct scholar of public policy at the Acton Institute.

Joan Frawley Desmond is a Catholic journalist; she blogs at The Cathoholic. A graduate of the Pontifical John Paul II Institute for Studies on Marriage and the Family, she leads Theology of the Body study groups.

Richard Doerflinger has a day job at the U.S. Conference of Catholic Bishops, which has not the remotest connection with his love for watching and talking about movies in his spare time.

Jean Duchesne is a writer and emeritus professor of English at Condorcet College in Paris. He has served as personal adviser to the archbishops of Paris since 1981 and is now secretary general

Contributors

of the French Catholic Academy and vice-president of the French bishops' Faith and Culture Observatory.

Mary Eberstadt is a Senior Fellow at the Ethics and Public Policy Center and author of several books including How the West Really Lost God, Adam and Eve after the Pill, *and* The Loser Letters.

Anthony Esolen is a lecturer, translator, and writer. His latest books are Reflections on the Christian Life: How Our Story Is God's Story *and* Ten Ways to Destroy the Imagination of Your Child. *He teaches at Providence College.*

Patrick Fagan is director of the Marriage and Religion Research Institute (MARRI) at Family Research Council whose project, Mapping America, charts social trends.

Sean Fieler, a money manager, writes in a private capacity.

Bruce Fingerhut is the founder and director of St. Augustine's Press, South Bend, Indiana.

Michael Foley is an associate professor of patristics in the Great Texts Program at Baylor University.

Karen Goodwin is a producer with over a dozen Broadway shows to her credit. She is founder of Fifth Avenue Entertainment and serves on the Department of Business and Economics Advisory Board of Catholic University of America where she is Adjunct Professor.

Matthew Hanley is, with Jokin de Irala, M.D., the author of Affirming Love, Avoiding AIDS: What Africa Can Teach the West, *which won a best-book award from the Catholic Press Association. His latest report,* The Catholic Church & The Global AIDS Crisis, *is available from the Catholic Truth Society.*

Todd Hartch teaches Latin American history at Eastern Kentucky University. He specializes in World Christianity, missions, and the religious history of Mexico.

Charlotte Hays is Director of Cultural Programs for the Independent Women's Forum and coauthor of Being Dead Is No Excuse: The Official Southern Ladies Guide to Hosting the Perfect Funeral *and author of* When Did White Trash Become the New Normal?

John Jay Hughes is a priest of the St. Louis archdiocese and the author, most recently, of the memoir: No Ordinary Fool: A Testimony to Grace.

Kristina Johannes is a registered nurse and a certified teacher of natural family planning. She has served as a spokeswoman for the Alaska Family Coalition, which successfully worked for passage of the marriage amendment to the Alaska Constitution.

George Sim Johnston is a free-lance writer living in New York. He is the author of Did Darwin Get It Right? Catholics and the Theory of Evolution.

Howard Kainz is emeritus professor of philosophy at Marquette University. His most recent publications include Natural Law: an Introduction and Reexamination, The Philosophy of Human Nature, *and* The Existence of God and the Faith-Instinct.

John B. Kienker is managing editor of the Claremont Review of Books.

Jeremy Lott is the founding editor of Real Clear Religion *and* Real Clear Books *and is the author of* William F. Buckley, *part of the Christian Encounters Series published by Thomas Nelson.*

Daniel J. Mahoney is Professor of Political Science at Assumption

College and editor, with Edward E. Ericson, Jr., of The Solzhenitsyn Reader: New And Essential Writings, 1947–2005. *His latest book is* The Conservative Foundations of the Liberal Order: Defending Democracy against Its Modern Enemies and Immoderate Friends.

George Marlin is an editor of The Quotable Fulton Sheen *and the author of* The American Catholic Voter. *His most recent book is* Narcissist Nation: Reflections of a Blue-State Conservative.

Fr. C. John McCloskey is a Church historian and research fellow at the Faith and Reason Institute in Washington, D. C.

Ralph McInerny was a prolific and celebrated writer of philosophy, fiction, and cultural criticism, who taught for many years at Notre Dame. He was a founding editor of The Catholic Thing *and died in 2010, full of years and honors.*

Emina Melonic immigrated to the U.S. in 1996 and became an American citizen in 2003. She received an M.A. in Humanities from the University of Chicago, an M.A. in Theology from Christ the King Seminary, and is currently completing a thesis on Bernard Lonergan and the Trinity. She is pursuing a Ph.D. in medieval philosophy at SUNY Buffalo.

Brad Miner is senior editor of The Catholic Thing, *senior fellow of the Faith & Reason Institute, and a board member of Aid to the Church in Need USA. He is the author of six books and is a former Literary Editor of* National Review.

Michael Novak is a prolific author and one of the most influential and honored Catholic intellectuals of his generation in America and the world. He is a founding editor of The Catholic Thing *and currently teaches at Ave Maria University.*

John O'Callaghan is Associate Professor of Philosophy and

Director of the Jacques Maritain Center at the University of Notre Dame.

Father Val J. Peter was Executive Director from 1985 to 2005 and is now Executive Director Emeritus of Girls and Boys Town, the original Father Flanagan's Boys' Home. He has served on the boards or committees of more than twenty national and local organizations, including the Parents Television Council, and has published eleven books and more than fifty scholarly articles. He holds doctorate degrees in canon law and theology.

Greg Pfundstein is the executive director of the Chiaroscuro Foundation.

Robert Reilly is a former director of the Voice of America. He has taught at the National Defense University and served in the White House and the Office of the Secretary of Defense. His most recent book is The Closing of the Muslim Mind: How Intellectual Suicide Created the Modern Islamist.

Dr. Damiano Rondelli is the Michael Reese Professor of Hematology at the University of Illinois at Chicago. He is the editor of Storia delle discipline mediche, *a history of the medical profession.*

Robert Royal is Editor-in-Chief of The Catholic Thing *and President of the Faith & Reason Institute. He is finishing a book on the Catholic intellectual tradition in the twentieth century.*

Austin Ruse is the President of the New York and Washington, D.C.-based Catholic Family & Human Rights Institute (C-FAM), a research institute that focuses on international social policy.

William Saunders is Senior Vice President of Legal Affairs at Americans United for Life. A graduate of the Harvard Law School, he writes frequently on a wide variety of legal and policy issues.

Appendix: In Memoriam

James V. Schall, S.J., , who served as a professor at Georgetown University for thirty-five years, is one of the most prolific Catholic writers in America. His most recent books are The Mind That Is Catholic *and* The Modern Age.

Randall B. Smith is Professor at the University of St. Thomas, where he has recently been appointed to the Scanlan Chair in Theology.

Michael Uhlmann, who teaches at the Claremont Graduate School, writes frequently in matters of law, culture, and politics.

Aaron Urbanczyck is Director of the Write Reason Plan and member of the Liberal Arts faculty at Aquinas College, Nashville, Tennessee.

David Warren is a former editor of the Idler *magazine and columnist with the* Ottawa Citizen. *He has extensive experience in the Near and Far East. His blog is called* Essays in Idleness.

Andreas Widmer, a former Swiss Guard, is Director of Entrepreneurship Programs at The Catholic University of America and President of The Carpenter's Fund.

Joseph Wood is a former White House official who teaches at the Institute of World Politics.